Challenging Slavery in the Chesapeake

Challenging Slavery

in the

Chesapeake

Black and White Resistance to

Human Bondage, 1775–1865

T. STEPHEN WHITMAN

BALTIMORE

MARYLAND HISTORICAL SOCIETY

2007

Maryland Historical Society
201 West Monument Street
Baltimore, Maryland, 21201
www.mdhs.org

Publication of this work was made possible
by the generous support of
The William L. & Victorine Q. Adams Foundation
and
The Rogers Family Fund.

ISBN 0-938420-96-8

CIP Data Pending

Manufactured in the United States of America.
The paper used in this book meets the minimum requirements of the
American National Standard for Information Sciences Permanence of Paper
for Printed Library Materials ANSI Z39.48-1984.

Contents

Acknowledgements

This book began as a project sponsored by the Maryland Historical Society, and I want to thank Dennis Fiori, Nancy Davis, and Ric Cottom for their support and encouragement. I am particularly indebted to Ric, as editor, for all his work on the text, images, and layout of the book, and to Bill Evitts for his incisive editing and historiographical insights. Kym Rice found and secured the use of most of the images between these pages, and has given me many invaluable suggestions on the text over the past few years; it would not be amiss to think of her as a virtual co-author.

Many people read parts or all of the manuscript at differing stages of its development and helped improve its arguments and accuracy. Among them are Christine Daniels, Peter Dorsey, Douglas Egerton, Ellen Eslinger, Curtis Johnson, Michael Johnson, Michael Nicholls, Christopher Phillips, James Sidbury, and Frank Towers.

Financial support for this work came from the Maryland Historical Society, as well as a Mellon Grant for a research stint at the Library Company of Philadelphia in the summer of 1999. Summer research grants from the National Endowment for the Humanities in 2002 and the Pennsylvania History and Museum Commission in 2003 also proved useful for this book. I am particularly grateful to Philip Lapsansky of the Library Company of Philadelphia for his insights during my stay there. I also received summer study grants from Mount St. Mary's College that forwarded this work.

Funding for the publication of this book was made possible by the generous support of the William L. & Victorine Q. Adams Foundation and the Rogers Family Fund.

My colleagues and students at the Mount have inspired me to keep working at this project. Notably, I learned a great deal from testing ideas with students in Race and Slavery seminars.

The last word goes to Nancy Fadel Whitman, for all her support and engagement. This book is dedicated to her.

T. Stephen Whitman
Emmitsburg, Maryland
December 1, 2006

Introduction

In 1775, American colonists took up arms against Britain in the name of freedom. Some scorned attempts to seek accommodation with Great Britain as acceptance of tyranny, of being reduced to "slavery." As Patrick Henry put it bluntly, "Give me liberty or give me death." Henry, of course, was himself a slaveholder, as were nearly all the revolutionary leaders in the southern colonies, and not a few in the northern colonies as well. From that moment when America's revolutionaries enshrined freedom as the highest good, to be cherished above life itself, they transformed slavery from an immutable fact into a festering, intractable contradiction.

Did the existence of slavery negate American claims to be the freest people on earth? Did commitment to freedom mean that black slaves should be liberated, or was freedom a condition for which only whites were fitted? Americans white and black struggled with these questions for ninety years, from the dawn of the Revolution until the end of the Civil War.

No place better exemplified the passions aroused by the words and deeds of those who challenged slavery than the Chesapeake. Virginia, the famed "cradle of liberty" of Jefferson and Washington, also first nurtured chattel slavery in British North America and was home to more slaves than any other state between the Revolution and the Civil War. Maryland, birthplace of Frederick Douglass and Harriet Tubman, eliminated slavery by a constitutional referendum during the Civil War but also supplied tens of thousands of troops to the Confederacy. Delaware's Caesar Rodney cast a swing vote for freedom in the debate over the Declaration of Independence, but slavery would linger on there until ended by the enactment of the Thirteenth Amendment in December 1865.

In all three states, African Americans shared goals and means in battling against slavery. Slaves opposed their bondage by purchasing their freedom and by suing for it in the courts. Some fled to free territory. Others battled for their liberty by serving in American wars or by rebelling against those who called themselves their masters. Free people of color from Norfolk to Baltimore to Wilmington clung to their hard-won status, resisting kidnappers who sought to re-enslave them, assisting fugitive slaves, and writing and speaking against efforts to deport African Americans to Africa under the aegis of "colonization." Black people, free and enslaved, strove to practice freedom in their daily lives by uniting families, by founding churches and schools, and by toiling to acquire homes, businesses, and land.

The context in which freedom could be lived and opposition to slavery could be expressed varied from state to state, and by region within each state. In the more northerly areas, free people of color were numerous and lived in communities that by 1860 were long established, however precariously. Slavery, by contrast, had become moribund in places like Wilmington or Baltimore, and clearly static or declining in most of northern Delaware, western and northern Maryland, and Virginia west of the Blue Ridge and at the state's northern border on the Potomac River. In more southerly areas, such as Delaware's Sussex County, Maryland's tobacco-growing counties on the lower Western Shore, or Virginia's "Southside"—Tidewater and Piedmont counties south of the James River—slavery still defined both state and society.

Sub-regions strongly committed to slavery meshed uneasily with neighboring counties drifting away from the peculiar institution. In large measure, the politics of slavery in each state turned on the relative size of these regions, as did the strength of white anti-slavery sentiments and reactions to them. In Delaware, Quakers and Methodists from the northern counties secured legislation banning the sale of slaves to Deep South states, crippling the economic viability of slavery, but they failed to muster legislative majorities to end slavery altogether. Maryland saw the rise of Baltimore as an island of freedom in a slave society and briefly witnessed the presence of an anti-slavery newspaper and political party. In Virginia, where far fewer blacks gained freedom, slaves nearly brought off the momentous rebellion that bears the name of its planner, Gabriel, and did unleash the far bloodier uprising led by Nat Turner. The latter event, in 1831, produced a major debate on gradual emancipation, but ultimately white Virginians turned to an ever more pro-slavery stance.

The coming of the Civil War and the destruction of slavery illustrate the depth and complexity of conflicts within and between the states of the Chesapeake. Virginians at first rejected secession in February of 1861, then endorsed it after Lincoln's call for soldiers to suppress rebellion two months later, only to split in two over whether to fight for slavery and southern rights. Maryland's loyalties wavered, but the state remained in the Union, while Delaware seems never to have seriously considered secession. African Americans from all three states served the Union cause and helped destroy slavery, but the death knell of bondage rang at different times and in different keys in each state. Virginia's slaves became legally free with the issuance of the Emancipation Proclamation in 1863, if they had not already liberated themselves as "contrabands" earlier in the war. Delaware, the least "disloyal" of the Chesapeake states, waited longest to end slavery. Its politicians refused Lincoln's compensated emancipation plan and allowed freedom to arrive only with the Thirteenth Amendment late in 1865. Marylanders in 1864 voted for a new constitution that abolished slavery, but some whites strove to apply apprenticeship laws to reinstitute slavery in all but name as late as 1868.

African Americans sought in nearly all places and times within the Chesapeake to replace a life in chains with the enjoyment of freedom, but no single trajectory captures the progress of white antislavery. In the 1780s and 1790s, antislavery commonly meant an individual's slow and selective withdrawal from the practice of buying, selling, and holding slaves. Slaveholders might consult their religious convictions, their political consciences, their pocketbooks, or all three in concluding that slavery was an evil for the enslaved and their owners alike. Groups of whites might seek societal reform through legislation or by moral suasion, aiming for slavery's abolition, immediately or gradually, often with accompanying plans to "colonize" freedpeople to Africa. Still others grew ever more attached to black slavery and began by the 1830s to develop comprehensive defenses of the institution as necessary to the preservation of a white republic. By the 1850s, white Virginians had become publicly committed to proslavery ideology, while Marylanders and Delawareans had all but ceased to discuss this most sensitive of issues.

In short, the story of "antislavery in the Chesapeake" is in fact several intertwined narratives. For African Americans, antislavery meant a long struggle to escape slavery and infuse freedom into one's life, in an atmosphere increasingly hostile after 1820 to the aspirations of free people of color. Still, that struggle concluded victoriously, with the final abolition of slavery. For whites, antislavery commenced with brave intentions, flowered momentarily, and then suffered a lingering death, kept barely alive for decades in the guise of colonization. Both the white and black stories, as noted above, display a range of intensity that varies by state and region.

This book relates these stories in a loosely chronological framework. Chapter One sketches the rise of slavery and the origins of a small free black population in the Chesapeake from the early 1600s to around 1770. Chapter Two examines the military and political impact of the American Revolution on slavery in the Chesapeake and asks whether the nation's founders can be credited with putting slavery on the road to extinction, or achieved little or nothing toward that end. Chapters Three and Four deal with opposition to slavery up to about 1815. Chapter Three treats white antislavery activism—religious movements, political antislavery at the state level, and the inchoate process of individual manumissions that freed thousands of blacks in the Chesapeake. Chapter Four's theme is black agency in achieving freedom, and it examines freedom suits, self-purchase, flight, rebellion, and black alliances with the British in the War of 1812 as efforts to achieve liberation.

Chapters Five through Seven cover the years from 1815 to 1860. Chapter Five features the central social expression of white "antislavery" in that period, the colonization movement, paradoxically championed by white antislaveryites while blacks fought determinedly against it. Chapter Six centers on black action against slavery, emphasizing the formation of black churches and the ways in which religious thought informed the actions of black abolitionists, evangelists, and the insurrectionary Nat Turner. Chapter Seven revolves around the "two underground railroads," i.e., slave flight to Canada and kidnapping of free blacks to the Deep South, and considers the importance of black fugitives and their white allies in sharpening tensions between North and South. Chapter Eight concludes the book with a treatment of secession sentiment in the Chesapeake, and the destruction of slavery in the ensuing Civil War.

The experience of the Chesapeake extends the story of antislavery beyond pious Quakers and unbending New England abolitionists like William Lloyd Garrison. The sheer existence of over 150,000 free people of color in the Chesapeake in 1860 constitutes undeniable testimony to the success of blacks and whites in undermining slavery and bringing freedom to at least some African Americans. However muted public expressions of antislavery had become in the late antebellum Chesapeake, two of the three Chesapeake states fought for the Union, as did a considerable portion of the third, that region we have ever since called West Virginia. By largely casting their lot with the Union in the 1860s, black and white citizens of the Chesapeake swung the weight of history in favor of American union and freedom. Perhaps the incessant pressure of antislavery throughout the preceding nine decades helped the nation hold together and resolve, at last, the contradiction of slavery in the land of liberty.

Challenging Slavery in the Chesapeake

CHAPTER 1

The First Africans in the Chesapeake

A CCOUNTS OF AMERICAN SLAVERY typically begin with the fateful episode of a Dutch ship putting in at Jamestown, Virginia, in 1619 and selling "twenty negars" to the colony. These were certainly not the very first enslaved Africans in America: slaves took part in the Spanish expeditions of Ponce de Leon, Narvaez, and Coronado as early as the 1520s.[1] Nonetheless, the events of 1619, like many foundational stories, transmit important truths about the origins of slavery in the territory of the future United States. The Dutch did play an important role in extending the Atlantic slave trade northward from its initial focus on Brazil and the Caribbean. And 1619 marked both the beginning of the tobacco boom that would shape the Chesapeake and the colonists' creation of a legislative body to regulate their affairs, Virginia's House of Burgesses. A tobacco-driven demand for laborers and colonists' ability to make their own laws would be critical in turning Virginia into the first slave society of Britain's mainland colonies.

Although 1619 approximates slavery's origins in North America, the moment of its end as a lawful institution is not in doubt: On December 18, 1865, the ratification of the Thirteenth Amendment to the Constitution terminated slavery's 246-year history. Only in the Chesapeake did slavery run this full historical course. By comparison, that emblematic image of slavery, the cotton plantation of the Deep South, endured no more than seventy-odd years, from around 1790 to 1865, and perhaps no more than forty years or so in the fabled black belts of Alabama and Mississippi. There, plantation slavery, no matter how powerful its stamp on society, was an affair of two or three generations, while in Virginia or Maryland it ran a course of eight or even ten generations, from its rise to prominence in the last quarter of the seventeenth century to its destruction in the 1860s.

Slavery's long history in the Chesapeake critically shaped how people in the region challenged human bondage. The major outbreaks of slave unrest of the revolutionary era came after blacks and whites had already been contending with each other for a century and a half.

The arrival of slaves early in Virginia's history typified the experience of its sister colonies. In Maryland, the first slave may have arrived with the founding voyage of the *Ark* and the *Dove* in 1634, in the person of a "black servant" belonging to Father Andrew White. Delaware, too, dated its initial encounter with slavery to the colony's very first year. A few months after New Sweden appeared with the erection of Fort Christina on the Christiana River in 1638, in today's northern Delaware, a Swedish vessel from the West Indies delivered a slave named Anthony. Sold to New Sweden's Governor Johan Printz, Anthony survived into the 1650s and may have witnessed the Dutch conquest of the colony in 1655.[2]

Dutch control of Delaware would last only nine years, ending with its transfer to England along with the larger New Netherland colony after the second Anglo-Dutch war of 1664–67. During that brief interval, the Dutch West India Company shipped slaves from its West African trading stations to its Caribbean entrepôt of Curacao, whence merchants sailed with mixed cargoes of newly enslaved Africans and slaves seasoned in the West Indies to New Amsterdam on Manhattan Island. From there, at least one group of seventy-odd slaves was marched across New Jersey in 1664 to their final destination in New Amstel, current day Newcastle, Delaware. At the time of the English takeover, there may have been 125 slaves in Delaware, representing as much as 20 per cent of the colony's tiny population.[3]

As the odyssey of the New Amstel slaves suggests, slave traders visited the Chesapeake only sporadically, regarding it as a marginal market where only relatively small lots of slaves could be sold, compared to shiploads of two or three hundred blacks auctioned in Barbados or Bahia. From a trader's perspective, the region lay at the far northwestern end of a long arc of potential destinations that began with the coastline of Brazil. There, sugar growers and later gold miners of the interior hungered for thousands of slaves and paid for them with the highly valuable goods they generated. Some landfalls in Brazil were less than two thousand miles from the Gold Coast, today's Ghana. This journey was short enough that even the horrifically unsafe conditions of the seventeenth century slave trade could generally yield a satisfactory profit, the deaths of one-fifth or more of the slave cargo notwithstanding.[4] In contrast, the Chesapeake lay four to six thousand miles from most of the slave trading ports, seriously increasing the risk that the Middle Passage would claim too many slaves' lives to render a voyage profitable. Besides, the tobacco growers of Maryland and Virginia were not yet rich enough to guarantee a ready market for a dealer's slaves. Planters could purchase the indentures of English or Irish servants far more cheaply, without having to surmount language and culture barriers that complicated making human contact with and extracting labor from Africans. Little wonder then that the Chesapeake attracted few slavers until the 1670s at least, even as English planters in Barbados, Nevis, and Antigua piled up fortunes from slave-grown sugar.

Those Africans who did turn up on the Chesapeake's shores before 1650 found a world in which the words "black" and "slave" had not yet become entirely synonymous. To be sure, Europeans regarded Africans as non-Christian "outsiders," so culturally different as to be potential slaves.[5] But a few, at least, of this "charter generation" of Africans in British North America could overcome perceptions of otherness. Able to easily learn new languages, possessed of valuable skills, and able to adapt culturally, they took advantage of a short-lived historical moment when Chesapeake society was still fluid.

Men like Anthony Johnson would win their way to freedom and even respectability.[6] Johnson appeared in Virginia in 1621, as "Antonio, a Negro," sold as a servant to a planter named Bennett. Through "hard work and known service" to the Bennetts, Antonio garnered the right to farm some land for his own benefit, married, and even baptized his children. By 1640 he had become free, had changed his name to its English style, and had moved across the bay to the Eastern Shore where he soon acquired land. By 1651, Johnson had obtained rights to 250 acres by sponsoring servants to come to Virginia. Eventually he would himself own slaves and would even file suit against a white neighbor who had harbored John Casar, a black slave who had absconded from him. At his death in 1670, Johnson left a substantial estate.[7]

Anthony Johnson and others of the charter generation could work their way out of slavery because it suited the interests of an emerging planter class to let them do so. Tobacco growers of the 1630s and 1640s typically commanded the labor of no more than a few servants or slaves, and these workers were often scattered across isolated patches of land suitable for to- bacco cultivation. Close supervision of servants would have been prohibi- tively expensive, if not impossible. Instead, masters and servants negotiated bargains in which workers traded steady and productive labor for the chance to accumulate property in their spare time. Francis Payne, a slave who ar- rived in the Chesapeake in 1637, freed himself and his wife by 1656 through a series of deals that sprang from Payne's promise to manage his mistress' plantation if she would let him "from tyme to tyme make good use of the ground" for his own benefit. Payne bought his freedom with profits he ex- tracted from the soil, money his mistress used to purchase replacement ser- vants. John Graweere, permitted to keep hogs for his own gain, sold the animals and purchased the freedom of his son. As Ira Berlin notes, men like Johnson, Payne, and Graweere had to combine determination, shrewdness, and the ability to attract the attention of and win the favor of a white pa- tron.[8] The odds against doing so were long: perhaps no more than a few dozen blacks succeeded in becoming free in the first half of the seventeenth century. But even this narrow window of opportunity would soon be shut.

From the 1660s onwards, demographic and economic factors in both the Chesapeake and England combined to spur the expansion of African slavery wherever tobacco could be grown. Planters cleared more land and planted more tobacco, increasing their need for labor. But the supply of indentured servants willing to come to the Chesapeake had begun to de- cline. The rapid population growth of late sixteenth- and early seventeenth-century England leveled off, improving economic opportunities there for young workers. In addition, the slackening stream of English migrants now had a wider array of colonies to choose from: by 1670, South Carolina, New Jersey, and New York were available as destinations, with Pennsylvania to follow in the 1680s. As a consequence of diminishing supply and rising demand, the price of servants rose and the length of their terms of servitude decreased. Simultaneously, the slave trade expanded, particularly the English trade, led by the newly founded Royal African Company, gradually making more slaves available in the Chesapeake. In addition, death rates on the Middle Passage declined in the late seventeenth and early eighteenth centuries, reducing the costs of shipping slaves and their price of purchase.

Slaves remained more expensive than servants, but they could be made to work harder and longer, precisely because they were complete "outsiders": few of the cultural limitations on the exploitation of Europeans by Europeans applied to them. For example, customary sanctions against compelling women to work in the tobacco fields, if imperfectly observed with respect to English servants, simply did not exist with regard to enslaved African women, making their purchase at lower prices than male slaves attractive. The view of black women as economically productive workers, in contradistinction to white women who were classified primarily as domestics, appeared in Virginia law as early as 1643. Free black women were classed with slaves and servants and declared subject to a head tax from which white women were exempted.[9]

The growing attractions of purchasing slaves generated gradual increases in the number of slaves imported to the Chesapeake in the last three decades of the seventeenth century, until it reached a level between three and four hundred a year. Immediately after 1700 this figure jumped to well over a thousand per year. In the region as a whole, the black population rose from perhaps two thousand in 1670 (about 6 per cent of the total) to thirteen thousand by 1700 (about 13 per cent.)[10] By 1720 the region was a quarter black, and by 1740 nearly two-fifths of all residents were slaves. In parts of tidewater Virginia and Maryland slaves were almost half the population.[11] The long term growth of slavery in the Chesapeake thus relied on falling shipping costs for slaves and a rise in their availability from West Africa that coincided with declining numbers of voluntary English migrants.

Before planters could convince themselves to seize on these developments and import Africans, an additional issue arose: investment in and control over human property had to be rendered secure. A successful slave regime required dealing with four questions. First, should servitude for blacks be a lifelong condition, as opposed to the limited terms applicable to indentured servants? Second, would the status of slavery be heritable, i.e., were the children of slaves born free or enslaved? Third, would baptism as a Christian, whereby an African slave crossed one of the cultural boundaries between himself and his master, lead to a slave's emancipation, or not? Finally, would government and society sustain slavery by granting masters broad authority to use violence to control their human chattels?[12]

On the first point, although Anthony Johnson left servitude behind after a term of years, many if not most Africans were treated as slaves for life as early as the 1620s: merchants and planters routinely bought and sold them, and testators devised them as legacies in their wills.[13] But statutory recognition of this practice did not arrive until the 1660s. In 1662, Virginia's House of Burgesses also decided that all children "borne in this country shal be held bond or free only according to the condition of the mother," probably to clarify the status of children with slave mothers and free white fathers, and also to underline that no child of a white woman, even by a slave father, would be a slave. Maryland passed similar statutes in the same decade. In the same vein, a 1667 law stipulated that conversion and baptism as a Christian "doth not alter the condition of a person as to his bondage or his freedom." Maryland followed suit in 1671; Delaware, then governed as part of the Duke of York's American holdings, closed this route of escape from slavery in 1665.[14]

With lifelong slavery established as an institution, lawmakers and courts faced the problem of how to discipline slaves. Extending the term of servitude, a common punishment for indentured servants, held no terrors for those already enslaved for life. In 1669, Virginia declared that if a slave resisted a master or anyone else punishing her or him on the master's orders, and if that slave died while undergoing such punishment, the death would not be a felony, "since it cannot be assumed that prepensed malice ... should induce any man to destroy his estate." By 1723 the few limitations on this already broad exemption from prosecution would be discarded, and there after masters could flog, mutilate, or shoot slaves with impunity. Colonial court records confirm that in fact whites were rarely tried for assaulting or murdering slaves. Eighteenth-century law stood fully behind the master's coercive power.[15]

The practice of using harsh physical punishment to control African servants possibly came to the Chesapeake with migrants from the sugar island of Barbados, who persuaded their neighbors to adopt the severity that was customary in the islands. If so, their suggestions fell on fertile ground, surely in part from the presence of substantial and potentially threatening black resistance to slavery. From the time Africans began to be held as slaves in the Chesapeake, masters complained of blacks who purposely broke tools, pretended illness, or indulged themselves in drunkenness to avoid work. And blacks, like white servants, frequently ran off. Sometimes they decamped together. As early as 1661 Virginia mandated that English indentured servants absconding with slaves have their term of servitude extended so that they could make up the slave's lost labor to his master.[16]

More alarmingly, slaves were clearly willing to fight for their freedom, as evidenced in Nathaniel Bacon's "Rebellion." When troubles with neighboring Indian tribes flared up in 1675, Bacon placed himself at the head of colonists dissatisfied with what they saw as the overly pacific responses of Virginia's royal governor William Berkeley. The dispute between Bacon and Berkeley escalated in 1676 and reached a kind of culmination when Bacon's men burned the capital at Jamestown. Bacon, seeking to strengthen his hand, offered to free and arm servants and slaves of men loyal to Berkeley. As was so often the case with civil wars in slave societies, hundreds of bound men seized the opportunity to break their chains, including at least eighty slaves. When Bacon died in October the rebellion collapsed, but a group of slaves and servants held out and surrendered only after accepting what turned out to be a false promise to honor their free status.[17]

With the specter of armed slave rebels fresh in their minds, white colonists' fears for their safety were further inflamed by the increased number of "outlandish" slaves shipped direct from Africa. Until 1680 most slaves arrived in Virginia or Maryland after spending time in the Caribbean, where many had acquired some familiarity with European cultures and languages. After that date, more and more Royal African Company slavers, as well as interlopers, sailed directly to the Chesapeake from Whydah on the Slave Coast or Calabar in the Bight of Benin.

More difficult to manage because they lacked prolonged contact with Europeans, the newly arrived Africans also encountered planters demanding more work and higher productivity. Faced with declines in the price of tobacco that became particularly severe in the late 1670s and 1680s, masters drove slaves and servants harder, hoping to squeeze from each worker larger amounts of tobacco grown, harvested, and stuffed into large barrels called hogsheads. Legally sanctioned violence against workers who resisted or simply did not understand soon became an integral part of the emerging Chesapeake slave society. Slaveholders hamstrung runaways or lopped off their toes. Blacks who returned a blow for a blow might be flogged to death or shot. Those who openly rebelled against authority could be burned or hung in chains for the crows to pick to pieces.[18]

In this charged atmosphere, social space for men like Anthony Johnson or Francis Payne steadily contracted. White Virginians began to view free blacks as anomalies that might weaken slavery's legitimacy. As part and parcel of slavery's evolving legal code, laws appeared throughout the Chesapeake that marginalized free blacks and firmly subordinated them to whites.[19] Routes to freedom closed. The Virginia burgesses imposed severe restrictions on private acts of manumission in 1691, to prevent individual slaveholders from blurring the image of bondage as lifelong and immutable. In the same year, marriage between a free black and a white person became a crime punishable by banishment from the colony. Should a white woman bear a child out of wedlock to a black man, both she and her child would become servants, the mother to be sold for a term of five years and the child bound out to the age of thirty-one.[20] Should that child herself bear children during her servitude, they, too, would be bound out for thirty-one years. In practice, once taken from their parents, unprotected mixed-race children often slipped into lifetime slavery to masters ever eager for more field hands.[21]

These efforts to prevent the growth of a free black population were matched by measures that circumscribed the lives of those already free. By 1723 free people of color could not legally hold office or vote in any election, nor could they bear arms in local militias. Blacks could not testify in court against whites, a proscription that made them vulnerable to fraud and chicanery in commercial transactions, labor contracts, or debt cases involving whites. Finally, any and all acts of violence against a white person were deemed criminal, even if undertaken in self-defense. Blacks who fell afoul of these laws, or who could not repay debts, were sold into servitude.[22]

Under these circumstances, many legally free blacks spent most of their lives in servitude. Others lost their freedom altogether. Jane Webb, born in the 1680s, was bound out for most of her childhood and had only recently gained her freedom when she chose to marry a slave named Left. Hoping to win her husband's emancipation, Webb agreed in 1703 to bind herself to Thomas Savage for seven years and also promised to bind any children born during her term until their eighteenth birthdays. When Jane's term expired in 1711, Savage refused to free Left. Jane challenged this violation of the agreement in court, but because she could produce no written contract the court accepted Savage's version of events, one that omitted any promise of manumission. When Savage died in 1728 he still possessed Left and several of Jane's children.[23]

Even blacks who held their freedom securely could be ensnared by white trickery and intimidation. When Robert Candlin, a white tenant farmer, told Peter George and Sarah Driggus in 1688 that the legislature had authorized the re-enslavement of all free blacks, the rumor seemed entirely plausible to them. They decided to flee northward from their Northampton County homes to Somerset County, Maryland, where some of Anthony Johnson's descendants had settled. Candlin agreed to hold George and Driggus's property in trust for them, so they signed over land and livestock to him before making good their escape. When the passage of time revealed that Candlin had concocted the re-enslavement story to terrify and defraud his black neighbors, George and Driggus returned and tried, with only limited success, to regain their property through the courts.[24] In this climate, free blacks would remain a tiny and insignificant element in Chesapeake society for most of the eighteenth century. Enslaved Africans and their American-born descendants would typify black life and culture in a crystallizing slave society.

For about two generations, from roughly 1680 to 1730, what might be called the Africanization of the Chesapeake roughly followed a path that had earlier transformed Caribbean islands into sugar-exporting slave societies.[25] Planters intent on increasing tobacco cultivation purchased twice as many male slaves as females. By 1700 that ratio was reflected in the entire slave population. This shortage of women meant that, as in the West Indies, children were few and the population did not replace itself. Deaths exceeded births. In addition to producing an imbalance between the sexes, the slave trade directly contributed to high black mortality rates in the Chesapeake. Men and women who had spent ninety days or longer, sometimes much longer, in the fetid holds of slave ships reached the Chesapeake physically and emotionally drained. Once on shore, they, like white immigrants, confronted a new environment. Newly arrived slaves fell prey to diseases against which they had no immunity, as witnessed by the fact that those who survived for a year were deemed "seasoned" and commanded a higher price if resold. High death rates, low birth rates, and periodic spurts of slave importation meant that by the 1720s, a substantial majority of blacks in the Chesapeake were African-born.[26] By that time, though, a creole generation, i.e., people of African culture but born in the Chesapeake, had come into being. That generation was more evenly balanced between males and females and possessed greater immunity to the endemic microbes of the region. Unlike slaves in the Caribbean they were spared the crushing work routines of the sugar plantations that kept mortality rates perennially high in the islands. For all these reasons, they proved capable of increasing their numbers, and as a result, the need to import slaves gradually abated.[27] By the eve of the

American Revolution perhaps no more than one-fifth of American slaves had begun life in Africa.

Enslaved and shipped across the Atlantic to meet the demands of tobacco cultivation, Africans and their descendants would be distributed across the Chesapeake by the specific demands of that crop. Where the best and most profitable sweet-scented tobacco thrived, in the York and Rappahannock River valleys, clamor for slaves to clear land and plant tobacco reached its highest pitch. Farther north, in the Potomac Valley, and in the counties of Maryland's lower Western and upper Eastern shore, cultivation of lower-priced but still valuable Oronoco tobacco also produced black majorities or near majorities. But in most of Delaware and on Maryland's lower Eastern Shore, the few suitable tobacco lands played out quickly. As planters there diversified into growing grain and raising livestock as early as the 1690s, their desire for slaves moderated and white majorities remained the rule. In Delaware itself, the slave population share peaked at about 25 per cent.[28] On Maryland's lower Eastern Shore, planters developed alternatives to tobacco by generating income through exports and used slaves in moderate numbers to grow grain and harvest timber.[29] As tidewater lands filled up and tobacco leached soils of fertility, settlers pushed westward into central Virginia and western Maryland. By the middle of the eighteenth century this Piedmont region also had substantial numbers of slaves.

What can we know of the lives of these Africans in America, beyond their numbers, geographic distribution, and work in the tobacco, wheat, and corn fields? How did the tenor of those lives inform resistance to enslavement? No brief sketch of slaves' culture can do justice to the varieties of experience that marked the lives of men and women thrown together in the Chesapeake from dozens of West African societies, or their encounters with European settlers of many different stripes. Nevertheless, it is possible to establish a few broad patterns of work, family life, culture, and resistance, as well as changes in those patterns over time, as a way of understanding the evolution and potentialities of slave life in the decades before the American Revolution.

First and foremost, slaves worked, primarily in agricultural labor that intensified and became more regimented over time. On older lands, planters struggled against diminishing yields from worn out soil. In more recently settled areas, clearing timber, pulling stumps, cutting brush, and erecting houses and barns were superimposed on the drudgery of the tobacco field. In the tidewater counties where planters shifted into grain and livestock production, male slaves might at least find variation in their tasks. Some would become plowmen or cowherds, while others sowed, mowed, and threshed grain. Still others mastered carpentry or toiled at the country forges that sharpened plowshares or repaired edge tools and log chains. Slave women, on the other hand, remained as hoe hands tending tobacco, with fewer opportunities to acquire new skills.[30]

Whether slaves took on new tasks or not, they found planters squeezing more time and work from them, especially night work. Hours of shucking corn, grinding grain into meal, carding wool, or retting and hackling flax might follow a sunup to sundown day in the fields. Reductions in rations or floggings loomed as threats for those who shirked. The seventeenth-century approach of encouraging slaves by offering partial control of one's time and a general absence of close supervision in return for productive labor largely fell into disuse. Correspondingly, slaves' ability to generate income through independent economic activity, as practiced by Anthony Johnson and his contemporaries, dwindled. Blacks continued to raise garden vegetables and to hunt and fish to supplement their rations, but few of these goods reached the market.[31]

Planters' demands for more work were not matched by improvements in blacks' material lives. For most of the eighteenth century, slaves lived in cramped, poorly built dwellings, wearing cheap, drab clothing that provided inadequate warmth in winter. They ate a monotonous diet in which corn meal fried into bread anchored a regimen high in starch, low in protein and vitamins. Conditions may have been somewhat better than average for slaves on the largest plantations, and somewhat worse for those who had the misfortune to be owned by small slaveholders who skimped on their workers in the hopes of amassing riches.[32]

Of course not all blacks toiled on plantations. Urban centers began to emerge in the eighteenth-century Chesapeake—capitals like Annapolis and Williamsburg, or entrepôts like Norfolk, Wilmington, and Baltimore. These towns needed workers, and a few blacks there learned crafts such as shipbuilding or ironworking and seized opportunities to engage in independent economic activity, garnering money for overwork, casual labor, or marketing the surpluses from their gardens and hen coops.

Whether in town or countryside, a life of hard work and poor living was not imposed on slaves without a struggle. Newly arrived Africans, at first genuinely unable to comprehend their masters' demands, soon learned to feign ignorance as a way of withholding coerced labor. As a Maryland observer noted of one "saltwater negro," "Let an hundred Men shew him how to hoe, or drive a Wheelbarrow, he'll still take the one by the bottom and the Other by the Wheel."[33] Others ran off, hoping to escape their oppression altogether for a day, a week, or with extraordinary good fortune, forever. Presaging nineteenth-century patterns, slaves with craft skills or knowledge of the roads and waterways were more likely to summon up the courage and self-confidence to flee their masters. Carpenters, smiths, wagoners, and especially boatmen appeared disproportionately often in runaway advertisements.[34] Some of these runaways formed permanent communities. Colonies of maroons maintained a shadowy existence in the Great Dismal Swamp, or in the backcountry mountains. One such outpost was discovered and broken up near modern day Lexington, Virginia, around 1730. Hiding out, though, became more difficult as the zone of settled territory expanded to embrace the Piedmont and the Shenandoah Valley by mid-century.[35]

Occasionally, slaves banded together and conspired to take back their freedom through rebellion. Virginia planters uncovered at least six such plots between 1709 and 1731. Tightened laws and increased night patrols reduced the number of insurrection scares: no slaves were prosecuted for such activity between 1731 and 1750. William Byrd II reflected the restored tranquility of those decades, and contrasted Virginia's situation to other slave societies, confidently asserting that "our negroes are not so numerous or so enterprizeing as to give us any apprehension or uneasiness." Yet, in the

1750s, court records show slaves again being convicted and whipped for insurrectionary talk, e.g., "being privy to an Opinion entertained among many Negroes of their having a Right to their Freedom and not making a discovery thereof."[36]

The outbreak of the French and Indian War in 1754 led Chesapeake slaves to hope that the "French will give them their freedom," and their behavior became "very audacious." Backcountry Maryland and Virginia reported insurrectionary movements among slaves after the French and their Ohio Valley Indian allies routed General Edward Braddock in 1755. These stirrings for liberty twenty years before the American Revolution suggest that blacks in the Chesapeake had deep seated desires for and claims to freedom long before the political conflicts of the 1770s.[37]

Not all challenges to enslavement took the form of confrontation with masters. The decades between 1730 and 1770 also witnessed the painstaking formation of black families and communities within the world of plantation slavery, institutions that bespoke slaves' determination to find and defend cultural spaces that could be both islands of refuge from the slaveholders' world and strong points from which to venture into that world in search of freedom.[38]

The gradual increase in the number of black women in the Chesapeake between 1720 and 1750 created greater possibilities for slaves to form families, though formidable obstacles remained. Slaves who were part of a large holding might hope to find a marital partner on the same plantation, but more commonly, marriage involved people with different masters. In such situations, the slave husband visited his wife by night or on Sundays, and their children for the most part experienced a single-parent household as the property of their mother's master. Slave "marriages" had no legal recognition. Slaves could not claim any of the rights to a spouse's property or support that in part define marriage. Masters could block cross-plantation marriages, and those allowed to exist could be easily destroyed if one partner's master relocated, sold, or hired out that person to a distant place. Even slaves owned by the Chesapeake's largest slaveholders, such as the Carrolls of Maryland or the Carters of Virginia, could be separated by a master's decision to scatter his workers over a host of different "quarters" in groups of eight to twenty, or by periodic reshufflings of the workforce to open up new estates far from one's family and spouse.[39]

One measure of slaves' tenacity in trying to maintain marital ties is that approximately one-third of advertisements for runaways mentioned that they had fled to avoid separation from families.[40]

These difficulties notwithstanding, in the fifty years or so that preceded the American Revolution slaves in the Chesapeake significantly deepened and broadened kinship networks through blood and marriage. If households with two parents and children did not become the norm, they became much more common and the existence of slaves living alone decreased.[41] Extended family connections also appear to have grown, along with the social and cultural resources represented by the presence of grandparents, uncles, aunts, and siblings. By 1800 the existence of slave families had drawn the attention of masters. Some slaveholders began to express and act on reservations against separating husbands and wives by sale. A much smaller number also had scruples about selling very young children apart from their mothers. As in most dealings with slaves, masters' motivations always included self-interest. If a slaveholder paused before selling a man or woman, perhaps it was because doing so would arouse discontent among kinfolk and affect production.[42] The same master might also threaten to sell the mother, wife, or child of any man who ran away. Like any other aspect of slave life, slaves' desires to maintain family ties could be manipulated to the master's advantage. Still, all of these developments, however tenuous and uneven, humanized and individualized slaves in the eyes of their masters, a necessary if not sufficient precondition before the latter considered manumission.

As the formation of families diminished the perception that slaves were "outlandish," so did familiarization with Anglo-American culture. Acculturation began with acquiring the rudiments of English, and soon extended to the whole range of interpersonal skills entailed in sizing up whites and presenting oneself to them. Many creoles—that is, blacks born in the Chesapeake—were described as smooth-tongued or fair-spoken in English and could be perceived as subtle, artful, cunning, ingenious, or shrewd. Slaves were also remarked upon as singers and balladeers, tobacco chewers, card players, or rum drinkers. A few had learned to read and write, and by mid-century, growing numbers took an interest in the practice of Christianity, especially with the advent of the first evangelical preachers. All in all, blacks born in the Chesapeake may have possessed a greater knowledge of the dominant culture of the slaveholders by the eve of the American Revolution than contemporary counterparts in the slave societies of South Carolina or the English Caribbean.[43] By the 1770s, the Africanization of the slave populace had ended, and had yielded to the formation of generations of African Americans.

Cultural influences flowed both ways across the racial boundary. European Americans in the eighteenth-century Chesapeake began to exhibit African cultural attributes in everything from the building of light-frame houses to the appearance of the "Southern" accent, to the popularity of call-and-response rhythms in the evangelical churches to which blacks and whites alike flocked.[44] If whites in the Chesapeake (and South Carolina) began to speak "like negroes" as European travelers noted, we should not assume that they consciously sought to emulate blacks or that they abandoned some or all of their own cultural practices. Likewise, black acquisition of white speech, habits, or vices should not be understood to imply that African ways of living and thinking about the world disappeared entirely or were rejected and replaced with European models.

Instead, it might be valuable to think of Virginia, Maryland, and Delaware as colonies in which enslaved black African Americans had been more thoroughly permeated by white culture than elsewhere. They had been immersed in the destructive element, so to speak, and that perilous experience would prepare them, when opportunity offered during the American Revolution, to seize the day and strive for freedom.

CHAPTER 2

Slavery and the American Revolution

W HAT IMPACT DID THE AMERICAN REVOLUTION have on slavery and what did it mean for slaves? Some historians argue that the revolution sparked an anti-slavery crusade that eventually led to destruction of the institution in the Civil War. They note that, under the pressure of Revolutionary idealism, by 1804 every state north of Maryland had either eliminated slavery altogether or set in motion the gradual emancipation of slaves over time. They point to the Northwest Ordinance's 1787 ban on taking slaves to territories north of the Ohio River. They cite the American abolition of the Atlantic slave trade in 1808. Most famously, the Declaration of Independence proclaimed all men born equal, sentiments Lincoln later invoked in making the Civil War into a war to end slavery. If the founders did not and could not end slavery with a few bold strokes, they did, in this reading of history, do everything within their power to put it on the road to extinction.[1]

An alternative view argues that the revolution resulted in slaveholders gaining political mastery of half of the new republic and using their power to fasten their grip more tightly on slaves. Independence insulated them from the effects of British anti-slavery movements of the nineteenth century, and ended British restraints on westward expansion, fostering the rapid growth of slavery in an empire stretching from Kentucky to Texas. If the Declaration trumpeted equality, the Constitution dealt matter-of-factly with slavery, contained a fugitive slave provision, and protected the importation of slaves for at least twenty years, even if it avoided using the word "slave."

The approximately half million enslaved African Americans of British North America, concentrated in five coastal colonies from Maryland to Georgia, swelled by 1860 to four million slaves in seventeen states and territories encompassing roughly a million square miles. Leaving aside demography, did not Jefferson Davis and his Confederate colleagues see themselves as the true heirs of the Revolution, fighting to defend its key political principle, the right of men to hold and use property as they saw fit, without governmental restraint?[2]

A more open-ended answer to the question is that the American Revolution made slavery into a problem.[3] Before the revolution, colonial Americans enthusiastically bought and sold slaves and employed them in a multitude of occupations. Only a handful of people, mostly Quakers, had even begun to question the morality of slaveholding. Up to the 1760s, the number of slaves grew in all of the North American colonies.[4] Then came the crisis in imperial relations with Great Britain, and a rising sense that American colonists faced so-called political slavery if they did not resist attempts by king and Parliament to encroach on their natural rights.

Natural rights philosophy was by no means new in the 1760s or 1770s, but its repeated invocation by Americans in defense of self-government, and the insistence that those deprived of natural rights were "slaves," made more and more Americans acutely aware that their practice contradicted their ideals. How could they answer Englishman Samuel Johnson's sarcastic question about why "the loudest yelps for liberty are heard from the drivers of negroes"?[1] During and after the Revolution, slaveholders needed to explain or surmount the "problem" of slavery in a land of liberty. Moreover, those who succeeded in persuading themselves that slaveholding was consistent with the ideals of freedom still faced the task of coercing submission from the enslaved, which now became far more difficult. African Americans could appropriate revolutionary concepts to break the chains that bound them. When colonial Americans marched and sang to praise liberty, or fought to defend it, some voices in the crowds—and fingers on musket triggers—were black.

If the ideas of the American Revolution made slavery problematic, far more so did the war itself. Americans won independence only after eight years in which the patriots, aided by the French, squared off against the British and their loyalist supporters. Early in the contest both sides, searching for more manpower, sought to draw slaves to their banners. Thousands of slaves headed for British lines seeking personal freedom as reward for their services, and perhaps hoping that a British victory might bring down the whole framework of slavery. Others thought their chances for liberation were better if they joined the American forces. By the end of the war in 1783, between fifty and one hundred thousand slaves had fled their masters, and untold thousands more had gained a measure of autonomy within slavery as the disruptions of war weakened owners' control. As John Francis Mercer of Virginia's Northern Neck remarked, it became prudent to improve the conditions of the slaves, lest no slaves remain.[5]

When American independence was at last recognized, slaveholders in large sections of the new nation discovered that their authority was now tenuous at best. They not only had to repair the breakdown in control over slaves, they also had to come to terms with a substantial and rapidly growing population of free people of color, people whose very existence threatened the fabric of slavery.

Finally, the separation of America from the British Empire removed the American economy from the confining but sheltering atmosphere of Britain's empire. British policies had encouraged production of slave-grown tobacco, rice, indigo, and naval stores by offering protected markets in the metropolis. The loss of those markets forced many to rethink the economic rationale of slaveholding and plantation agriculture.

In short, the Revolution undermined slavery by impeaching it on philosophical grounds, by momentarily shattering slaveholders' political and social control, and by removing some of its economic underpinnings. Where slaves and their allies could exploit all these weaknesses, slavery was killed off, as in the Northeast.[6] In the Deep South, by contrast, slaveholders quickly rallied their forces, hunted down fugitives and maroons, found new lands and crops with which to prosper, and crafted a new ideology that championed African slavery as the foundation for white American liberty. Slavery took on renewed strength there and flourished from the late 1780s onward.[7]

In the middle ground of the Chesapeake, struggles over slavery generated by the Revolution produced no decisive outcome. To be sure, Virginia,
Maryland, and Delaware remained slaveholding states down to the Civil
War, turning aside calls for gradual emancipation. In many ways, slavery
grew stronger in the decades after the revolution, not least because slaveholders adapted successfully to postwar conditions. When stagnant tobacco
markets drained Chesapeake slavery of its first and greatest source of profits, slaveowners in the Piedmont and on the Eastern Shore rebounded by
raising new crops. Surplus agricultural workers were put to work in crafts
and manufacturing, or as casual laborers in the cities and towns that grew
up in response to economic diversification. Slavery gradually regained a
firm economic foundation, especially when new settlements in the booming Southwest began to provide reliable markets for surplus slaves from the
Chesapeake.

If slavery did not wither in the revolutionary Chesapeake, neither could
the door to freedom be kept firmly shut. Substantial numbers of African
Americans in all three states gained freedom through manumission and
self-purchase, taking advantage of opportunities to earn money in the
region's changing economy and buying themselves out of slavery during
downturns in the domestic slave trade. Once free, they carved out lives for
themselves in an often hostile legal and social climate. Many more lived free
by fleeing their masters and swelling the black populations not only of free-
state cities and towns like New York, Philadelphia, Lancaster, and Harrisburg, but also the major towns of the Chesapeake—Baltimore, Wilmington,
Richmond, and Norfolk. By 1815 free people of color had constructed large
communities in a region of the new republic that nonetheless remained
firmly under the direction and control of slaveholders.[8]

Blacks' efforts to stake their own claims to liberty, like those of America's
white revolutionaries, can be traced to the very beginnings of the imperial
crisis with Britain. In some parts of the American colonies, white resistance
to British plans for governmental control and increased taxation quickly
generated a resonating black response. Residents of Charleston, South Carolina, protesting the Stamp Act in January 1766, were surprised and disturbed

to see slaves joining the crowds in the streets chanting for liberty. Beginning in 1770, free people of color and slaves in Massachusetts sought to turn the imperial crisis to their benefit. Some, including Prince Hall, petitioned the Massachusetts legislature for an end to African chattel slavery, in consonance with that body's resistance to the political enslavement of white citizens. Others hoped to liberate themselves by bearing arms should fighting break out. One group offered its services to General Thomas Gage, the royal governor of Massachusetts.[9]

In Virginia, home to 180,000 slaves in the 1770s, concern about slave unrest long predated the imperial crisis. During the French and Indian War (1754–63) and in the ensuing conflict with Indians known as Pontiac's War (1763–65) white Virginians feared that slaves would make common cause with the Indians. Rumors of conspiracies and prosecutions for slave insurrections rose in volume through the late 1760s and early 1770s. By 1772 the Virginia House of Burgesses sought to tax the slave trade to reduce the number of blacks entering the colony and thereby diminish fears of slave rebellion. Acting on royal instructions aimed at protecting English merchants, Virginia's new governor, John Murray, Earl of Dunmore, vetoed this restriction on the slave trade.[10]

Black stirrings continued unabated as relations between Britain and the North American colonies worsened. By late 1774, Parliament had passed the Coercive Acts to punish Boston for its famous Tea Party. The Continental Congress responded with a call to boycott exports and imports to and from Britain. Blacks began taking their own measures in anticipation of open conflict. "If American and Britain should come to an hostile rupture, an insurrection among the slaves may and will be promoted," James Madison reported in November. "In one of our counties lately a few of those unhappy wretches met together and chose a leader who was to conduct them when the British Troops should arrive."[11] In the spring of 1775 murmurs of a possible black rising came from Maryland's Eastern Shore. A Dorchester County grand jury learned that a disaffected wheelwright, John Simmons, believing that "the gentlemen were intending to make us all fight for their lands and negroes," had said, "damn them if I had a few more white people to join me I could get all the negroes in the county to back us, and they would do more good in the night than the white people could do in the day." In the fall of that year, the county's Committee of Inspection ordered a sweep through slave quarters that netted more than eighty guns, swords, and other weapons.[12] Slaves listening to the intensifying argument between Britain and America applied the rhetoric of resistance to their own situation.

Blacks advanced from watchful waiting to open resistance thanks to Governor Dunmore's actions in Williamsburg. In 1774, Dunmore had momentarily won the applause of Virginians with the successful prosecution of an Indian war in the Ohio Valley, where his victories improved prospects for settlement in Kentucky and western Virginia, but by the spring of 1775, Dunmore and the House of Burgesses were at loggerheads over the larger issues of the imperial crisis. Sensing threat, Dunmore on April 21, 1775, had all the gunpowder removed from the colonial magazine in Williamsburg to a royal navy ship, HMS *Magdalen*. Gathering near the governor's palace to protest the action, a hostile crowd quieted hopefully as a delegation of colonial legislators led by Peyton Randolph, Speaker of the House of Burgesses, went inside to parley with Dunmore. Hope turned to dismay when the delegates reappeared without a deal to get the gunpowder back. Then dismay turned to anger as word spread that Dunmore had threatened to arm and perhaps to free blacks who came to his banner, should the dispute escalate into a military confrontation. The governor's desperate move hit its mark. Legislators retreated in the face of possible black insurrection. That same month conspiracy rumors and insurrection trials popped up in Prince Edward County, Chesterfield County, and Williamsburg itself. The legislators allowed Dunmore to hang onto the munitions for the time being.

Upcountry reaction to Dunmore's seizure of the powder provoked yet another showdown. Militia companies from the Northern Neck, Albemarle County, and elsewhere voted to march on Williamsburg to recover the powder. When a Hanover County group led by Patrick Henry began tramping towards the capital, Dunmore publicly warned on April 28 that if any armed men came within thirty miles of Williamsburg he would raise the slaves to defend his position. Once again legislative leaders retreated, this time convincing the Hanover County men to stop their advance. Dunmore had secured his gunpowder and faced down his opposition, but any chance that he could repair his relations with the Virginia populace was rapidly evaporating.

White Virginians were enraged and terrified by the prospect of a black rebellion fomented by a British governor and aided by British arms. From tutor-diarist Philip Fithian to rebel leader Richard Henry Lee, observers agreed that Dunmore's move to unleash slaves upon their masters drove many ambivalent Virginians toward open confrontation and permanent separation from England. Revolutionary committees in Richmond and Louisa Counties, for example, noted the importance of clashes at Lexington and Concord and Dunmore's seizure of the gunpowder, but they were especially alarmed at "the declaration . . . made for raising and freeing the slaves."[13] When the colonists proclaimed their independence in 1776, one of the gravest charges they laid against King George III was that he had "raised insurrections" amongst the slaves against his own subjects. The bitterness in that clause of the Declaration of Independence cannot be dismissed as the exaggerated fears of overwrought white Virginians or brushed aside as propaganda ornamented with Jeffersonian rhetorical flourish. Both Dunmore and his opponents had learned by 1776 that slaves would fight for their freedom.

As early as April 1775 slaves offered Dunmore their services should fighting erupt. Dunmore at first turned them away, but after he abandoned the governor's palace for the safety of the HMS *Fowey*, on June 8, he began to welcome the blacks who flocked to his standard. By mid-summer more than three hundred slaves had reached Dunmore, and Virginia vessels had intercepted many more en route in canoes, rowboats, and cutters. When a detachment of British regulars and a few ships reached Norfolk on July 31, black sailors and pilots immediately came forward to join them. Demands by Norfolk slaveholders for return of such fugitives were met by ambiguous promises that of course the property of loyal subjects would be rendered up.[14]

Men like Joseph Harris, a slave pilot who escaped to the British in July 1775, aided Dunmore in controlling the mouth of the Chesapeake from a

1775

By His Excellency the Right Honorable JOHN Earl of DUNMORE, His
Majesty's Lieutenant and Governor General of the Colony and Dominion of
VIRGINIA, and Vice Admiral of the fame.

A PROCLAMATION.

AS I have ever entertained Hopes, that an Accommodation might have
taken Place between GREAT-BRITAIN and this Colony, without being
compelled by my Duty to this most disagreeable but now absolutely neceſſary
Step, rendered ſo by a Body of armed Men unlawfully aſſembled, firing on His
MAJESTY's Tenders, and the formation of an Army, and that Army now on
their March to attack His Majesty's Troops and destroy the well diſpoſed Subjects of this Colony. To defeat ſuch treaſonable Purpoſes, and that all ſuch
Traitors, and their Abettors, may be brought to Juſtice, and that the Peace, and
good Order of this Colony may be again reſtored, which the ordinary Courſe
of the Civil Law is unable to effect; I have thought fit to iſſue this my Proclamation, hereby declaring, that until the aforeſaid good Purpoſes can be obtained, I do in Virtue of the Power and Authority to ME given, by His MAJE-
STY, determine to execute Martial Law, and cauſe the ſame to be executed
throughout this Colony: and to the end that Peace and good Order may the
ſooner be reſtored, I do require every Perſon capable of bearing Arms, to reſort
to His MAJESTY's STANDARD, or be looked upon as Traitors to His
MAJESTY's Crown and Government, and thereby become liable to the Penalty
the Law inflicts upon ſuch Offences; ſuch as forfeiture of Life, confiſcation of
Lands, &c. &c. And I do hereby further declare all indented Servants, Negroes,
or others, (appertaining to Rebels,) free that are able and willing to bear Arms,
they joining His MAJESTY's Troops as ſoon as may be, for the more ſpeedily
reducing this Colony to a proper Senſe of their Duty, to His MAJESTY's
Crown and Dignity. I do further order, and require, all His MAJESTY's Leige
Subjects, to retain their Quitrents, or any other Taxes due or that may become
due, in their own Cuſtody, till ſuch Time as Peace may be again reſtored to this
at preſent moſt unhappy Country, or demanded of them for their former ſalu-
tary Purpoſes, by Officers properly authoriſed to receive the ſame.

GIVEN under my Hand on board the Ship WILLIAM, off Norfolk,
the 7th Day of NOVEMBER, in the SIXTEENTH Year of His Majesty's Reign.

DUNMORE.

(GOD ſave the KING.)

base at Norfolk. Harris guided British raids against rebel-held plantations, ships, and stores. Like Harris, many of the raiders were former slaves who knew the local territory thoroughly, and who used that knowledge to help still more blacks flee to the British. As a Norfolk correspondent wrote, "Dunmore sails up and down the river and where he finds a defenceless place, he lands, plunders the plantation and carries off the negroes." These forays typically attracted one or two runaways at a time, but sometimes achieved more dramatic results. In April 1776, John Willoughby reported the loss of all of his eighty-seven slaves shortly after a local committee of safety had ordered that slaves in areas threatened by Dunmore's raids be removed inland. The people on Willoughby's plantation passed up earlier opportunities to join Dunmore, but when faced with the possibility of being separated by relocation, in addition to losing their option to run to the British, they abandoned caution and fled.[15]

In addition to taking part in harassing raids, African American pioneer companies fortified and defended Dunmore's position in and around Norfolk. Only in autumn did Dunmore obtain enough muskets to outfit several companies of black soldiers and take the offensive. On November 15 a mixed force of British regulars and blacks fought a sharp skirmish with patriot militia of Princess Anne County at Kemp's Landing. In the rapid rout of the militia, one ex-slave had the satisfaction of capturing his former master, Colonel Joseph Hutchings.[16]

With a victory to bolster his position, Dunmore ordered the printing of a proclamation composed on November 7, declaring "all indented servants, Negroes, or others (appertaining to Rebels,) free, that are able and willing to bear arms, they joining His Majesty's Troops, as soon as may be, for the more speedily reducing the Colony to a proper sense of their duty, to His Majesty's crown and dignity." Dunmore no doubt hoped to cow American rebels while attracting enough loyalists and disaffected servants and

Opposite: Lord Dunmore's Proclamation of November 1775 offered to free and arm slaves who rallied to his banner. (The Albert and Shirley Small Special Collections Library, University of Virginia Library.)

slaves to reassert control of Virginia, or at least to maintain his base in Norfolk. He certainly did not intend to end slavery. After all, the principal value of the colonies to Britain lay in their exports of slave-grown produce.

Virginia's revolutionary leaders quickly saw the danger in Dunmore's proclamation and reacted with a mixed volley of threat and persuasion to forestall slave escapes. The *Virginia Gazette* of November 23, 1775, spoke directly to slaves contemplating flight, telling them of the horrors to expect "should they be so weak and wicked as to comply with what lord Dunmore requires." The writer of the article, a vice-president of the Virginia Committee of Safety named John Page, predicted that the British would use slaves and then sell them to the West Indies when the crisis was over, or return them to their masters. At least one black observer agreed with Page. John Hope, also known as Barber Caesar or Caesar Hope, wondered aloud in the pages of the *Gazette* why any slave would join Dunmore when the governor had not freed his own slaves. Page noted that Dunmore promised freedom only to arms-bearing men and that men who went to Dunmore would be leaving their wives and children in the hands of "an enraged and injured people."

Virginians also enacted laws to punish and intimidate fugitives. They decreed the death penalty for ex-slaves taken captive while bearing arms for the British, and sale to the West Indies or punitive labor in the colony's lead mines in other cases. On the other hand they promised mercy to those who returned on their own within ten days of absconding. These laws were not mere bluster. Two runaways who mistook a Virginia ship for one of the British fleet and declared their sympathies with Dunmore were captured, tried, and summarily executed to discourage others from emulating them. In Maryland, royal governor Robert Eden reported that revolutionary leaders attempted to cut off all correspondence with Virginia, to prevent slaves from learning of Dunmore's proclamation.[17]

Despite the risks, blacks responded to Dunmore's offer. Nearly one thousand blacks joined the "Ethiopian Regiment," donning uniforms emblazoned with the slogan "Liberty to Slaves." Though not specifically promised freedom, many women and other non-combatants also flocked to Dunmore's camp.[18] Word of his plan to enlist blacks as soldiers spread well beyond the

Sketch of an African American soldier in the Revolutionary War, by DeVerger. (Anne S. K. Brown Military Collection, Brown University Library.)

Chesapeake by December. A Philadelphia newspaper reported a clash between a "gentlewoman" and a black man who refused to yield the sidewalk to her. When she reprimanded him for insulting behavior, the black jeered, "Stay you d[amne]d white bitch 'till Lord Dunmore and his black regiment come, and then we will see who is to take the wall." By 1776 slaveowners as far west as Frederick County, Maryland, reported flights. In troubled Dorchester County, three slaves were hanged, drawn, and quartered for killing a white in a failed attempt to reach Dunmore.[19]

A few new recruits arrived in time to participate in the battle of Great Bridge, on December 9, fought at a crossing of the Elizabeth River ten miles below Norfolk. Here Virginians turned the tables, defeating Dunmore and compelling him to abandon the town. After Great Bridge, the British would experience difficulty in maintaining any kind of land base. Successively driven from islands near the mouths of the Rappahannock and Potomac, Dunmore's men spent many weeks cooped up on the ships, where fevers and small pox ravaged them. In August 1776, Dunmore finally abandoned the Chesapeake, sailing for New York with several hundred black survivors.

While the Ethiopian Regiment melted away as an official military unit, ex-slaves from the Chesapeake continued to fight for the British as partisans and raiders, particularly around New York City, the largest British base. When the British evacuated New York in 1783, blacks from the Chesapeake joined the large stream of loyalists who departed with the British army and fleet for Nova Scotia and New Brunswick.

Lord Dunmore's attempt to suppress American rebels with liberated black soldiers set a pattern for future British campaigns in the Chesapeake, Carolinas, and Georgia. Needing substantial local support to reassert control over the colonies, the British looked first to free white colonists. When loyalists proved too weak a force to rely upon, British commanders turned with some reluctance to the use of African Americans as military laborers and, more rarely, gun-carrying soldiers. At no point did they conceive of encouraging a full-scale slave insurrection, or of creating a slave army, as opposed to detachments of pioneers, rangers, and marines.

The British had to strike a delicate balance. Their mission in America depended on restoring the colonies to their former role as loyal and submissive producers of tropical staples and consumers of British manufactures. Fomenting a slave insurrection might defeat the Americans but would surely also destroy the plantation economy that made the southern colonies in particular so valuable a possession. Accordingly, the British sought to obtain the maximum military and propaganda value from black allies with the minimum disruption, offering freedom selectively, but only to men fleeing masters in rebellion. No general emancipation was contemplated. Dunmore himself freed none of the slaves he owned.[20]

This British policy compelled Maryland, Virginia, and other slave-filled colonies to commit more men to maintaining control of slaves and fewer to fighting the redcoats. It may also have dampened the response of black people to British freedom proclamations. Many, perhaps the majority, adopted a "wait-and-see" attitude, striving above all to avoid separation from home and family. Still, slaves raced to the British wherever troops or ships flying His Majesty's colors appeared, undeterred by stories of captives being sold to the West Indies. Nor were runaways dissuaded by the knowledge that short rations, hard labor, and a variety of camp fevers awaited most who reached the British, with eventual freedom a distant and extremely uncertain prospect. No matter how assiduously American newspapers, militia leaders, and public officials spread word of the ill-treatment and death awaiting those who joined the British, escape and insurrection attempts mushroomed whenever military operations returned to the Chesapeake.

In February 1777, a small British fleet operating in the lower Chesapeake took on board some three hundred runaways from Northumberland, Gloucester, and Lancaster Counties. A month later, Toney, Ben and eight other African Americans in Essex County were tried on charges of conspiracy and insurrection. Anticipating further British activity in the bay, these ten held secret meetings to recruit slaves "for purposes unknown and training them to arms and instructing them in Military Discipline." Historian Philip Schwarz has concluded that the men were trying to create a guerrilla force to battle the local militia. Four of the conspirators were hanged; six others were whipped or had their ears cropped.[21]

In the summer the Chesapeake briefly became the most active theater of the war as General Howe sailed his army up the bay, heading for Philadelphia. Keeping his warships and troop transports well away from shore to avoid the shoals, Howe at first attracted relatively few fugitives. Once his fleet passed the mouth of the Patuxent, though, where the bay narrows, slaves could reach Howe more easily. Local militias in Maryland tried to block such escapes, intercepting canoes and skiffs, and burning unsecured small boats. When Howe's men landed at the head of the bay, Delaware militias joined the effort to stem the flow of disaffected blacks. Maryland officials complained that in addition to the lure of the British army and navy, they had to contend with privateers who trailed in Howe's wake, making forays into the tidal rivers and taking on board slaves from the interior. Many of these luckless people were sold into slavery in the West Indies. Those fortunate enough to reach Howe advanced with him to Philadelphia, where the British formed black pioneer companies to construct defenses, clean the streets, and remove public nuisances during their occupation of the city.[22]

The British next invaded the Chesapeake in 1779. A raiding expedition entered the bay to seize food, supplies, and horses and to divert possible reinforcements to American troops in South Carolina. Admiral Collier and General Matthews quickly seized Portsmouth, then systematically plundered the surrounding area. When they departed in August, they took at least a thousand ex-slaves with them, including many women and children. Farther north, residents of the Eastern Shore town of Salisbury, Maryland, reported Negroes embarking on British boats that had come twenty miles up the Wicomico River. The appearance of British ships off St. Mary's County on Maryland's lower Western Shore likewise led blacks to "abandon the Service of their Masters who live on the Waters."[23]

At the end of 1780 yet another British force appeared off the Virginia Capes, this time led by Benedict Arnold, a few months after his change of sides in the war. Arnold, like Matthews, aimed to prevent Virginians from assisting General Nathanael Greene's southern Continental army and thereby to give General Cornwallis a freer hand in his North Carolina campaign. Unopposed, Arnold swept up the James River as far as Richmond. Meanwhile, renewed naval raids struck hard at the tidewater plantations. In April 1781, when a British sloop of war anchored in the Potomac near Mount Vernon, seventeen of George Washington's slaves at least temporarily obtained their freedom by rowing out to the ship. Despite entreaties from Lund Washington, a cousin of the general's who managed the estate throughout the war, none of the fourteen men and three women voluntarily returned. In other upriver raids, largely black-crewed barges worked up the Patuxent to Benedict and Lower Marlboro, looting the town and aiding slaves in escaping from the surrounding countryside. Similar attacks repeatedly hit Dorchester, Somerset, and Worcester Counties on the Eastern Shore.[24]

In May, Cornwallis brought his army north into Virginia, ranging inland to Petersburg, Richmond, and Albemarle Courthouse before taking position at Yorktown in early August. Large numbers of blacks joined Cornwallis, despite efforts by slaveholders to "refugee" their chattels by taking them upcountry. Estimates are imprecise, but General Henry Clinton, Cornwallis's superior, thought "thousands of poor blacks" were with him.

Cornwallis put these runaways to work serving British officers, maintaining latrines, slaughtering cattle, cooking, or digging trenches for the army's defense as Washington and Rochambeau surrounded and besieged Yorktown. According to Lafayette, blacks proved skillful at impressing patriot horses. "Nothing but a treaty of alliance with the Negroes can find us dragoon horses. . . . It is by this means the enemy have so formidable a Cavalry," he informed Washington.[25]

Like most American slaveholders, Cornwallis saw Africans as better able than whites to bear heavy work in the hot weather of summer, but, unlike the Virginians, Cornwallis could not supply his black workers with adequate food. As the British withdrew from positions in Portsmouth, concentrating their forces at Yorktown, black rations were reduced. Smallpox swept through the besieged camp, hitting undernourished blacks especially hard. Finally, in early October, Cornwallis expelled many erstwhile black allies from his lines. "We had used them to good advantage," Hessian officer Johann Ewald observed, "and now with fear and trembling, they had to face the reward of their cruel masters."[26]

When the British surrendered, African Americans who had cast their lot with Cornwallis faced chaotic uncertainty. Some were returned to service with former owners, including three or four of the runaways from Mount Vernon. Others were peremptorily seized as spoils of war by American soldiers, despite orders to the contrary from Washington. Still others made their way to British ships in the bay, exploiting a loophole in the articles of capitulation that provided for the return of American property in the hands of the British garrison but said nothing about navy vessels.

The departing French army under Count Rochambeau offered another chance to escape reenslavement. Sustained correspondence between Rochambeau and Washington, and also with Virginia governor Benjamin Harrison, suggests that French officers and men were reluctant to hand over black people who had come within their lines. In July 1782, Harrison, dismayed at French unwillingness to render up slaves, complained to Washington: "I am wearied out without being able to procure them." Blacks were remaining with the French, "either for want of their owners having any

The Marquis de Lafayette with James, who took the surname Lafayette after obtaining his freedom in recognition for his services to the American cause. Oil portrait, Jean-Baptiste Le Paon. (Lafayette College.)

proof at hand or the negroes declaring themselves free." Yet some who found a haven with Rochambeau's men ultimately traded slavery in Virginia tobacco fields for a worse fate on sugar plantations in St. Domingue or

Martinique, for many French soldiers had no more aversion than Americans or the British to "putting slaves in their pocket." Nonetheless, both at Yorktown and during the French army's march north to New York in 1782, its ranks proved a magnet for blacks seeking freedom in the turmoil of revolution, as runaway advertisements from Baltimore and Annapolis slaveowners testify.[27]

As the war wound down to its conclusion in late 1782, British and American negotiators in Paris signed preliminary articles of peace committing the British to leave all the places they occupied without "carrying away any negroes" belonging to Americans. Slaveholders from Virginia, Maryland, and elsewhere congregated in New York, one of the last major British strongholds, "seizing upon their slaves in the streets . . . or even dragging them from their beds." Yet revolutionaries hoping to recover their slaves in New York or elsewhere would be largely disappointed. British General Guy Carleton interpreted the treaty as applying only to African Americans who had joined the British after the signing of the articles, on November 30, 1782. Despite strong objections from Washington, Carleton held to this view, "fill[ing] us with joy and gratitude" according to one black fugitive.[28] By the time the last British soldiers left New York on November 25, 1783, between three and five thousand African Americans had departed with them, many of them former slaves of Chesapeake masters. Similar evacuations of Charleston, Savannah, and East Florida provided a passage to freedom for another ten to twelve thousand blacks.[29]

Some of the emigrants had fought to win personal liberty for as long as eight years; others had perhaps slipped inside the British lines only days before embarkation and managed to pass as free. A few had been free before the war began. Shadrack Furman, a onetime farmer in Accomac County on Virginia's Eastern Shore, would secure a pension from the British government for his loyalty to the crown and for services during the war, including the capture of American spies in Portsmouth during Dunmore's time there in 1776.[30]

Those who landed in Nova Scotia would endure many years of frustration before realizing dreams of independence. Blacks, like other loyalists, were promised land in Nova Scotia as a reward for service or compensation for losses. Veterans were entitled to one hundred acres of land, at no cost. Colonial officials in Nova Scotia, though, overwhelmed by having to absorb more than thirty thousand new settlers, moved slowly. Blacks were among the last to be situated and often received tracts too stony to farm. By 1791 more than a thousand black emigrants were ready to abandon Nova Scotia and to accept abolitionist Thomas Clarkson's offer of resettlement in a proposed new colony in West Africa. In 1792, black loyalists took ship once more, bound for Sierra Leone, where their descendants still reside.[31] Still other blacks settled and remained in England after the war, chiefly in London and other seaports, while some returned to Germany with regiments from Brunswick or Hesse to which they had attached themselves.

The freed slaves who sailed with the British evacuation fleets made up only a fraction of the total losses to American slaveholders during the Revolution. Contemporaries estimated that as many as 55,000 blacks had joined or been captured by the British, or about one in ten slaves in the former colonies.[32] Thousands more had fled to towns and cities to pass as free, or had lost their lives during the conflict. Jefferson gave the number of fugitives from Virginia alone at 30,000, a claim regarded by some historians as hyperbolic. Perhaps Jefferson extrapolated from his own losses: no fewer than thirty of his slaves ran to or were taken by the British.[33]

These departures, catastrophic though they were for some slaveholders, clearly did not destroy the viability of slavery in the Chesapeake. Indeed, moving slaves to the backcountry speeded the institution's penetration of the Piedmont and the Shenandoah Valley and shored up white political support for slavery by creating new constituencies who owned or hired slaves.

Blacks fleeing to British forces risked all to gain all. If they reached British lines they had a chance to gain legally recognized freedom. They might even become soldiers and be given land of their own after the war. But this path to freedom and respectability lay strewn with obstacles. Many owners removed slaves from the coast to the Piedmont to discourage flight. In the tidewater counties, militias, patrols, and state navies guarded roads and rivers. If caught by patriots, runaways might be consigned to the state lead mines or worse, sold to be cane cutters or salt rakers in the Indies. Reaching the British safely brought no guarantee of freedom, either. Escapees were snatched by British officers and resold, or distributed to loyalists as rewards for faithful service. Those who did establish themselves as free persons still had to face the perils of battle, the wasting diseases of army camp life, and the very real possibility of re-enslavement or execution if recaptured by the Americans. Under these daunting circumstances, the fact that so many ran to the British offers strong testimony for the breadth and depth of the black drive for independence.

Not all blacks pursued freedom by supporting the British, of course. According to historian Benjamin Quarles, as many as five thousand African Americans fought for the patriot cause. Most of them hailed from northern colonies with relatively few slaves. They served in Continental army regiments, as militia men, and as sailors in the American and state navies. Thousands more, like counterparts with British forces, performed military labor, piloted ships, guided troops, delivered messages, and spied on the enemy. Many of those who bore arms were free people of color who enlisted or were drafted into a military unit. Other free blacks accepted bounties from white draftees and served as substitutes for them.

For slaves, military service could hold out the prospect of freedom. Some northern colonies accepted black recruits on the condition that military service would release them from servitude. In Virginia, unwillingness to arm or emancipate slaves dictated that only free blacks could join state regiments. Blacks who volunteered were required by a 1777 law to show recruiting officers a certificate of freedom signed by a magistrate, a measure aimed at preventing slaves from running away to join the army in the hopes of passing as free.[34]

At least one slave successfully evaded the law. William Ferguson, formerly known as Toby, ran from his master, James Wimbish, in 1773. Remaining at large for five years, he then enlisted as a free man in a Virginia regiment and served until legally discharged. When Wimbish finally tracked down his ex-slave in 1785, he did the handsome thing, formally manumitting Ferguson in recognition of his services to the revolutionary cause.[35]

Owners, too, connived at undercutting the ban on slave enlistments. A slaveholder who sought to avoid being called up could present one of his slaves as a free person for substitute service, perhaps privately promising to free the man in question at the end of the war. Some owners failed to keep their end of these bargains, as evidenced by a 1783 Virginia statute mandating freedom to slave veterans who had served as substitutes.[36]

Still other slaves labored for the revolution as publicly owned workers, either bought from their masters or impressed into service in much the same manner used to obtain foodstuffs or horses. Virginia used public slaves extensively as military laborers, and Maryland in 1781 actually impressed slaves into its armed forces, compensating owners for their loss but making no promises of freedom to black men thus drafted.[37] Finally, some slaves, particularly those confiscated from loyalist slaveholders, found themselves offered up as enlistment bonuses to white soldiers toward the end of the eight-year war, as disillusionment with the long conflict made securing replacements for state regiments ever more difficult. In sum, most black people who aided the Revolution hefted axes or spades rather than shouldering muskets, or drove supply wagons rather than mounting cavalry horses.

A few African Americans managed to earn praise, glory, and the reward of individual freedom for their wartime accomplishments. James, slave of William Armistead of New Kent County, Virginia, enlisted in 1781 with his master's permission and served with the young Marquis de Lafayette, who employed him as a spy and to commandeer horses. Impressed by James's acumen and courage, Lafayette wrote a testimonial that helped influence the Virginia legislature to free him after the war. Renaming himself James Lafayette, the freedman lived into the 1820s, eventually receiving a war pension and renewing his acquaintance with the marquis on his return visit to the United States in 1824.[38] Saul Matthews, another slave spy, repeatedly penetrated Cornwallis's lines in the Norfolk-Portsmouth theatre during the 1781 campaign, securing intelligence that contributed to successful American forays against the British. Though highly praised by his superior officer, Colonel Josiah Parker, Matthews only gained his freedom twelve years later with a petition to the Virginia legislature. Although most African Americans who saw combat in Virginia did so in and around the bay itself, Richard Pointer earned plaudits for heroic actions in defending a frontier fort in Greenbrier County, Virginia, against Indian attack in 1778. Pointer's liberation, also achieved by special legislative act, waited until 1795.[39]

Slave pilots who gained freedom included Caesar Tarrant, who steered the Virginia navy sloop *Patriot* for four years until it sank in 1781. Tarrant, too, was enfranchised by legislative acceptance of his petition in 1789, and settled down to life in Hampton. In a final recognition of his services, Virginia granted land from a veteran's tract in Ohio to his daughter in 1831.[40]

Black men like Tarrant who enlisted in the state navies of Maryland or Virginia fought both to free themselves from slavery and to prevent Britain from "enslaving" Anglo-American rebels, to use the patriotic rhetoric of the day. Ironically, no small part of navy duty consisted of patrolling rivers and harbors to prevent other slaves from fleeing to the British to pursue their dreams of freedom. For blacks as well as whites, the Revolutionary War could be a civil war. Blacks were pitted against each other on land as well as at sea. When Dunmore's Ethiopians went down to defeat at Great Bridge, one of their conquerors was William Flora, a free person of color who distinguished himself in turning back the initial British assault. Later in the war, African American soldiers fighting in Maryland and Virginia regiments in Washington's Continental army took part in battles at Brandywine, Germantown, and Monmouth in 1777 and 1778, where they may well have clashed with veterans of Dunmore's Ethiopians.[41]

The black experience of war during the American Revolution, as distinct from the ideological and social impact of revolutionary ideas, resembled that of slaves caught up in a host of colonial wars between European powers. Blacks in the Chesapeake tidewater could fight for or flee to the British, much as earlier runaways from colonial South Carolina had enlisted under the Spanish banner in Florida, or as blacks in South America would do in the early nineteenth century wars of liberation against Spain.[42] Like the Spanish in St. Augustine, the British tried to overcome manpower shortages by making free allies of slaves. When pressed for men, the Americans likewise armed slaves and sometimes offered freedom selectively to bolster their forces. Though African Americans participated in the Revolutionary War on a larger scale than in earlier colonial conflicts, the structure of the situation was the same. Thousands of slaves achieved a hard fought freedom, but none of the warring powers actually aimed to end slavery.

Independence achieved, Americans came to grips with restoring a war-torn economy and also creating a government for their new nation. Slavery soon came to be controversial in addressing each of these issues. Concerns about slavery and the economy centered on whether the Atlantic slave trade should be revived or abolished. Questions about the compatibility of slavery with natural rights philosophy played out in political battles over writing the Constitution and, subsequently, operating the new federal government.

In practice, debates about slavery rarely fit neatly into compartments of liberty versus servitude. The same natural rights that buttressed personal freedom also upheld the prerogatives of white property holders to purchase or trade slaves. As at least one scholar has noted, the concept of freedom embodies not only being free from others' exercise of power over oneself, but also the ability to direct and control the activities of others.[43] Similarly, a resolute defender of slaveholders' property rights might side with antislavery advocates in favoring restrictions on slave trading because an indiscriminate flow of slaves imported from Africa could glut the market and reduce the value of slaves as property.

George Mason of Virginia, for one, refused to sign the Constitution at the close of the convention in Philadelphia and opposed ratification by Virginia because it did not at once ban the slave trade. South Carolina and Georgia, eager to purchase slaves to replace losses in the war, had secured language preventing Congress from legislating on this subject for twenty years after ratification. Mason combined opposition to this proviso with a denunciation of the Constitution's inadequate protection of slavery itself. "And though this infamous traffic be continued, we have no security for the property of that kind we have already. There is no clause in this Constitution to secure it; for [Congress] may lay such a tax as will amount to manumission." In reply, James Madison touted the Constitution's protections for slavery, e.g., its mandating the return of fugitives who flee to free states, and by allowing for a nationwide ban on the African slave trade eventually, if not at once. Ending the slave trade was clearly dissociated from ending slavery in Mason's mind, and apparently that of most delegates to Virginia's ratification convention.[44]

Opponents of the slave trade had long warned that it discouraged the immigration of poor whites and thereby retarded economic development, an argument first advanced in the late colonial period by merchants engaged in shipping English convicts to Maryland and selling their labor as indentured servants.[45] By the early 1770s, slave imports had waned in the region, perhaps because of stagnating European demand for slave-grown tobacco. After the Revolution, Chesapeake slaveholders who had lost thousands of slaves during the war tended to disagree with their Deep South counterparts in one respect—they had little faith that renewing the importation of slaves would result in either short term profit or long term development. For them, devotion to protecting property rights combined protection of slavery as it existed with prohibition of the trade that had created it.

Social and philosophical reactions to the slave trade showed the same overlapping of short and longer term perspectives. Jefferson's *Notes on Virginia*, written in the early 1780s, displayed a deep fear of black insurrection juxtaposed with a wish for slavery's ultimate demise over the very long run. Eliminating the slave trade would diminish black-white ratios and thus reduce the chances of a successful black rebellion, and might even speed the withering away of slavery itself. With the explosion of the slave revolution in St. Domingue in 1791 that culminated in the creation of Haiti in 1804, Jefferson's fears and hopes acquired new urgency.

For all of these reasons, the three Chesapeake states outlawed the African slave trade without significant opposition, and no movement to reopen the trade ever developed. Virginia ended the importation of slaves in 1778, Maryland in 1783, and Delaware in 1787. Interfering with the export of slaves, though, was a far different matter. Slaveholders wanted the option of converting slaves to cash by selling them to planters in the Carolinas and Geor-

gia, and later in Kentucky, Tennessee, and the Gulf States. Market considerations drove thinking on these issues: those with more slaves than they could
profitably employ favored creating a large and unrestricted "home" market
for slave sales, and also smiled on the elimination of "foreign competition"
from importers of slaves.

Opposition to the Atlantic slave trade could combine reservations about
slavery in the abstract with a determination to protect the value of existing
slave property and the social status of slaveowners. When Congress debated
abolition of the Atlantic slave trade in 1807, Chesapeake legislators supported the idea, but many opposed any attempt to free illegally imported
slaves, and all objected to moral denunciations of those who bought and
sold slaves.[46] At the state level, opposition to importing slaves coexisted com-
fortably with legislation allowing Chesapeake slaveholders to move slaves
from one state to another. Maryland amended its ban on slave imports and
authorized owners to bring into the state slaves acquired by inheritance or
marriage. Residents of other states could also bring slaves into Maryland to
labor so long as they annually registered such slaves and promised not to
sell them in the state. When white refugees from the Haitian revolution
began arriving in Maryland ports in the early 1790s, legislators quickly authorized them to bring in their slaves, provided that they did not sell any of
those slaves for at least three years. Cases not covered by these broad exemptions could be addressed through private bills, of which Maryland legislators passed more than four hundred between 1800 and 1860.[47] Ending the
Atlantic slave trade was meant to protect slaveholders of the region in the
here and now. If it also blazed a path toward the eventual end of slavery and
the concomitant whitening of America, so much the better.

Whether acting in the Continental Congress, in the debates surrounding writing and ratifying the Constitution, or in matters brought before the
first federal Congresses of the 1790s, Chesapeake legislators worked to keep
slaveholding safe and secure in their region. They did not oppose regulating
the slave trade, so long as the mode thereof enhanced the value of slaves in
Maryland and Virginia. They generally favored the expansion of slavery
westward into areas that would become Kentucky, Tennessee, Alabama, and

Mississippi—until it appeared that opening new territory to slaves might lead to direct competition with Chesapeake planters. They then swiftly changed course. Fearing that the fresher soils of Ohio might produce cheaper and better tobacco than the tidewater, Virginians accepted the Northwest Ordinance's 1787 ban on bringing slaves into land that soon would become Ohio, Indiana, Illinois, and Michigan. Years later, when emigrants from the Chesapeake to Indiana, led by Virginia-born territorial governor William Henry Harrison, sought repeal of the ordinance, a congressional committee chaired by Virginian John Randolph of Roanoke quietly killed their proslavery, and potentially competitive, petition.[48]

Comfortable with limited, strategic curbs on slavery's expansion, men like Randolph were adamantly opposed to any government actions that might restrict slavery itself or, worse, encourage emancipation. When Philadelphia Quakers urged anti-slavery petitions upon the First Congress in 1790, representatives from Virginia and Maryland objected strenuously, arguing that the Constitution gave the federal government no power of any kind to legislate on the domestic institution of slavery in the existing states. Should Congress even consider such petitions it would unwisely open the door for a dangerous and pernicious misreading of the law.[49]

Also important was ensuring that the new federal government did not inadvertently undermine slavery by appearing to endorse equality for free people of color. The existence of free blacks, a lamentable necessity of the post-revolutionary economy, threatened control over slaves. At the very least, they had to be excluded from the militias, one of whose duties was the suppression of slave revolts. Planting-state legislators ensured that the federal Militia Act of 1790 barred people of color, a precursor to later laws that disparaged black testimony in federal trials and discriminated against employment of free blacks in federal government jobs such as mail carriers.

Chesapeake congressmen also saw a need for federal action in the matter of interstate runaways. The Constitution required states to co-operate with each other in restoring fugitive slaves, but the provision had no administrative teeth. Stung by the flight of slaves to Pennsylvania and by that state's perceived unwillingness to cooperate in the rendition of fugitives, representatives from Maryland and Virginia took the lead in passing the Fugitive Slave Act of 1793.

Both white and black Americans in the Chesapeake wrestled with the local and national questions surrounding slavery. Planters labored to reinvigorate their slaveholding regime. They recaptured runaways and mounted military expeditions against hidden bands of maroons, some of which still roamed remote forests and swamps for years after peace returned in 1783. Though planters did not shrink from brutal means to restore control, they faced new challenges they could not resolve with the cowhide alone.

To diversify beyond tobacco, reduce their dependence on imported manufactures, and increase their slaves' value, more planters trained their slaves in skilled labor. This strategy required more than intimidation; masters had to promote co-operative behavior and steady labor from enslaved coopers, shoemakers, blacksmiths, and shipbuilders. At times the owner's interest in increasing a slave's value might overlap with that slave's desire to free himself. Both might find manumission through self-purchase attractive, provided masters could structure such transactions in ways that stabilized slavery rather than eroding it.

Planters also had to confront a new threat to slavery, the first to come from within Anglo-American society itself. Even before the end of the Revolutionary War, a white anti-slavery movement launched religious, political, and economic attacks on the practice of human bondage. This rising dispute over slavery would roil the Chesapeake during the infant years of the new republic.

CHAPTER 3

Manumitters and Would-Be Emancipators

WHITE OPPOSITION TO SLAVERY in the mid-Atlantic began with the Quakers, who painstakingly worked out a stand against slaveholding as a violent activity that promoted pride and arrogance and thereby endangered the souls of those who owned human chattel.[1]

Warner Mifflin's story is illustrative. A leading Quaker opponent of slavery in Virginia and Delaware in the last quarter of the eighteenth century, he grew up on Virginia's Eastern Shore in the 1750s as part of "the only Quaker family within sixty miles." Surrounded by a slaveholding community that had formed before the Society of Friends condemned slavery, Mifflin's father owned as many as a hundred slaves. When he was fourteen, Warner Mifflin was asked by one of those slaves "Whether I thought it could be right, that they should be toiling to raise me, and I sent to school, and that by and by their children must do so for mine also?" Though initially "irritated" by this question, Mifflin began to reflect deeply on the matter the "idea of losing so much property . . . seemed hard at first" but he resolved not to be a slaveholder.

This resolution proved hard to keep. As a wealthy young man in a slaveholding society, Mifflin faced repeated temptations to "[sit] down quiet in the use of [slaves]." Marriage brought him slaves as part of his wife's dowry. Slaves of his father or from his mother's family in Maryland came to his plantation on "various errands" and then stayed on, with his parents' permission, to live with him. Appointment as a justice of the peace excited a "considerable thirst for preferment" and a supposed "necessity for slaves to support me in that mode of life." Named as executor to an estate, Mifflin was obliged to supervise the distribution of slaves to heirs.[2]

In short, Mifflin discovered that it was virtually impossible to be a leader in his community without surrendering to the blandishments of slave-holding. Ultimately, he chose to free his slaves and give up his pursuit of distinction in society. Going even further, Mifflin "engaged to make restitutions to those I had held in a State of bondage, according to the judgment of indifferent men, agreed on by myself and the blacks," an action that roughly paralleled the payment of freedom dues to apprentices who concluded a period of indenture. Mifflin also bought and freed slaves he had earlier had a hand in selling, and worked on a committee to persuade other Friends to liberate their slaves. Few slaveholders, even among Quakers, went to such lengths. The "freedom dues" that accompanied manumission far more often passed from black to white hands in the form of payments for purchasing oneself.[3]

Mifflin's doings made a "great stir" among his slaveholding neighbors. Conventional wisdom, supported by law, held that "Negroes were such thieves that they would not do to be free." Only two dozen Virginia slaves won legally sanctioned manumission in the fifty years preceding the Revolution.[4] Disapproving neighbors at first contended that Mifflin was simply an unsuccessful manager of slaves who had liberated a "parcel of lazy, worthless Negroes" because "he could make nothing by them." When Mifflin then entered into new arrangements with some of the freedmen, offering them land to work on shares, he was accused of "making more money by his Negroes than ever, and keeping them in more abject slavery, under the pretence of their being free."

During the Revolution antislavery Quakers like Mifflin were suspected of being "Tories" whose manumission of their slaves concealed a stratagem to ally them with the British. Supporters of the Revolution also harassed the pacifist Quakers for failing to fight and refusing to support the war financially. This wartime hostility toward Quakers may in fact have helped prompt them to manumit their slaves. Both they and their bondsmen knew that Patriot governments were unlikely to expend much effort in securing the return of runaways from "disloyal" masters.

The sporadic presence of the British in the region made a difference, too, by destabilizing slavery and perhaps pushing ambivalent slaveholders toward manumission as a way to forestall slave flight. In several Maryland Eastern Shore counties the first waves of Quaker liberations, mostly promises of future freedom, neatly coincided with the presence of British forces around Philadelphia in 1777–78, or at the southern tip of the bay in 1780–81.[5] Yet by the end of war, the Quakers' stubborn neutrality had won grudging respect, and "sour looks and threats abated." Mifflin now embarked on the next stage in his antislavery career, joining other Quaker leaders throughout the Chesapeake as an antislavery agitator.[6]

Opponents of slavery attacked the institution at some or all of four points. First, to halt slavery's continued growth, they sought to ban the importation of slaves from Africa and elsewhere in the Americas. In a companion measure, antislavery men strove to bar slaveholders from selling blacks away from the Chesapeake to ostensibly harsher slave regimes such as the West Indies, South Carolina, or Georgia. Third, they tried to ease legislative restrictions on private acts of manumission. In Virginia, for example, Mifflin's manumissions in the 1770s lacked legal standing, because private acts of manumission had been barred since 1723. Slaves could only legally be freed with the approval of the governor and his council. Mifflin's "freedmen" were in legal fact abandoned Negroes, subject to seizure and sale by churchwardens for the support of the established Anglican church. In this case, external pressure hastened the arrival of freedom. Mifflin carried out his unauthorized manumissions just as war was breaking out with Britain, and the government was fully occupied with the crisis. Fourth, and most ambitiously, opponents of slavery urged state legislatures to adopt gradual emancipation statutes. Typically, such bills copied Pennsylvania's *post nati* emancipation of 1780, proposing to phase out slavery by prospectively freeing children of slave mothers. George Buchanan, speaking to a Maryland abolition society in 1791, advised that emancipation "be done gradually; let the children for one or two generations be liberated at a certain age, and in less than half a century the plague will be totally rooted out." The Pennsylvania law freed such "after born" African Americans at age twenty-eight. Other proposals would set the age of liberation anywhere from eighteen to thirty.[7]

In the years following the Revolution, all three states around the Chesapeake banned the importation of Africans and eased their manumission laws. Virginia ended its ban on private manumissions in 1782, and Maryland legitimized manumission by last will and testament in 1790. Delaware loosened requirements that manumitters post bonds and accept financial responsibility for ex-slaves in 1787. Significantly, all three states retained upper and lower age limits on manumission, lest slaveholders "dump" young children or aged slaves unable to support themselves who might then become public charges. But only Delaware banned out-of-state slave sales, and no Chesapeake state adopted a gradual emancipation law.[8]

The historical moment in which public authority in the Chesapeake favored manumission was brief—virtually all the significant measures passed between 1782 and 1790. At no point, even in the immediate afterglow of the Revolution, did the further step of state-mandated gradual emancipation attract widespread support. After 1790 slaveholders regained lost ground on all fronts, hedging manumission laws with new restrictions and passing legislation hostile to free people of color, who were increasingly described as a "demoralizing" influence on slaves. By 1800 antislavery was a spent force in the Chesapeake. In the words of one contemporary, "the emancipation fume has long evaporated, and not a word is now said about it." Most whites had quickly come to view freedom for people of color as a failed experiment, and free blacks themselves as a "subversive element" in a resurgent slave society.[9]

These outcomes were forged by three loosely defined and overlapping groups of whites and their corresponding attitudes toward the antislavery effort: defenders of slavery, religious opponents of slavery, and politicians and officeholders.

Slavery's defenders wanted state power used to uphold the institution and slaveholders' interests. For such persons, the right to hold, buy, and sell slave property formed a defining element of the very liberty they had fought to preserve in the Revolution. They were reluctant to declare that "all men are by nature equally free and independent," in the words proposed by George Mason's Declaration of Rights at Virginia's state constitutional convention in 1776, but not because they believed blacks possessed such rights. The issue was how to clarify that only whites should be free and independent. Properly understood, freedom and independence could be claimed as rights only "when [men] enter into a state of society," which Africans, brought to Virginia already enslaved, had not done. Once this language had been inserted into the document, Mason's Declaration of Rights sailed through to adoption. When Virginia jurist George Wythe, Jefferson's instructor in law at William and Mary, attempted to interpret the Declaration of Rights as an antislavery text some years later, his opinion was promptly overturned on appeal.[10]

For defenders of slavery, gradual emancipation was an unthinkable violation of slaveholders' property rights, and manumission was almost equally suspect. Permitting individuals to free their slaves threatened to create a free black population whose very existence would erode the stability of slavery and thereby destroy the value of slave property. Governments, created to protect property, had no business authorizing such misguided actions. Petitioners opposed to legalizing manumissions repeatedly made that argument to their lawmakers in Virginia and Maryland in the 1780s.[11]

Slavery's opponents were also inspired by religious feeling. The Quakers were foremost, though Methodists also figured in the argument, primarily in Delaware and on Maryland's Eastern Shore. Many Christian churches had at some point wrestled with the question of whether buying, selling, and holding other humans in slavery constituted sin. Most had long made their peace with the institution itself from the time of its rise to prominence in the sixteenth century, with occasional expressions of doubt about the morality of the slave trade.[12] For Quakers, though, the issue took on great significance in the second half of the eighteenth century. They believed that one's salvation depended upon receiving grace through the operations of the Inner Light, a kind of direct communication between the

Elisha Tyson (1749–1824), a Quaker merchant of Baltimore, devoted forty years to anti-slavery causes. Oil portrait. (Maryland Historical Society.)

believer and the Holy Spirit. Since man was made in God's image, and the Inner Light was available to all, this led them to a radical egalitarianism. Prompted by antislavery activists such as Anthony Benezet, Quakers began to ponder whether slaveholders, caught up in the violence and disorder that inevitably accompanied the buying and holding of slaves, could hope to experience the redemptive power of the Inner Light. After reflection and debate through the middle decades of the eighteenth century, they answered this question in the negative. Selling or holding slaves ensnared masters in sinfulness and precluded the reception of grace. Slaveholding Quakers must be persuaded to free their chattels, and if they refused, they must be "disowned," that is, expelled from fellowship with other Friends. By the 1780s, the process of cleansing Quakers from the stain of slavery was largely complete, though not without the loss of some who left the church and kept their slaves.[13]

Moving beyond their own religious community, Chesapeake Quakers urged other Christians to sever their ties with slavery. These Quaker abolitionists included Warner Mifflin (who had relocated to Delaware by the late 1780s), Maryland's Elisha Tyson, and Robert Pleasants in Virginia. Pleasants, a principal sponsor of that state's 1782 law legalizing private manumission, had inherited his opposition to slavery from his father, John, who died in

1771, leaving a will that distributed slaves to his children but also enjoined them to free all such slaves at age thirty, if or when a change in the Virginia manumission laws authorized such liberations. Acting as his father's executor, Robert Pleasants set to work to change Virginia law. In 1777, he appealed to Governor Patrick Henry, urging Henry's support both for a voluntary manumission law and for a gradual emancipation act that would free future slave children at age twenty-one if male, and eighteen if female, ages at which apprentices commonly completed their indentures and attained freedom. Pleasants drafted and circulated petitions for gradual emancipation through the 1780s and into the 1790s to the Virginia General Assembly and sought support for the concept in letters to Washington, Madison, and Jefferson.[14]

In the late 1780s, Elisha Tyson helped found a Quaker-dominated abolition society in Maryland that urged its legislature to take up the subject of gradual emancipation. Tyson, unlike many contemporaries, never wavered from his anti-slavery activism. Shortly before his death in 1824, in a self-styled farewell address to the "people of color, in the United States of America," Tyson summed up his life as one in which, "I have, for the last forty years, sustained many trying conflicts on your account; but . . . I have the consolation of believing myself to have been imperiously called upon to espouse your cause; and I now feel the reward of an approving conscience, under the reflection that I may, in some degree, have been instrumental in promoting the melioration of your condition."[15]

Two abolition societies sprang up in Delaware in the late 1780s. The Wilmington-based Delaware Society for the Gradual Abolition of Slavery began meeting in 1789. A year earlier a group of Quakers in and around Dover had founded the "Delaware Society for Promoting the Abolition of Slavery, for Superintending the Cultivation of Young Free Negroes, and for the Relief of Those Who May Be Unlawfully Held in Bondage." Both groups corresponded with the Philadelphia-based Pennsylvania Abolition Society and sent delegates to the American Convention of abolition societies starting in 1794. Delaware abolitionists, reorganized more than once, would continue to maintain an active society into the early 1800s.[16]

Formation of the societies may have been spurred by the success of antislavery laws pushed through the Delaware legislature in 1787. Petition drives spearheaded by Warner Mifflin and Methodist Richard Bassett led to liberalized manumission and a ban on the slave trade, though companion efforts to secure a gradual emancipation law failed. Private manumissions had been possible in late colonial Delaware, but the law required would-be manumitters to post costly indemnity bonds for the maintenance of those they intended to free. This provision dissuaded slaveholders from using manumission to shift costs of providing for old or disabled slaves to the public. The law was stiffened in 1767 to require bonds of sixty pounds for the freeing of any slave, regardless of age or condition. It discouraged manumission so effectively that less than 5 per cent of Delaware's blacks were free circa 1770.[17]

With the onset of the Revolutionary War and disruption of Delaware's exports of corn, wheat, and timber, economically challenged slaveholders began freeing slaves informally, without filing documents or posting bonds, in a manner akin to what Warner Mifflin had done earlier in Virginia. Following the war, the successful campaign of 1787 amended the manumission law so that no bond need be posted to free a slave between the ages of eighteen and thirty-five. In the same session, Delaware's legislature banned the sale of slaves to the West Indies, the Carolinas, or Georgia. Forbidden to sell slaves to locales where they would have little or no chance of freedom, masters found it easier to free them instead. With the urging of Mifflin and others, the ban was extended in 1789 to cover sales to Maryland and Virginia, as a way of dealing with the rapidly developed loophole of selling slaves to Maryland dealers who then shipped them to Charleston or Savannah. Another amendment adopted in the 1790s specified that a slave illegally sold to someone not a resident of Delaware would be set free, and the seller would face criminal penalties.[18] In driving for this important legislation, Mifflin and Bassett drew significant support from political leaders outside their faiths. Both Caesar Rodney and John Dickinson lent their support to measures to suppress the African slave trade, and Dickinson advocated a ban on slave export sales as early as 1775.[19]

Criminalizing out-of-state sales was a blow to slavery in Delaware, constricting its profitability. Just as in Maryland, Delaware planters could manage the size of an enslaved workforce by a judicious mix of field or craft work on one's own plantation combined with hiring surplus workers out to neighbors or in nearby towns or cities. They could also trim the numbers of African Americans they held by selling slaves locally or by offering delayed manumission to selected individuals. Manumissions could be written to tailor a term of service required to earn freedom to the master's work needs, or might allow a slave to "cash out" through self-purchase. But only the Maryland slaveowner could readily sell large numbers of slaves at high prices, because only interstate slave dealers looked to buy blacks in volume with payment in cash.

With "Georgia men," as slaves called them, ruled out as buyers, prices for slaves in Delaware lagged well behind those in nearby Eastern Shore Maryland or Virginia. As a result, black people more easily bargained for their freedom, and the proportion of free blacks in Delaware soared. In 1790, 30 per cent of blacks in the state were free, compared to 8 per cent in neighboring Maryland. By 1810, fully 76 per cent of Delaware's African Americans were out of slavery, compared to Maryland's 23 per cent, and less than 10 per cent in Virginia. In fact, a smaller proportion of Delaware blacks were enslaved in 1810 than in New York or New Jersey, years after the passage of gradual emancipation laws in those states.[20]

Some Delaware slave owners tried to circumvent the laws, typically by illegal removal of slaves for sale to the Deep South, or by reneging on promises of freedom via manumission or self-purchase. Delaware abolitionists spent much of their energy combating such activities, as well as trying to prevent the outright kidnapping of free people of color. In 1802 society members Moses Rea and Hezekiah Niles took on the case of Lowden Williams, who had purchased his freedom for fifty dollars but had not been released by his master, Joseph Ross. By turning up a signed agreement that bore out Williams's claim, Rea and Niles were able to win his freedom. In other cases, abolitionists intervened to compel reluctant heirs and executors to make good on testators' wills promising freedom.[21]

The temptation of higher prices for slaves in nearby Maryland proved an irresistible lure to the unscrupulous. If a black person could be spirited out of Delaware, it mattered little whether he or she was legally free, promised freedom via manumission, or a slave. There were always buyers willing to accept black persons offered for sale without asking embarrassing questions. Abolitionists had to work fast, ride hard, and face threats and violence to redeem smuggled captives. For perhaps a dozen years, the Delaware Abolition Society intervened frequently and effectively on behalf of blacks. By 1810 it had lost members and become moribund, but the track record of early white antislavery was more impressive in Delaware than elsewhere in the Chesapeake.

Aiding black individuals seeking freedom also constituted a major activity of the "Maryland Society for promoting the abolition of slavery, and the relief of poor negroes and others unlawfully held in bondage," a group with some two hundred fifty members in the 1790s, preponderantly merchants and professionals from Baltimore and its environs.[22] Slaves lacked legal standing to sue or be sued, but they could petition or plead a court to recognize that they were wrongfully held as slaves and entitled to freedom. Typically, petitioners sought to trace their descent from a free female ancestor, relying on statutes dating from the 1660s that inflicted slave status only on persons born to enslaved women. The presence of thousands of white indentured servants in the Chesapeake even after the rise of slavery in the late seventeenth century had resulted in substantial numbers of children of mixed parentage. Many slaves therefore could hope to advance claims to having white foremothers whose mulatto children had illegally been treated as slaves.

In the 1780s and 1790s a spate of petitions flooded Maryland, Delaware, and Virginia courts, often turning on the status of a claimant's great or great-great grandmother.[23] Others hoped to shed their chains by showing that they had been sold or transported across state lines in violation of newly legislated restrictions on the domestic slave trade. In relying on the courts, blacks in the Chesapeake brandished a weapon that yielded dramatic results elsewhere, notably in Massachusetts and New Hampshire, where judges used petitions for freedom to rule slavery unconstitutional.[24] That no such outcome developed in the Chesapeake forms one part of the story of how defenders of slavery gradually rallied their forces to withstand all assaults. In Maryland, judges did not seize on freedom petitions as a tool to rule against the legitimacy of slavery. Instead, Maryland cases turned only on the particular claims of people seeking to prove free female ancestry.

In 1792 the Maryland Abolition Society sustained Jonathan and David Fortune's attempt to establish freeborn lineage through two years of litigation, eliciting a shrill protest from the Fortunes' ostensible owners, Ezekiel and Edward Dorsey of Anne Arundel County. The Dorseys complained to a Maryland House of Delegates committee of having expended more than six hundred dollars contesting the freedom petitions, more than the slaves were worth. Agreeing wholeheartedly with the Dorseys' self-serving portrayal of themselves as innocent victims of "improper interference" with their slaves, the Committee of Grievances flayed the abolition society for that heinous sin against true republican values, the exercise of arbitrary power. "From the numbers, wealth, influence, and industry of the society, with their extensive connexions, an individual has but a slender chance of encountering them; and that if interest only was to be considered, he had better content to give up a slave . . . their conduct has been unjust and oppressive."[25]

Four years later, as part of an overhaul of the state's laws on slaves and free negroes, the assembly rallied to protect slaveholders by requiring that costs of unsuccessful petitions be paid before appeals could be filed.[26] Subsequent laws would strike directly at antislavery advocates for blacks by making petitioners' attorneys responsible for the court costs of unsuccessful freedom suits. Thus burdened, freedom suits became less common after 1800.

Practical politicians in Maryland and Virginia were wary of committing themselves to antislavery measures, even during the years immediately after the Revolution. In Maryland the young William Pinkney, a future U.S. Senator, did successfully urge passage of a bill in 1790 allowing manumissions by last will and testament. He succeeded by arguing that testators should be able to dispose of property as they wished, so long as creditors were not defrauded.[27] But proposals for gradual emancipation received a frosty reception.

Marylanders rarely debated manumission and emancipation laws in their newspapers, but an exchange in the *Maryland Gazette* in late 1790 affords a glimpse of the ideas in play. Ezekiel Cooper, a Methodist preacher writing under the pseudonym "A Freeman," presented the libertarian argument that Americans' claims to cherish liberty were inconsistent with the continuation of Negro slavery. He challenged the claim that slavery's longstanding existence demonstrated its providential nature, by noting that the same could be said for the "impious" Algerine practice of capturing and enslaving European and American sailors in the Mediterranean. Nor did slavery's ubiquity in ancient Greece or Rome provide precedent for its legitimacy. Could not the same plausible but false claims be made on behalf of monarchy? Cooper urged that slaveholders free their chattels in obedience to the Golden Rule.[28]

Two weeks later, "A True Friend to the Union" responded. Although slavery "ha[d] been a curse to the southern states," it was "entailed" on them for some time to come. Blaming slavery's introduction on British merchants, this writer insisted that, "As the evil came among us slowly . . . so must it be done away, almost as gradually as it came on." Fear of free blacks demanded delay: "You could not with propriety, let all loose among us at once." Besides, if emancipation came rapidly, financial "ruin to white inhabitants would ensue." Citing the "convenience" of fathers leaving slaves to their daughters, whose "hire, with the industry of their mistresses, yields a competency for the support of all," True Friend linked the survival of slavery to sustaining the genteel status of white women. Finally, he chided would-be emancipators who had "never considered the political state of the union, with respect to the southern states, otherwise they would not have proposed a matter that might tend to create confusion." Even state-level consideration of emancipation could threaten national harmony, a warning that would be echoed by southern proslavery men in later debates.[29]

The Freeman admitted in a rejoinder that many free blacks "would abuse their freedom and render themselves more miserable than they are in bondage" but restated the moral necessity of liberating bondspeople. True Friend's rebuttal hammered away at the point that "a general manumission" would be dangerous without "exportation. . . . It would not do to keep them among us."[30] Four weeks later a scornful poem by "Abaris" lampooned Freeman as a "monarch of the blacks," ruling subjects characterized by filth, dirt, poverty, and dishonesty. It evoked the horror of miscegenation by reference to "sable concubines," a rare reversal of the proslavery favorite image of emancipation's consequences, that free black men would marry white men's daughters. Taking up the cudgels again, Freeman eruditely noted that Abaris had been a priest of Apollo with a gift of prophecy, and challenged the appropriateness of the pen name. Moving to his main task, Freeman entered a carefully qualified class-oriented defense of free blacks, claiming that their "industry and honesty" would equal that of whites "of a similar station" in life.[31]

The debate between True Friend and Freeman turned chiefly on the criteria for evaluating the desirability of emancipation for white society. Freeman claimed no great gains to be won by liberating the slaves but argued that True Friend and Abaris's claims were exaggerated, and that free blacks would implicitly be no more harmful to society than whites who lacked property. Freeman was scarcely unique in his cautious advocacy. At least one contemporary combined a call for immediate abolition with a demand for colonization of all freed blacks. "Othello," in a pair of letters to the *American Museum* in 1788, urged that "we should set all our slaves at liberty, immediately, and colonize them in the western territory." Othello thought that emancipation would encourage industry among whites and make America "a richer and more happy country," because "our lands would not then be cut down for the support of a train of useless inhabitants," whose existence inspired only "sloth and voluptuousness among our young farmers and planters."[32] In common with opponents of emancipation, Othello saw free blacks as potential contaminants to be removed from America.

Othello, Freeman, Abaris, and True Friend thus positioned themselves along a spectrum ranging from ambivalence through pessimism to negative certainty regarding the prospects of free blacks. They all harbored doubts about the capacity of black people to improve themselves and drew on the idea, still prevalent in the late eighteenth century, of work as a divinely ordained curse on sinful man that most persons naturally sought to avoid. Even white Americans might sink into indolence because of the supposed ease of satisfying basic wants and needs in a bountiful country. James Madison, for one, feared that Americans in the western settlements would succumb to the temptation to enjoy the produce of rich new lands without having to labor extensively. Their resulting torpor would unfit them for the stern responsibilities of citizenship, thus threatening the stability of the republic.[33]

To some worried about white industriousness, the "sloth and voluptuousness" encouraged by slavery's presence in Maryland were equally threatening to republican virtue, making the extinction of slavery desirable. But given such concerns about preserving a sturdy, working, white citizenry, the notion that black ex-slaves would exhibit self-reliance and industry seemed unlikely. Slaves who had lived with little ability to accumulate property would not acquire the urge to do so when their chains were struck off. Claims of "shirking" by slaves or free blacks do not appear to have been based on any detailed observation. Instead, theoretical concerns dominated. Late eighteenth-century stereotypes of "lazy" free blacks as a "useless" caste pre-dated the presence of any substantial population of free people of color on which to base such characterizations.[34]

In this atmosphere, measures to compel slaveholders to give up chattels went nowhere. When an obscure state legislator proposed to the Maryland House of Delegates in 1789 to ban slave export sales and to pass a *post nati* emancipation law, the bill was quickly tabled by a 39–15 vote. A similar measure was rejected by the Maryland Senate in 1797, despite support from Charles Carroll of Carrollton. One last attempt in 1798 created such a hostile uproar that only the withdrawal of the bill before its formal presentation restored order in the House.[35] By 1798, Governor John Henry carried opposition to emancipation a step further, denouncing private abolition societies as contrary to the settled wisdom of the political community on the subject of slavery.[36] As in Delaware, manumission of slaves unable to support themselves was forbidden, as was the liberation of any enslaved person over the age of forty-five.

Though Virginians authorized private manumissions in 1782, rescinding an earlier law requiring them to be approved by the governor and council, they sternly refused to go any farther. Robert Pleasants's letters to the state's political leaders on emancipation all met the same fate. In 1777, Patrick Henry informed Pleasants of his support for manumission, but balked at supporting state-mandated emancipation. Madison straightforwardly responded to a similar query by noting that many of his constituents viewed slaveholding as a key property right and would be horrified if he were to oppose their wishes. A few years later, as a member of the First Congress, Madison would decline to present a petition against the slave trade because, "animadversions, such as it contains . . . on the slavery existing in our country, are supposed by the holders of that species of property to lessen the value by weakening the tenure of it."[37] Washington in 1785 assured Pleasants of his personal sympathy but deemed the times unpropitious for public advocacy of antislavery views. Approached in the same year by Methodist leaders Francis Asbury and Thomas Coke, Washington promised to signify his sentiments on slavery by a letter, if the Virginia General Assembly actually took up consideration of their petition calling for gradual emancipation. No letter ever came from Mount Vernon. When the petition was presented to the Assembly no one would vote to consider the subject, perhaps not least because more than twelve hundred citizens endorsed counter-petitions opposing emancipation.[38] According to Madison, one member moved that antislavery petitions be thrown under the table rather than simply laid upon it, an idea "regarded with as much indignation on one side as the petition itself was on the other."[39]

Jefferson, serving as minister to France at the time, had no need to get on the record on the question. This no doubt suited his purposes, given his assiduous efforts to avoid public expression of his views on slavery, at least in America, throughout most of his political career.[40] As a young member of the House of Burgesses in 1769, Jefferson co-sponsored a bill introduced by Colonel Richard Bland that aimed at loosening the restrictions against private acts of manumission. Like other antislavery legislation, this proposal generated vitriolic protest, most of it directed at Bland. Jefferson never forgot this incident. When he chaired a legislative committee on revisal of Virginia's laws in 1779, Jefferson worked quietly for consideration of a *post-nati* emancipation law but did not include such a measure in the revised code. Instead, he suggested that proponents offer the idea as an amendment during debate on the revisions. No such amendment was ever offered.

Writing in the early 1780s for an intended French audience in his *Notes on the State of Virginia*, Jefferson sketched out a plan for emancipation of the most gradual kind. He suggested that *post nati* rules be drawn up for births occurring after 1800, granting slaveholders nearly twenty years to convert their human property into cash or take it out of Virginia to points west or south. Jefferson also stipulated that onetime slaves who did gain freedom must be removed from the state. Like many if not most of his contemporaries, Jefferson's antislavery had as much to do with whitening the new republic as with ending injustice to blacks. Jefferson simply could not and did not see black people, free or enslaved, as desirable members of the American nation.[41]

Although it has been tempting for some historians to condemn Jefferson for equivocation and apparent contradiction regarding slavery, he was not alone. Four astute politicians, arguably the four most famous Virginians of the revolutionary age, men who clashed on a host of other important issues, united in their extreme caution and circumspection on the subject.[42] For them, as for most political leaders, slavery was a bad thing in the abstract, but the idea of using state power to take slave property away from its owners seemed a far worse evil.

Nor did their personal choices, for the most part, indicate any deep-seated desire to act to end slavery. Patrick Henry, who had praised the Quakers for their "noble effort to abolish slavery," died possessed of more than thirty adult slaves. His will permitted his widow, "if she chooses . . . to free one or two of my slaves." Jefferson freed only five persons of the more than two hundred he owned, all of them related to Sally Hemings. Madison, longest to survive of the four, died in 1836. Urged by his one time protégé and friend Edward Coles to free his slaves, Madison made no provisions to do so in his will. Only Washington acted to free his chattels, liberating more than one hundred people that he personally owned, effective on the death of his widow Martha. The remainder of Washington's slaves, nearly two hundred people, had come under his control as part of Martha's dowry. They and their progeny remained enslaved to Martha Washington and her heirs. Perhaps "the general inconvenience of living without [slaves], as Henry put it, carried the day for most of Virginia's slaveholding gentry.[43]

Large-scale manumissions like Washington's clearly did not sway many other Virginians and indeed often generated hostility among local slaveholders who viewed the presence of free black people as threats to the stability of slavery. Robert Carter's 1791 plan for the gradual emancipation of his more than four hundred slaves aroused intense opposition from his prospective heirs and from his white tenants and neighbors. Likewise, Richard Randolph's emancipation of some ninety people whom he settled at Israel Hill, in Prince Edward County, though successful in creating a self-sustaining community, generated anger from nearby slaveholders.[44]

Only in Delaware did opponents of slavery come close to eliminating it. In comparing the vigor of antislavery in Delaware with its political weakness in Virginia and Maryland, two explanations can be advanced to account for the insistence in the latter states on rebuilding a war-battered institution. First and foremost, Virginians could hope to rejuvenate slavery in new western lands that the Old Dominion controlled at the close of the Revolution: the Piedmont, the Shenandoah Valley, and the future state of Kentucky all offered rich acres suitable for plantation slavery. Under such circumstances, few slaveholders thought in terms of cutting ties with the institution, preferring to regain the whip hand over blacks and then head west, or at least sell some of their chattels there. As one traveler put it in 1792, "To talk of Manumitting Slaves to a Virginian would be attempting to reason him out of what he believes to be his living, and his senses."[45]

Marylanders, though not so favorably endowed with new lands as Virginians, did have a small backcountry in modern day Frederick, Washington, Allegany, and Garrett Counties that, in the 1780s, had yet to be fully exploited by slaveholders. Well into the 1820s those western counties would witness a steady influx of slaveholders putting slaves to work clearing land

and planting crops. These western Maryland counties saw their slave populations more than double between 1790 and 1820, compared to a slight decline in slave numbers in the remainder of the state. In these same years, the ratio of slaves to whites in the western counties increased from 1:9 to 1:6.[46] Only in Delaware, completely lacking a western outlet, could slavery's opponents even partially overcome slaveholder opposition.

Virginia slaveholders enjoyed another significant advantage over most Delawareans and many Marylanders besides superior access to western lands. Geography placed them and their slaves much farther from free Pennsylvania than their northern Chesapeake counterparts, rendering slave escape more difficult and profits from slavery more viable. African Americans in most of Delaware and Maryland's counties could plausibly contemplate a flight to freedom, and they and their owners knew it. Little wonder, then, that far more slaveholders in Maryland and Delaware than in Virginia allowed slaves to purchase freedom or to earn it through delayed manumissions contingent on a term of faithful service. In a variation on this theme, slaveholders who lived near the Pennsylvania border often cashed out an investment in slavery, while simultaneously granting freedom, by selling blacks as indentured servants to Pennsylvania farmers and craftsmen. This practice, particularly popular with Delaware slaveholders in the early nineteenth century, afforded Pennsylvanians a chance to command adult labor for several years at prices well below waged labor. Slaves had a stake in co-operating with this arrangement because their relocation to Pennsylvania constituted a stronger legal guarantee of freedom than reliance on a slaveholder's informal promise of eventual manumission.[47]

The economic pressures against slavery's expansion and profitable maintenance in Delaware and northern Maryland, in combination with religious or egalitarian manumissions, helped prevent the growth of slavery and lessen the proportion of slaves in each state's population from the 1780s onward. In Virginia, where a similar stream of manumissions driven by white conscience was augmented much less strongly by profit-driven actions, slavery soon regained the ground lost in the Revolutionary era, rendering political opposition to it first marginal, and then unacceptable.

Virginians dealt with freedom suits in much the same manner as Marylanders. An initial willingness to consider black claims to liberation in the 1780s quickly gave way to concern that petitions might threaten slavery's foundations. Manumission as the "gift" of a master to a slave could be tolerated, but having blacks hale their owners into court and vindicate their claims to freedom was deeply unsettling.[48] Before long, legislation systematically restricted freedom suits, and courts retreated from favorable construction of law and evidence in petition cases. As in Maryland, the turn against freedom suits began in the 1790s and hardened into resolute hostility by the first decade of the nineteenth century.[49]

A few black war veterans won cases in the 1780s by demonstrating that their owners had promised to free them as a reward for service in the Revolutionary War, and others successfully traced themselves to a white or Indian female ancestor.[50] Slaves were sometimes assisted financially or in the courtroom by Quakers, some of whom acted through the offices of the short-lived Virginia Abolition Society.

These efforts soon generated petitions of another kind to the Virginia General Assembly from slaveholders outraged at organized intervention on the slaves' behalf. Seized with the subject, the Assembly pointed to "great and alarming mischiefs" caused by "voluntary associations" who "under cover of effecting that justice towards persons unwarrantably held in slavery, which the sovereignty and duty of society alone ought to afford; have in many instances been the means of depriving masters of their property in slaves, and in others occasioned them heavy expenses in tedious and unfounded lawsuits."

Determined to thwart such self-appointed meddlers, the legislature mandated new procedures for freedom suits in a 1795 statute. Slaves could still petition, and magistrates could, if they chose, require a slaveholder to post bond for the appearance of the slave in court. But slaves could no longer choose their legal representatives: the court would appoint counsel, who would serve *without* "fee or reward" of any kind. Finally, the law targeted Quakers directly, imposing a fine of one hundred dollars on any person aiding an ultimately unsuccessful petitioner. Three years later an amendment to the act barred abolitionists from sitting on juries trying freedom suits.[51] The new laws apparently reflected public opinion accurately and drove fledgling abolition societies into retreat. In 1796 the Winchester Society for the Abolition of Slavery and the Relief of Free Negroes Unlawfully Held in Bondage issued a careful disclaimer against the notion that it might "take advantage of those who through ignorance or inattention . . . have suffered their slaves to become entitled to their freedom by the strict letter of [Virginia's] laws."[52] After 1798 slaves would have much more difficulty finding allies in or outside the courtroom.

In tandem with statutory restrictions, Virginia's courts moved to limit the grounds on which black petitioners could prevail in freedom suits. In 1794 a district judge on an Eastern Shore circuit ruled against a disputed manumission in *Tom v. Roberts*, a case that strikingly illustrates the leanings of the Virginia judiciary towards the protection of property rights at the expense of claims to liberty.

Tom, a twenty-two-year-old black man, had been prospectively manumitted in 1782 by his mistress, Anne Roberts. Her deed of manumission had freed adult slaves at once and slated male children like Tom to be free at age twenty-one, females at eighteen. Roberts, like her cousin Warner Mifflin, acted without full legal authority, freeing her chattels four months before passage of the 1782 manumission law. In itself, this action did not invalidate her act; hundreds of other similar manumissions had gone unchallenged. Tom's attorney argued at trial that Roberts' manumissions had the sanction of the community and ought to be respected, in that the churchwardens of Northampton County had declined to exercise their option to round up and sell Roberts' ex-slaves.

The fundamental legal challenge to the manumission came from another source: Anne Roberts had been married, a *feme covert* in the eyes of the law, when she drafted and signed her deed of manumission. Even though she had owned the slaves before her marriage to Humphrey Roberts, she had no authority to dispose of property that had rightfully become her husband's. Tom's lawyer nonetheless insisted that Anne Roberts's action be upheld, noting that her husband had been a notorious loyalist during the war, a man who had fled wife, home, and slaves to join the British in 1775. When Humphrey Roberts returned after peace was restored in 1783, he had declared his wife's manumissions nullified and sold Tom to a relative, Edward Roberts. Tom had bided his time and filed his petition in 1793, on reaching his twenty-first birthday.

Presiding over this tangled case was none other than St. George Tucker, a distinguished jurist perhaps best known today for his plan for the gradual emancipation of slaves in Virginia, proposed only two years later, in 1796. Though he may have been Virginia's most prominent white advocate of antislavery, Tucker came down strongly in defense of Humphrey Roberts's rights to his property: Tom remained a slave. Tucker so found despite his awareness of Roberts's status as a loyalist who had "abjured the realm" by his actions in 1775, an action that made him liable to the forfeiture of his property rights. Statute and case law in Virginia supported this point, as could commentary from Blackstone, the great eighteenth-century authority on the English common law.

Tucker, a learned legal scholar who would go on to publish treatises on Blackstone's work, surely knew that he had an opportunity to affirm revolutionary principles of liberty in a way that need not fatally undermine slavery. Still, to have freed Tom would have rejected the traditional claims of husbands to the property of their wives under the doctrine of coverture, and would also have departed from the emergent custom of freeing slaves only on the basis of white or Indian ancestry.[53] Tucker's judicial conservatism could not embrace such a decision.

In 1806, while sitting on the state's Supreme Court of Appeals, Tucker made plain the racial logic that underpinned Virginia judges' mode of resolving freedom suits. In *Hudgins v. Wright*, the appeals court upheld an 1804 decision by Chancellor George Wythe that set free a "perfectly white" looking slave family. But the court struck down Wythe's opinion that slaveholders should carry the burden of proof in petition cases. For Tucker, slavery and not freedom was the normal condition of African Americans in Virginia. Tucker's opinion argued that petitioners had to prove their freedom and that the burden of proof weighed most heavily on dark-skinned plaintiffs. Hypothesizing three claimants of uncertain lineage, a "black or mulatto," a "copper-coloured" person, and "one with a fair complexion," Tucker believed that the last two should go free, presumptively having white or Indian blood, while the black or mulatto remained a slave. Tucker's colleague, Justice Spencer Roane, agreed, and noted that visual evaluation of racial characteristics had long been practiced. Under this test, few petitioners were likely to gain freedom. The Virginia bench plumped for upholding property rights with only a narrow path to liberty remaining selectively open to light-skinned African Americans.[54]

Tucker's reasoning evinced a deep-seated pessimism about the prospects for people of color mingling with whites in free society, as an examination of his *Dissertation on Slavery* reveals. Published in 1796, this hundred-page pamphlet offered a proposal for the gradual abolition of slavery in Virginia for consideration by the state legislature. Tucker's scheme, like Pennsylvania's *post nati* law of 1780 or Jefferson's ideas in the *Notes on the State of Virginia*, freed only the unborn. All living slaves and all future sons of slave mothers would remain slaves for life. Daughters of slave mothers born after adoption of the plan would be prospectively free but would serve their mothers' owners until age twenty-eight as compensation for their upbringing. The children of this transitional generation would be born free. Under these rules, no black person would gain freedom for the first thirty years of the plan. Females born just before the act's passage would give birth to sons enslaved for life as much as forty years in the future. All told, slavery would theoretically live on in Virginia for about one hundred years, a span roughly equal to its previous life as an important labor institution in the commonwealth. Had the plan been adopted, it is entirely possible that emancipation would have arrived far sooner. In Pennsylvania, for example, slavery dwindled much more rapidly than mandated by the state's 1780 gradual emancipation law, a fact of which the well-read Tucker was no doubt aware.

Attempting to anticipate objections, Tucker strongly asserted his plan's respects for property rights: "The abolition of slavery may be effected without the *emancipation* of a single slave; without depriving any man of the *property* which he *possesses*, and without defrauding a creditor who has trusted him on the faith of that property."[55] As a member of America's Revolutionary generation, Tucker hoped to achieve eventual liberty for all without compromising property rights, and to paper over the potential contradiction inherent in being a slaveholding republican. In crafting this slow-moving solution, Tucker also attempted to accommodate leading Virginians' reliance on slaves as income-generating property by affording them decades to convert their holdings into other forms of wealth. Sympathy with black desires for freedom had little influence in Tucker's thinking. Tucker sold slaves to dealers, manumitted few or none, and opposed the efforts of his step-son to liberate slaves inherited from Tucker's wife.[56]

Even with a grindingly slow transition from slavery to freedom, Tucker's scheme would eventually create a substantial free black population. This prospect was anathema to most Virginia whites, who viscerally feared blacks who, after gaining their freedom, had migrated to the towns where their presence as independent people unknown to and unrecognized by locals generated deep suspicion. Three years before Tucker's *Dissertation* appeared in 1793, the Virginia legislature had responded to these fears, banning the migration of blacks into the state and requiring the annual registration of urban blacks.[57] Choosing to "accommodate" rather than "encounter" such prejudice, Tucker considered ideas already in circulation for the removal of freed blacks outside the United States. While such deportation was undoubtedly desirable, the expense entailed in relocating twelve to twenty thousand freedpeople a year would be prohibitive. Accordingly, Tucker urged Virginia to toughen existing laws that discriminated against people of color as an "inducement" for them to migrate voluntarily to Spanish Louisiana or Florida. Free black people should be forbidden to own land, to hold office, sit on juries, or engage in any legal action against a white person. They should be compelled to hire themselves out to whites on annual labor contracts, with violators to be bound out by the overseers of the poor. "The seeds of ambition" would thus "be buried too deep, ever to germinate," and the danger that ex-slaves might aspire to equality with whites could be contained.[58]

Despite its glacial pace of emancipation, and its efforts to assure per-

manent white supremacy over blacks, the plan met with the same swift and
angry rejection in the House of Delegates as the Quaker and Methodist
petitions of 1785, with some members again voting against having an antislavery measure even lie on the table. Considering Tucker's studied defer-
ence to white racial prejudice, the intensely hostile reception of these plans
suggests that in Virginia at least, there was no "revolutionary moment" in
which an opportunity to end slavery could have been exploited.[59]

If the Chesapeake's climate of opinion toward emancipation seemed
chilly in the 1780s and 1790s, it soon turned frigid. As whites grew ever more
fearful of the presence of free people of color in their midst, they backpedaled
on manumission. The successful slave rebellion against the French in St.
Domingue beginning in 1791 resulted in the birth of the black-led nation of
Haiti and spread alarms of slave insurrections everywhere in the Atlantic
world. These fears heightened with the discovery of Gabriel's Rebellion in
1800 in Richmond. By 1806, Virginia legislators sought to stem the tide of
freedom with new laws that required African Americans manumitted in
the future to leave the commonwealth within a year of their liberation. The
immigration of free blacks from other states had been banned earlier, in
1793. Maryland and Delaware also tried to restrict the ingress of free people
of color.

These developments discouraged opponents of slavery, many of whom
began to resign themselves to its permanence in the region. Short-lived abolition societies in Maryland and Virginia had wilted under legislative censure in the late 1790s and disbanded.[60] The same decade saw the departure
of antislavery activists like Baptist ministers John Leland and David Bar-
row. The latter, who freed his slaves in 1784 on the grounds that slaveholding
was inconsistent with republican principles, left Virginia for Kentucky in
1798 to seek a more receptive atmosphere for his antislavery sentiments. A
few years later, John Parrish, a Quaker, called attention to slavery's rein-
vigoration in the Chesapeake in a pamphlet that catalogued kidnappings of
free blacks and the spread of slave traders from Georgia and South Carolina. P. E. Thomas of Maryland concurred, noting in an 1806 letter that "the
practice of slavery is becoming daily less obnoxious to the feelings of the

mass of people in these parts," with "many who some years ago saw the iniquity of it . . . relapsing so far . . . as to have purchased other slaves." Thomas concluded that "hopes . . . that these people would be liberated by the voluntary efforts of their own masters will prove delusive."[61] As Thomas suspected, many who had manumitted blacks subsequently acquired more slaves. To take but one example, Harry Dorsey Gough, a wealthy convert to Methodism from the Baltimore area, had freed forty-five slaves in 1780, noting his religious convictions in the deed of manumission he executed; when Gough died in 1808, he disposed of fifty-one slaves in his will.[62]

One analysis estimates that perhaps twenty to forty per cent of Marylanders who manumitted their slaves subsequently purchased more slaves between 1790 and 1830, often commuting their status to "term slavery" in the process. Slaveholders of this sort promised to free slaves after eight to twelve years of service, hoping to forestall flight or malingering by a would be freedman. Toward the end of the slave's term, the slaveholder could purchase a replacement and repeat the process. For example, John Kelso, a Baltimore butcher, purchased and prospectively manumitted three teenaged boys over a twenty-year period, each of whom served eight to ten years before being freed. Used in this manner, manumission resembled indentured servitude or apprenticeship to a degree, but with significant comparative advantages for the master. Slaves for a term of years could be sold to another master if desired, apprentices could not. Nor were term slaves parties to labor contracts like apprentices: they had accordingly less access to courts respecting the enforcement of the master's promises to them. Indeed, if the master had only stated his intent to liberate a slave, rather than recording a manumission deed with a county court, the slave had no enforceable claims at all.

Term slavery enjoyed considerable popularity among urban craftsmen and manufacturers in Baltimore, where more than 20 per cent of all slave sales involved blacks who were not slaves for life. All of this suggests that these slaveowners offered freedom as a way to insure steady and productive labor from slaves rather than being moved primarily by religious or philosophical opposition to slavery. In Virginia's towns, by contrast, where the danger of slave flight counted for less in the master's calculus, term slavery played a less prominent role.[63]

In this climate, the political influence of Quaker antislavery activists waned. By the late 1780s most Quakers in the Chesapeake had either ceased owning slaves or had ceased to be Quakers to retain their slaves. In one notable case, Robert Pleasants, acting as executor of his father John's will, had to sue several relatives to enforce a provision granting freedom to Pleasants's slaves when they reached the age of thirty. Only in 1799, twenty-eight years after Pleasants's death, was the issue legally resolved.[64] By this time, few manumissions stemmed from Quaker action, not least because the Quakers' inveterate hostility to slavery discouraged potential converts.

By contrast, the Methodists became the fastest growing religious denomination in the Chesapeake in no small measure because they muted their early testimony against slavery.[65] In 1780 a General Conference of Methodists held at Baltimore under the leadership of Francis Asbury and Thomas Coke, with fiery antislavery stalwarts like Freeborn Garrettson in attendance, had drawn up a discipline for church members that required itinerant preachers to provide for the gradual emancipation of any slaves they held and advised all Methodists to do so as well. The next conference in 1784 strengthened this stand, mandating manumissions upon penalty of expulsion from the church for defiant slaveholders. Within a year, a flood of protests from southern Maryland, Virginia, and points south had caused reconsideration. Coke, for one, had been mobbed and threatened with violence in Virginia for voicing his opposition to slavery. Virginia Methodists urged rescission of the ban on slaveholding, arguing that it would cripple efforts to bring the Methodist message to slaveholders and to their slaves. Enforcement of the discipline was first delayed, then suspended, and finally left in limbo, as a matter to be determined by local conferences. A compromise measure that would have barred new members from holding slaves while grandfathering existing members was defeated at the 1800 General Conference, and 1804 saw the repeal of a longstanding recommendation that Methodists petition their state legislatures to end slavery by gradual emancipation. By 1808 the Methodists published separate church disciplines

for northern and southern congregations. As elder Jesse Lee noted with resignation, "a long experience has taught us, that the various rules which have
been made on this business have not been attended with that success which
was expected." And Francis Asbury, thirty years after his bold stand against
slavery in the 1780 conference, concluded that "We are defrauded of great
numbers by the pains that are taken to keep the blacks from us; their masters are afraid of the influence of our principles. Would not an *amelioration*
in the condition and treatment of slaves have produced more practical good
to the poor Africans than any attempt at their *emancipation*?" Faced with a
choice between compromising their ability to make new converts and sac-
rificing their antislavery principles, Methodists chose the latter course.[66]

A few local conferences of Methodists in Baltimore, Wilmington, and
northern Maryland and Delaware continued to challenge slaveholding into
the early 1830s and occasionally expelled a member for selling a slave for
life, but in most of the Chesapeake, the local option approach quickly led to
the virtual abandonment of strictures on slaveholding.[67] Methodism, by
accommodating the perquisites of planters, merchants, and well-to-do craftsmen who wished to own slaves, surged into prominence within the region.[68]

Still, despite the later retreat of the Methodist Church, early itinerants
and their converts contributed significantly to transforming the nature of
slavery in the Chesapeake by manumitting hundreds of African Americans,
thereby helping to create a community of free people of color. The experience of Freeborn Garrettson, who freed his slaves at the moment of his
conversion in 1775, would serve as a model for Methodist circuit-riders,
with Garrettson himself becoming perhaps the most famous Methodist
abolitionist. Raised in Harford County, Maryland, Garrettson responded
to an inner voice telling him that, "it is not the will of the Lord that you
should keep your fellow creatures in bondage." Announcing that "the op-
pressed shall go free," Garrettson proclaimed the freedom of his slaves, after
which "a divine sweetness ran through my whole frame." Only twenty-two
when converted, he would relate his antislavery epiphany to thousands of
listeners for decades to come.

Nor was Garrettson alone. Woolman Hickson, an itinerant on the Baltimore circuit, emulated the Quaker antislavery missionary John Woolman, trying "by the moste earnest application" to convince individual slaveholders that slavery was a sin, and urging upon them blank manumission forms. Hickson was credited with spurring the manumission of more than two hundred slaves in the Baltimore area by the late 1780s. Another staunch opponent of slavery, William Colbert, preached against slaveholding and threatened slave sellers with damnation during his tenure on circuits on the Eastern Shore of Maryland and in Delaware.[69] According to one study, these testimonies against slavery yielded more than seven hundred manumissions by Methodists in Talbot County alone between 1783 and 1800, or about one-eighth of all slaves in the county.[70]

Baptists in the Chesapeake described a similar trajectory on the slavery issue. Early Baptists sought black converts and even welcomed a few black preachers to their ranks in the late eighteenth century. Some white leaders, such as David Barrows, freed their slaves, but, as among the Methodists, efforts to achieve a broad antislavery policy failed. In 1785 the General Committee of Virginia Baptists tabled a proposed resolution characterizing hereditary slavery as "contrary to the word of God." Attempts to revive the measure in 1790 and 1793 failed, despite the support of prestigious leaders like John Leland. The Roanoke Association captured the mood of most Baptists in responding to Leland's proposed condemnation of slaveholding. While agreeing to "remonstrate" against all forms of oppression, they nonetheless felt that to "emancipate slaves promiscuously without means or visible prospects of . . . support" would be inhumane. Like many, perhaps most, whites in the Chesapeake, the Roanoke Baptists believed that black people would not work without compulsion, and they concluded that retaining blacks in slavery was necessary for their own benefit. From this point onward, Baptists in the region concentrated on ensuring slaves' access to religious instruction, and fell silent on the question of emancipation.[71]

Whites' embrace of antislavery in the late eighteenth and early nineteenth centuries was thus tentative, feeble, and quickly withdrawn. That was not the case among blacks.

CHAPTER 4

Early Black Challenges to Slavery

WHITE AMBIVALENCE ABOUT SLAVERY shaped the ways in which black people pursued liberty in the Chesapeake. During the Revolution groups of slaves could challenge the whole framework of slave society through rebellion or by allying with the enemies of the slave regime. An individual could run away and pass as free, or stay within the law and custom by working toward manumission or self-purchase, or petitioning a court for freedom. Those blacks who achieved emancipation then had to consider how to give meaning to their freedom and the extent to which emerging black communities should, and could, continue to bear witness against slavery.

Except for taking up arms against whites, these courses of action were not mutually exclusive. One strategy for slaves, then, was entrepreneurial—pursue freedom the way a capitalist chases wealth, assessing the risks and potential gains of different moves, evaluating one's assets and the surrounding environment, and periodically "repositioning" oneself when circumstances changed. When considered this way from the slave's perspective, stories of manumission take on a different look and feel than from the viewpoint of the white master, as the following examples illustrate.

Stokeley Sturgis, a white farmer living near Dover, Delaware, converted to Methodism in the early 1780s, stirred by the preaching of the redoubtable Methodist itinerant Freeborn Garrettson. Shortly afterward, Sturgis decided to free himself from the sin of slaveholding. He accordingly offered two young men he owned the chance to purchase their freedom. Within two years Sturgis received the agreed upon price and the two freedmen migrated north to Philadelphia to find work and make new lives in a free state. Sturgis's story is a simple but classic example of the antislavery impact of evangelical religion on the Delmarva peninsula. Newfound piety blossoming in the age of the Revolution led humane whites gradually to withdraw from slaveholding. Seen from the vantage point of the two young black men, though, the same story enriches and adds nuance to our understanding of slavery, religion, and the emergence of free people of color in the early republic.

The younger of the two liberated brothers, Richard Allen, would go on to become a founder and first bishop of the African Methodist Episcopal Church. In a brief autobiography written in 1831, Allen recalled having been sold to Sturgis along with his mother and several siblings, probably around 1768. A few years later, Sturgis was embroiled in financial difficulties, perhaps because of disruptions to commerce during the war with Britain. Despite being "what the world calls a good master," and a genuinely humane man in Allen's recollection, he sold Allen's mother and three brothers and sisters to a planter in Kent County, Maryland, in 1776.[1]

Soon thereafter, perhaps to rescue themselves from despair at the family's breakup, Allen and a brother still with Sturgis "embraced religion" and began attending Methodist society classes. Sturgis's neighbors "clucked at this," saying his "negroes would soon ruin him." The Allens resolved "to attend more faithfully to our master's business" to counter such gossip. Sturgis concluded that, contrary to popular wisdom, "religion makes slaves better, not worse." Capitalizing on his receptivity, Richard Allen now asked his master to allow Methodist preachers to come to his house. Sturgis agreed, and "some months" later, at Allen's invitation, Freeborn Garrettson rode through on his circuit and preached on the text, "Thou art weighed in the balance and found wanting," interpreting it as a dire prediction of the fate of slaveholders on Judgment Day. Shaken to the core of his being, Sturgis decided to free the Allens, and in January 1780 arranged for them to purchase their liberty for "sixty pounds in gold and silver or two thousand Continental dollars," to be paid in five annual installments beginning in 1781. By 1783 the brothers' strenuous labors had paid for their liberation, though not without a gnawing fear that Sturgis might die before they could fulfill the terms of their bargain. Had this occurred, the executors of the debt-ridden estate would have been compelled to sell the Allens. The claims of creditors would have outweighed their prospective entitlement to freedom.

Allen's account of his manumission does not detract from Sturgis's Christian piety or the importance of itinerant preaching as the lever that moved him to action, but we now see other sides of Sturgis, and by implication, of early antislavery as well. Though a good-hearted man, he had no moral difficulty in buying or selling slaves, including a transaction that broke up a family. After his conversion, his need for money still shaped his actions: he *sold* the Allens their liberty.

Allen and his brother actively maneuvered to obtain their freedom. They decided to work harder—to quell rumors that religious slaves are poorer laborers than the unconverted. They conscientiously balanced their need to produce for Sturgis with their religious desires, refusing to attend Thursday night meetings when "behind in work," despite his urgings. Did this insistence on rendering what was due to Sturgis before ministering to their own spiritual needs perhaps subtly hint that slaveholders were selfish sinners, placing their needs first? Then the Allens suggested that preachers come to Sturgis's house. Seeing that this arrangement would allow them to worship while reducing their travel time to distant class meetings, and correspondingly would increase the time the brothers could work for him, Sturgis agreed. Soon afterward, the formidable Garrettson appeared and went to work on the slaveholder, with the happy result of an offer of self-purchase to the Allens. Did Richard Allen orchestrate this sequence of events? He does not claim as much in the autobiography, but its overall tone of reticence about personal motivation is such that speculation along these lines can not be ruled out.

We will never know precisely how antislavery inspired by religious leaders like Garrettson, Sturgis's economic woes, the social tensions and disruptions of wartime, and the Allens' initiative blended to produce their liberation. We can see that these were the forces driving the substantial rise in manumissions that began in the 1770s and 1780s.[2] To be sure, slaves could not compel masters to free them. Liberation represented an alliance of spirit or interests, or both, however temporary, between slaveowner and slave.

In the Allens' case, other factors helped their interests to overlap with Sturgis's: they lived on the Eastern Shore and were freed during the Revolutionary conflict. Not only was the Eastern Shore home to substantial numbers of Quakers and converts to Methodism, it also harbored a large proportion of loyalists and neutrals who wanted nothing to do with the war. Patriot leaders in Maryland and Delaware struggled continually to maintain even a semblance of control over the region, wary that enforcing the laws or mustering militia might trigger loyalist reactions and plunge the region into a civil conflict like those that racked southern New York, northern New Jersey, or the Carolina backcountry.

The resulting breakdown in civil order rendered slaveholders' control over their chattels far from secure. Runaways knew that the danger of recapture and remission to a slaveholder by slave patrols, courts, and jails on the Eastern Shore was less than it had been before the war.[3] So did men like Sturgis, trying to manage young adult male slaves who were perhaps already separated from their families. Such men might well take it into their heads to flee, so why not give them a reason to remain with the promise of legal enfranchisement via self-purchase that would also put some money in the manumitter's pockets?

For Richard Allen, fulfilling his self-purchase bargain would be the first chapter of a classic success story, both spiritually and economically. Not all blacks seeking freedom would tread so smooth a path. Allen himself helped record a story of another kind: the cautionary tale delivered by a condemned man from the gallows.

On March 14, 1808, Peter Matthias, about to be executed as an accessory to a murder in Philadelphia, offered this account of his journey to freedom. Born into slavery in Queen Anne's County on Maryland's Eastern Shore, he worked until age twenty-three for John Mead. When Mead died, his widow "gave me an opportunity of purchasing my liberty for $200, on six years credit." Matthias eagerly accepted this offer and paid part of his purchase price at the close of the first year of his term. Then he took a job as a gardener near Dover, Delaware, followed by a stint on a "bay shallop," sailing cargoes of grain and timber to Wilmington and Philadelphia. Next, Matthias found work in Philadelphia, where he easily passed as a free man, without paying the balance of his self-purchase agreement to Mrs. Mead. Matthias may have felt that his uncompensated labors as a slave and his initial payment to the widow were more than adequate compensation. Perhaps he had never intended to make full payment and used his distant employment as a ruse to slip entirely from his master's control.

Mrs. Mead, no doubt chagrined at her financial loss, might still have consoled herself with having made the best of a difficult situation. Riding herd on a young adult male slave was no easy task, particularly one with few family ties to bind him to the area. (Matthias made no mention of a wife or sweetheart in his execution narrative, and described his mother as deceased.) Like many others so situated, she tried to trade a slave's eventual freedom for a flow of income from self-purchase. Women in early national Maryland granted a disproportionately large share of manumissions.[4]

Unfortunately for Mead, Matthias realized at some point in the process that he could improve the terms of the deal by disappearing into the anonymity of a large city like Philadelphia. Certainly, he could also have been taking precautions against Mrs. Mead's reneging on her side of the bargain and selling him to another master. She had not registered Matthias's prospective manumission with the Queen Anne's County court, and he had no means of enforcing their verbal agreement. A few years later, Matthias accompanied a friend, John Joyce, to the home of Sarah Cross, a widow who kept a store in their Philadelphia neighborhood. Joyce and Cross argued over a debt and Joyce killed her. An eyewitness implicated Matthias, and both men were hanged.

The uncertainties and shifting circumstances attending self-purchase led more than one slave to skip out on a partially completed agreement, and many a master to "put [the slave] in his pocket" by selling a prospective freedman as a slave for life. Slaveholders could also turn the tables on a would-be self-purchaser by accepting installment payments, then insisting on their legal right to keep a slave's earnings without recompense. Moses Grandy was twice defrauded of his freedom by masters employing this stratagem. His third attempt succeeded when he employed a white intermediary who purchased him and set him free.[5]

Another execution narrative, offered by Abraham Johnstone, testified to the importance of the right master for a slave seeking liberation, and to potential pitfalls on the path to freedom. Johnstone was born near "Possom Town" in Sussex County, Delaware, and trained as a blacksmith. Having gained value as a skilled hand, Johnstone was sold to Edward Callaghan, whom "I did not like, therefore I would not live with him, and insisted on having another master." Johnstone says little about why he could not get along with Callaghan, but it is reasonable to infer that unwillingness on Callaghan's part to discuss self-purchase contributed to his resentment. Still, his claim seems like mere bravado. Surely a slave could not dictate a choice of owners.

In fact, circumstances did afford slaves some control. Advertisements testify that many masters would only sell a slave to a local buyer, and many more authorized dissatisfied slaves to identify a potential new master of their own choosing. Slaveholders made wills, placed newspaper advertisements, or issued passes allowing slaves to travel and seek new masters. In addition, some buyers and sellers agreed on "trial sales," an agreement allowing a buyer to keep a slave for several months and then return him and recoup the purchase price if dissatisfied. All of these measures afforded slaves at least some influence over whom they would serve and thereby made resistance or flight less likely.[6]

Johnstone had not chosen Callaghan as a master. Nor could Callaghan avail himself of the slaveholder's favorite weapon to extract co-operation from a recalcitrant worker, threat of sale to a distant locale, because of Delaware's newly passed ban on out-of-state sales. Brutalizing Johnstone would be unlikely to make him a better blacksmith either, so Callaghan prudently acceded to Johnstone's request and sold him to John Craig. By provoking his sale as a slave for life to Craig, Johnstone hoped to give himself a better chance at manumission.

Pleased with Craig, Johnstone became "a very handy hard working black" and got a lucky break. When a knife-wielding slave attacked Craig, Johnstone disarmed the assailant. Craig "owned that he owed his life to me" and offered freedom, at a price, after a specified further term of service. As Johnstone put it, "Shortly after he sold my time to myself, and gave me a considerable length of time to pay the money in." If Johnstone failed to pay up by the end of the term, he would remain a slave, and forfeit any partial payments.

Johnstone now took up the task of earning his freedom but fell afoul of one of life's unpleasant realities for blacks in the Chesapeake. While seeking work in the boomtown of Baltimore, he was "taken up as a runaway." With no one to vouch for him there, and lacking documents to prove he was a free person of color, he languished in the Baltimore jail. When at last he managed to get word to Craig, who arranged to have him transferred to the Dover jail, it was too late. Before he could pay the required fees to Johnstone's jailors, Craig died. The disadvantages of Johnstone's self-purchase agreement quickly became evident. Craig's "executors then wanted to have me a slave," to sell for the benefit of the heirs. Johnstone found witnesses who could verify the existence of his self-purchase agreement with Craig and temporarily forestalled his sale. In the meantime, Dover's jailors wanted money for feeding and housing Johnstone. They accordingly sold him as a servant to James Clements, a Dover area merchant, who in return obtained Johnstone's labor for a "stated time."

Once he had worked out his time with Clements, Craig's executors reappeared and sent him to chop wood on Craig's estate. To propitiate men with whom he had still to reach an agreement about his freedom, Johnstone went off to the woodlot, but he had fallen into a trap: "They came with two Georgia men (to whom they had sold me) and tied me." Somehow, Johnstone found a way to slip a dinner knife into his clothes. He cut his cords and fled into the night. The fugitive sought out Clements, who "advised him to apply to Mr. Warner Mifflin of Dover." Mifflin secured Johnstone a legal manumission, but Craig's executors harbored resentment. Fearing another kidnapping attempt, Johnstone relocated to New Jersey in 1792. Five years later,

Abraham Johnstone was convicted of murdering "Tom, a Guinea negro" and was hanged at Woodbury. Johnstone maintained his innocence, but claimed that Tom had been "procured" to steal Johnstone's copy of a lease on his farm, so that a white landlord could evict him. Perhaps Johnstone's earlier experiences of having been cheated by whites drove him over the edge, resulting in a black man's death.

The complexities of Johnstone's efforts to buy his freedom were by no means atypical. Self-purchase, delayed manumission, and slave sale could be used separately or in combination. Masters who had entered into an informal self-purchase agreement with a slave could realize the cash promised to them by the slave by granting a prospective manumission, then selling the slave for a term of years sufficient to raise the unpaid balance of the self-purchase price. In all of these situations, slaveholders traded off the maximum potential gain available from lifelong labor from a slave or from selling him to a dealer. In return, they minimized the risk of loss associated with flight. Enslaved people accepted the risks of failing to complete self-purchase or of being cheated by a slaveholder in return for a prospect of gaining freedom that white society would legally recognize. The vast majority of manumissions in the Chesapeake appear to have been driven primarily by considerations of this kind, rather than by slaveholders' religious or libertarian motivations, particularly after 1790, by which time the Quakers had largely freed their slaves.[7]

Not all African Americans chose such slow-paced measures. Soon after the Revolutionary War, African Americans, with help from Quakers, began filing petitions for freedom in state courts. In Maryland's most celebrated case, Mary Butler obtained her freedom in 1787 when whites on nearby plantations vouched for her descent from Eleanor or "Irish Nell" Butler, who had come to Maryland in 1681 as the servant of the proprietor, Lord Baltimore, and then married an enslaved black man. Under the 1663 Act Concerning Negroes, her marriage made Butler and her children slaves for life.[8] When the proprietor learned of this, he secured a repeal of the 1663 act, replacing it with a law that banned marriages between female servants and slaves. The new law imposed a staggering fine of ten thousand pounds of tobacco on any master permitting such a marriage and freed the woman and her issue.[9] Lord Baltimore then returned to England, but back in Maryland, Nell Butler and her descendants would be treated as slaves because her marriage had occurred while the law of 1663 was still in force.

In 1770, William and Mary Butler, the latter a great grand-daughter of Nell Butler, and the parents of the 1787 petitioner, had filed petitions for freedom, arguing that the 1681 act should be construed to effect their liberation, as Lord Baltimore had presumably intended. The Provincial Court ruled against them, interpreting the 1681 statute as preserving the property rights of Nell Butler's master and his descendants. The court also opined that this decision made sense from "a political point of view. Many of these people, if turned loose, cannot mix with us and become members of society. What may be the effects cannot perhaps be fully pointed out; but as much inconvenience may reasonably be expected, their title to freedom ought to be made out very clearly."[10] The pre-revolutionary Provincial Court thus evinced early hostility to free people of color that would become a reigning passion for whites in the early national era. Blacks, even if free, "cannot mix with us and become members of society." Any "inconvenience" that whites might experience outweighed black claims to the natural right of liberty, which should be granted only electively for meritorious individuals.

Mary Butler's successful freedom petition of 1787 must be understood against this background. Her attorney sought a flat affirmation that descent from a white woman entitled one to freedom. The defendant contended that the long possession of Nell Butler's descendants as slaves was proof of title and urged that the 1770 opinion be upheld. The Appeals Court affirmed Mary Butler to be free but not solely because of her ancestry. Rather, the judges found that as no documentary proof existed that Nell Butler had ever been convicted of marrying a slave, she could not have forfeited her freedom.[11] By the same token, mere descent from a white woman did not automatically grant freedom.[12] The court seized on a procedural point that only minimally disturbed property rights. Nevertheless, several hundred African Americans used the precedent to gain freedom by claiming descent from Nell Butler.

In another landmark case filed in 1791, the brothers Mahoney sought freedom as descendants of a Negro woman named Ann Joice, arguing that she had become free when her master took her as a slave from Barbados to England in the late 1670s, where she then resided for three years. The Mahoneys based their claim on a 1772 ruling in an English court in which Lord Mansfield had released Somerset, a similarly circumstanced black man. After eleven years of litigation the Court of Appeals denied freedom, ruling that as Ann Joice had never formally been declared free, slavery "reattached" to her when she accompanied her master to Maryland. Another avenue of legal assault on slaveholding was blocked.[13]

In the Butler and Mahoney cases, the courts admitted hearsay evidence on the ancestry of petitioners, believing that the general reputation of the petitioner in his or her neighborhood as to descent would often be the only reliable evidence. In the Mahoney case, for example, the trial court permitted Henry Davis to give evidence to the effect that his deceased uncle David Davis had said "that it was the report of the neighbourhood that if she [Ann Joice] had justice done her, she ought to have been free."[14] This attitude offered possibilities to blacks attempting to show descent from white women or Indians.[15] In a different vein, runaway bondsmen could improve their chances of passing as free by "claim[ing] to be descended from the famous and prolific Nell Butler," as one slaveholder wryly noted in a 1792 advertisement for a runaway.[16]

Allowing juries to weigh hearsay testimony as competent evidence troubled many lawyers and judges. Maryland Attorney General Luther Martin angrily characterized the practice as "giving the power to ignorant persons to judge of rights" and spluttered that "hundreds of negroes have been let loose upon the community by the hearsay testimony of an obscure illiterate individual."[17] Gradually Martin's views gained ground, and in 1813 the United States Supreme Court ruled against admitting hearsay testimony, further whittling away at opportunities to win freedom through the courts.[18]

Despite these restrictions, freedom petitions offered slaves a bit of bargaining leverage, and they assiduously informed themselves about their petition rights. The Butler case originated in St. Mary's County, at the southern tip of Maryland's Western Shore, but within a few years the torrent of white complaints about freedom petitioners came from Baltimore, Anne Arundel, and Prince George's. Slaves also were quick to challenge masters who transported them into or out of Maryland in violation of the state's ban on slave importation, knowing they might well have legally forfeited title to such slaves.[19] Moreover, masters knew that contesting a freedom suit brought its own troubles. They could lose a slave's labor for months or years while the court considered the petition. Even a victory in court could bring new difficulties, as Gassaway Rawlings of Anne Arundel County learned. He first advertised to recover his slave Ephraim in 1797, noting that he was contesting Ephraim's freedom petition. In October 1800, Rawlings sought Ephraim again, declaring that he had run away immediately after the courts rejected that petition.[20]

Faced with these undesirable possibilities, some masters chose to manumit freedom petitioners. Although the Reverend John Ashton finally triumphed in court over the Mahoneys in 1802, by 1808 at least six of the seven brothers had been freed by Ashton or by Charles Carroll of Carrollton after he purchased some of the Mahoneys from Ashton. As an owner of more than two hundred slaves, including a number of Joices whose freedom might also be at stake, Carroll was intensely interested in the outcome of the case. He may have thought it wise to dampen discontent amongst his own bondspeople over rejection of the Mahoneys' petition by purchasing them in order to grant them eventual freedom six years after their final defeat in court. In a similar move, Carroll, who otherwise granted very few manumissions, sold John Joice his freedom for two hundred dollars immediately after the Ashton-Mahoney decision.[21]

At least one master explicitly manumitted a slave on the condition that the slave file no petition for freedom during the eight-year term he would serve before gaining liberty. Other deeds hint at similar bargains.[22] The promised emancipation of an individual, rather than weakening the social fabric of slavery, may in fact have reinforced it by providing an outlet for resistant or troublesome slaves. Still, freedom petitions constituted a major irritant to slaveowners, at least into the 1790s, one that loomed larger in and around

Baltimore than in more rural areas, given the greater flow of information among city residents and the fact that the abolition society had its headquarters there.

Those who petitioned for freedom or negotiated for self-purchase opted for gradual change in their lives. Others chose to speed up their liberation by relocating northward, like Peter Matthias. Still others may have decided to run away as a result of religious experience with white evangelicals, like the Maryland slave raised in a Methodist family on "terms of PERFECT EQUAL-ITY" who fled when hired out to someone who refused to treat him that way. Perhaps, like Alley, a Maryland woman who ran off in 1790, one might try to pass as free by claiming to have been freed by a Methodist preacher.[23]

Neither manumission nor flight posed fundamental challenges to a white-dominated society that accepted slavery. In the northern Chesapeake, where chances of thus gaining freedom were fairly high, the violent alternative of immediate and collective assaults on bondage through rebellion was unheard of. But farther south things were different.

In Richmond, as in Baltimore and Wilmington, the close of the eighteenth century saw a growing demand for skilled workers, coupled with stagnation in the tobacco trade. Opportunities increased for slaves to learn a trade, or to become carters and boatmen to keep goods moving. Like their northern counterparts, these men were hired out, or even hired their own time, turning over a stipulated weekly or monthly sum to a master but ordering their day-to-day business with little or no white supervision. This opportunity to exercise a degree of control over one's work and income appears linked to the ability to purchase freedom in many slave societies.

Opportunities to parlay autonomy at work into freedom arose less often in Virginia. Blacks lacked the leverage that borderlands and tidewater geography conveyed in Baltimore, and consequently the threat of flight weighed more lightly in Richmond slaveowners' calculations. In the late 1790s, manumissions through self-purchase remained a trickle, and chances to win freedom through the petition route had dwindled. As for the prospect of legislated emancipation, the adoption of a gradual abolition statute in New York in 1799 only underlined to Afro-Virginians how remote a prospect such legislation remained in Virginia. Black men hungering for control of their lives considered securing it by force.

Early in the year 1800, a twenty-four-year-old enslaved blacksmith named Gabriel, living near Richmond, began planning an armed uprising. A skilled craftsman, literate, and granted the privilege of moving about the countryside in his free time, Gabriel's circumstances underscored how changes in Afro-Virginian society had created people capable of challenging slavery in ways slaveowners had never encountered before. Gabriel's open resistance to white domination first surfaced in 1799, when he and two other black men were convicted of stealing hogs. Gabriel was also found guilty of assaulting the white who had discovered the theft, a capital crime for a slave. Because Gabriel was a first-time offender, he was granted benefit of clergy, a holdover from medieval law that Virginia law had applied to slaves since 1732. The grant spared his life and commuted his sentence to burning in the hand, some time in jail, and a requirement that his owner post a bond for his good behavior.[24]

We have no way of knowing if the humiliation of conviction and branding drove Gabriel to plot an insurrection, but the following spring he roamed the area around his home, visiting religious meetings, barbecues, and fish feasts where slaves gathered, and talking quietly about the "business" of rebellion. During the spring and early summer, Gabriel and a widening circle of lieutenants recruited hundreds of men from Richmond and nearby counties to take part in an elaborate plot to attack and seize the capital. One group of slaves was to set fires in the tobacco warehouse district at the eastern end of the city. When white citizens rushed there to put out the flames, a second detachment would seize the state armory in the capitol building at on the west side. Once armed, they would capture or kill the governor and as many legislators as possible. Meanwhile, a third body of men would take and hold Mayo's bridge over the James River, to prevent whites from the countryside retaking the town. Gabriel and his soldiers would then use surviving hostages to bargain for their freedom.

Such plans no doubt sounded fantastic to some who were invited to join the plot, but Gabriel made a convincing case. In 1800 slaves composed the greater part of the population in Richmond and its environs. Once begun, a revolt could not automatically be snuffed out by overpowering numbers of whites. Further, Gabriel and his men had a chance to overcome the lack of weapons that normally hamstrung slave rebellions. Robert Cowley, the doorkeeper of the General Assembly and a free person of color, held the keys to the armory. Gabriel believed that Cowley would open the armory and allow his men to arm themselves.

The odds were long, but circumstances made the times as propitious as they ever would be. In 1800 America was engaged in a naval war with France, which though formally undeclared still held out the prospect that foreign whites might lend aid to a slave insurrection. At the same time, bitter struggles between Federalists and Republicans divided white Americans approaching the presidential race between incumbent John Adams and Thomas Jefferson. To Gabriel and many of his adherents, the atmosphere was perhaps reminiscent of the fruitful turmoil of the 1770s and early 1780s. As in the Revolution, some whites might align themselves against the wealthy planters and merchants who led Virginia. Those known to be "friendly to liberty"— Quakers, Methodists, and Frenchmen—were to be spared when the coup succeeded, as were "poor white women who had no slaves." Whatever support might be expected from these groups, at the very least divisions and distractions could weaken white countermeasures against Gabriel's scheme.

The conspirators undoubtedly also drew inspiration from the still unfolding black rebellion in St. Domingue. Since 1791 slaves there had been battling to win independence and end slavery in what would become the nation of Haiti. Under the brilliant leadership of Toussaint L'Ouverture, they had overthrown the rule of colonial slaveholders and had beaten back English and Spanish efforts at reconquest. Throughout the 1790s white refugees from St. Domingue had fled to the United States and many other locations in and around the Caribbean, often taking slaves with them. Word of the slaves' revolution in St. Domingue, disseminated in part by the refugees, helped inspire a wave of rebellions in slave societies in the 1790s. By 1800 the Chesapeake was home to several thousand "French negroes" who could testify directly to the potential of a slave rebellion.[25]

By June 1800, Gabriel's plans had matured, and recruiting had spread twenty miles south of Richmond to Petersburg, where another band of black men stood ready to mount a diversionary disturbance or perhaps march to Richmond as reinforcements. Gabriel, his brother Solomon, and a third smith began to forge weapons. Scythe blades, symbolic of slaves' status as field hands, were hammered into swords, the weapons of white gentlemen, to be carried on the march to Richmond until the guns in the armory could be seized.

Indeed, much of Gabriel's presentation of himself to his followers demonstrates the emergence of a genuinely African American culture. Gabriel and his inner circle made lists of conspirators' names and brandished them at recruiting meetings. The risks that such lists might fall into hostile hands paled in comparison to Gabriel's desire to show his mastery of literacy and to tap the enormous psychological power such displays evoked for men with no access to the written word. Men joined the conspiracy, not as Africans taking an oath of blood or participating in a ring shout, but as Americans, enrolling their names on paper.[26]

Meanwhile, events in white Virginia continued to augur well. A contingent of U.S. Army troops stationed in Richmond was disbanded in June. At more or less the same time, Governor James Monroe ordered the guns of a number of county militia units brought to the armory in Richmond for repairs and cleaning. If Gabriel could take the armory, local militias would have nothing in their arsenals with which to fight back.

By early August, Gabriel and a half-dozen other leaders had agreed on the night of Saturday, August 30 for the attack on Richmond. Many slaves in the area had Saturday afternoon and evening to themselves. Their appearance on roads to Richmond would be a normal event that aroused no suspicion among whites. At a final meeting of the leadership group at Prosser's blacksmith shop on August 25, Gabriel estimated the strength of the conspiracy at five to six hundred men. Despite the breadth of the plot and its long gestation, whites suspected little. A few vague rumors had reached authorities in Petersburg in mid-August, and had been passed on to Richmond mayor James McClurg, who in turn had informed Monroe. Yet, other than a modest strengthening of patrols in Richmond, the government took no measures to secure the city.

Late in the afternoon of August 30, the weather turned violent. A ferocious thunderstorm brought torrential rains to the Richmond area, washing out bridges and preventing insurgent slaves from reaching their assembly points for the attack. Only a handful turned up. Gabriel and his cohorts hoped to pass the word for a new attack date, but the delay caused by the "providential" storm, as relieved whites would later call it, proved fatal to their plans. A recently recruited conspirator, Pharaoh, had decided to pursue his own interests by informing on the conspirators. After consulting with a fellow slave who was not involved in the plot, Pharaoh told what he knew to his owner's brother, Mosby Sheppard, on the afternoon of August 30, only hours before the planned assault. Sheppard quickly got word to the governor.

This time, with further confirmation of the conspiracy's existence coming in from Petersburg as well, Monroe did not hesitate. He had muskets transferred from the capitol to the more defensible state penitentiary, and patrols took to the roads. The dragnet quickly picked up a number of key conspirators and a grim business of extracting confessions, identifying additional plotters, and hanging would-be rebels commenced.

Gabriel went into hiding, then escaped from Richmond on the schooner *Mary*, with the apparent collusion of its master, Richardson Taylor, a white Methodist. Billy, a slave sailor on the vessel, recognized Gabriel and urged Taylor to turn him in to authorities. Taylor refused and sailed to Norfolk. Billy, who no doubt hoped to collect the three hundred dollar reward being offered for Gabriel's capture, went ashore at Norfolk and told what he knew to the sheriff. Gabriel was taken, returned to Richmond, convicted of insurrection, and hanged on October 10, the last of twenty-seven slaves to be executed. To the end, Gabriel refused to show remorse or to implicate others. His sentiments can be summed up in the words of another conspirator, who may have startled the whites of Richmond with language that hearkened back to the rhetoric of the Revolution: "I have nothing more to offer than what General Washington would have had to offer had he been taken by the British. . . . I have adventured my life . . . to obtain the liberty of my countrymen, and am a willing sacrifice in their cause."[27]

At Monroe's urging, the legislature authorized Pharaoh's purchase at public expense in order to free him. Pharaoh subsequently bought the freedom of his wife and son. For him, co-operation and pursuit of self-interest paid off. Billy received only fifty dollars for his role in Gabriel's capture and was unable to buy his freedom. Richardson Taylor was released on bail, left Virginia, and never stood trial for his effort to assist Gabriel.

With the conspiracy thwarted, and slaveholders' control of Virginia vividly displayed at public hangings, whites meditated on the narrowness of their escape and the meaning of the conspiracy. Thomas Jefferson, writing within weeks of the plot's discovery, urged deportation of conspirators not already brought to trial and sentenced to death. His letter to Monroe hinted at the idea that the uprising could not be treated as a simple crime, and that punishments were only justifiable under the doctrine of self-preservation.[28] John Randolph of Roanoke judged that Gabriel would have succeeded but for the storm—there were too few armed whites in Richmond to have resisted successfully.[29] What troubled him most was the conspirators' "contempt of danger" and "sense of their [natural] rights." George Tucker, cousin of the gradual emancipationist St. George Tucker, agreed in a disturbing comparison of the rebellion to black deeds in the American Revolution. Then, "a few solitary individuals flocked to [Dunmore's] standard, under which they are sure to find protection." In Gabriel's case, "they . . . of their own accord, combine a plan for asserting their claims, and rest their safety on success alone." For Tucker the alarming difference in slaves' outlook was that "then they fought for freedom as a good; now they also claim it as a right."[30]

Tucker argued that white Virginians had loosened their grip on slaves and discounted the possibility of rebellion with a misplaced "reliance on the difficulty of their acting in concert." Gabriel's rebellion had shattered the comfortable illusion that slavery could exist without complication within a republican society that championed liberty and equality. Tucker described three choices now open to Virginians. They could attempt to impose harsher controls on blacks to maintain slavery with safety, a course he dismissed out of hand. A "love of freedom," said Tucker, was an "inborn sentiment" that would continually be kindled into flame by the "advancement of knowledge among the negroes of this country," a process fostered by the growth of towns that "tend a thousand ways to enlighten and inform them." This was a process that could be "retarded, but which nothing could arrest." Those who "flatter themselves that a few cautionary laws, joined to a seasonable rigour" would end the danger of rebellion were deluded, because the Revolution had given birth to "an immense change in the opinions of men" that could not be reversed. Repression would fail, and fail bloodily.[31]

As a second alternative, Tucker posed that slaves might be emancipated to end the danger of insurrection. Could blacks and whites then live in harmony? No one imagined that the white body politic would end slavery on terms that would convey "the most important privileges of a citizen" to blacks, such as voting, office-holding, or any claims to social equality. Would men like Gabriel, who had planned to symbolize white acceptance of his equal status by "din[ing] and drink[ing] with the merchants of the city" settle for freedom without full civil and political rights?[32] Tucker thought not. He reasoned that a general emancipation of blacks would lead to the creation of social and economic distinctions among them, with "those who ... became rich ... form[ing] an intermediate class, which would be a fence against the possible enterprises of the rest." But playing one set of blacks against another to maintain white dominance was "one of those schemes ... which do more honour to the heart than to the head." Black people would "never rest satisfied with anything short of perfect equality." Hence the only safe solution was Tucker's third alternative—to emancipate and then transport the slaves elsewhere, to "colonize" them.

Plans for removing blacks for the good of white Virginians ranged from banishment of a handful of convicted rebel slaves to the wholesale relocation of all African Americans. The volume of deportation deemed desirable depended on the risk of insurrection, the cost of transporting blacks, and the purported economic and social gains to be realized by whitening the commonwealth. Proposed destinations for those to be colonized included Spanish territories in North America, West Africa, and eventually, any number of

Caribbean islands. Tucker's letter to the legislature ultimately called for transportation of all Virginia slaves to the trans-Mississippi region, or possibly
"the western lands of Georgia" (present day Alabama or Mississippi).

Presenting colonization as a safe passage between the Scylla of inaction
and the Charybdis of emancipated blacks loose in society, Tucker invoked
images of a horrific race war as the price to be paid if the ship of state went
off course. He did not speak for the majority. Letters to the *Virginia Gazette*
and to the *Fredericksburg Virginia Herald* acknowledged the difficulty of
maintaining slavery in a free republic, but their solution was to retrench
liberty to protect slaveholding.[33] The legislature agreed in part, quickly passing
laws to strengthen the militia and slave patrols and authorizing public purchase of slaves sentenced to death for the purpose of transporting and selling them outside the United States. This new law would be used in 1801 to
send one of Gabriel's lieutenants, Jack Ditcher, and a few other surviving
rebels to Spanish New Orleans.[34]

The legislators opened up the subject of colonization, passing a resolution that urged Governor Monroe to correspond with President-elect Thomas Jefferson regarding the purchase of land outside Virginia "whither persons obnoxious to the laws, or dangerous to the peace of society" might be
removed. This cautious proposal stopped well short of what George Tucker
had hoped for, and it also disappointed Jefferson, whose carefully guarded
views on slavery had long favored gradual emancipation coupled with colonization. Jefferson asked Monroe and the legislature to clarify their intentions, and to do so confidentially.

Over the next five years Virginia's white elite would struggle unsuccessfully to reconcile colonization with a host of ultimately irreconcilable needs.
In 1802 the discovery of another slave conspiracy, this one plotted by river
and ferrymen along the Roanoke River in Virginia and North Carolina,
spurred further legislative deliberations. Both houses passed proposals requiring free Negroes and those who might in the future be emancipated to
be colonized as soon as a suitable location was found. Western America
now seemed uncomfortably close for a colony of free blacks; this time Africa or South America were suggested to Jefferson as prospective sites.

At Jefferson's request, the American minister to Great Britain, Rufus King, pursued the option of sending black Virginians to Sierra Leone, a colony for freedpeople directed by British antislavery men. The company's directors turned King away. Sierra Leone already had black ex-slaves from the Americas, including Jamaican maroons resettled after the Maroon Wars of the 1790s and veterans of Lord Dunmore's regiment, who had arrived in West Africa following a long and unfruitful sojourn in Nova Scotia. Both groups had proved jealous of their liberties and unwilling to accept control of the colony by white leadership, which accordingly refused to consider taking on more black rebels.

When word of this rebuff reached Virginia, the legislature reverted to the notion of colonizing free blacks in western lands, pressing Jefferson with still more resolutions in 1804 and 1805. By then the Louisiana Purchase had made the trans-Mississippi American territory, and Jefferson refused to consider creating a black colony from any portion of it. In 1806, Virginia's lawmakers finally gave up on the idea of a federally sponsored colony. They settled instead for a law requiring slaves emancipated after its passage to leave Virginia within one year, subject to re-enslavement if they stayed in the state. This law, though frequently ignored or weakened by exemptions, remained on the books, registering most white Virginians' abiding distrust and fear of free people of color, until the end of slavery.

At first glance, the legislators' dogged focus on free blacks as the source of trouble seems incomprehensible. Gabriel's rebellion had been led by enslaved men, as had the subsequent conspiracy of 1802. Few if any free blacks had participated in either plot. Why target them in seeking to repress further insurrections? Either the thoroughgoing removal of all African Americans, as proposed by George Tucker, or the unflinching imposition of harsher control on slaves, as suggested by the correspondents to the *Gazette* or the *Herald,* would appear to have been more logical. Yet full-scale emancipation and colonization, as St. George Tucker had realized in 1796, was unthinkable because it would deprive planters of the cheap labor they absolutely needed. On the other hand, admitting that Virginia could protect slavery only through repression and relinquishing its place in the vanguard of free societies was equally unacceptable. As historian James Sidbury has suggested, Virginians instead chose to engage in a form of denial, displacing blame for slave conspiracies onto free blacks and soothing themselves with the thought that a limited relocation of this small element of society would solve all problems.[35] Colonization or banishment of free blacks would cost relatively little and would leave planters with their slave work force and their republican sensibilities relatively intact. It was a theory altogether more appealing than the alternatives.

The same black desires for independence and self-respect that drove Gabriel and his cohorts to rebel could find other expressions, particularly with the emergence of communities of free people of color. The decades between the close of the Revolution and the War of 1812 witnessed both the emancipation of thousands of African Americans in the Chesapeake and the creation of black Christian communities springing from conversions to evangelical sects, especially the Methodists and Baptists. These two crucial developments reinforced each other. Whites attracted by evangelical spiritual messages played an initially important role in proselytizing and freeing slaves. African Americans for their part seized the opportunity that conversion to Christianity afforded to assert one's humanity and spiritual equality, joining churches, forming congregations, and preaching to the unconverted. When white evangelicals pulled back from their religious challenge to slavery and demanded black subordination in biracial churches, blacks took matters into their own hands and formed the first African American–led churches and congregations, bulwarks that would help the black community to survive the post-1815 hardening of proslavery sentiment in the region.

The flowering of black Christianity and converts' relations with whites followed a path parallel to that of the secular liberation of slaves. The process began with individual black actions taken in alliance with principled whites, to achieve manumission on the one hand, or conversion on the other. The next step involved blacks attempting to bend institutions to their ends—using the law to file freedom petitions in the secular world, or asserting black rights to preach or to organize congregations in the spiritual world.

Finally, the withdrawal of white support for black objectives created conditions that fostered outright black assertiveness to achieve what had been
perceived as shared goals. Gabriel's Rebellion to achieve political and social
equality would find a spiritual counterpart thirty years later in Nat Turner's
fateful attempt to hasten the arrival of Judgment Day.

For all their significance, neither Gabriel nor Turner epitomized the
complex, intertwined nature of the black struggle to achieve both temporal
and spiritual freedom. If anyone could do so, it would surely be Richard
Allen, whose life touched on all the major elements of Christianizing the
black Chesapeake. Allen's religious conversion informed and facilitated his
manumission. After paying off his purchase price in 1783, Allen left Delaware for New Jersey, where he met the charismatic preacher Benjamin Abbott.
Traveling with Abbott as an exhorter, Allen preached to Indians in the Carolinas, to Germans in Lancaster County, Pennsylvania, and to white and black
audiences in and around Philadelphia and Baltimore. By 1785 he had joined
a group of Methodists in Fell's Point, Baltimore's ship-building area, and
had taken part as an observer at the 1784 Methodist conference in that city.

Allen had already attracted attention from white leaders, too. No less a
person than Bishop Francis Asbury asked Allen to accompany him as an
exhorter on a journey to the South. Asbury perhaps saw Allen following in
the footsteps of other early black preachers such as Harry Hosier, who had
achieved fame speaking to white audiences in Virginia, or Jacob Toogood, a
onetime slave from Frederick County, Maryland, who became a notable
itinerant in that state in the 1770s and 1780s.[36] But Asbury also made it clear
that white sensibilities would circumscribe Allen's ability to preach to slaves,
and that social convention would deny Allen hospitality in the white homes
where Asbury slept, requiring him to bed down in the bishop's carriage.
Even in the 1780s the marriage of white and black enterprise in Methodism
was an uneasy one.[37]

Allen turned down Asbury's offer and continued to travel the mid-
Atlantic, eventually settling in Philadelphia, where the blacks he brought
into Methodist congregations and religion classes included many ex-slaves
from Delaware or Maryland. But the success of Allen and men like Absalom

Jones, another freedman from Delaware, made white church leaders uneasy. Black efforts to create a separate African chapel in the late 1780s were rebuffed. Yet when the white trustees of St. George's chapel, the principal Methodist church in Philadelphia, expanded their church they insisted on segregating black worshippers in a second floor gallery. Unaware of the new rules, Allen, Jones, and other blacks took their accustomed places on the main floor at a service in June of 1792. The trustees demanded that they leave: Absalom Jones was pulled away while kneeling to pray. As Allen reported, "we all went out of the church in a body, and they were not more plagued with us in the church."[38]

Blacks now bent all their efforts to establishing their own chapel with their own ministers. White Methodist leaders disapproved of this course as well. The hierarchy did not trust blacks to provide spiritual guidance or manage church affairs without white supervision. Over the next twenty years, Allen and his parishioners would struggle to assert their autonomy within the Methodist church, fending off efforts by whites to seize legal control of the black-funded chapel and defeating attempts to place white preachers in the pulpit. The issue would be resolved only by separation. In 1816 black Methodists in the mid-Atlantic convened in Baltimore and created the African Methodist Episcopal church with Richard Allen as its first bishop.

Throughout the Delmarva region whites who had welcomed the first black converts reacted negatively to dramatic increases in the number of blacks in their congregations. Wherever blacks attained what whites deemed a "critical mass," segregation was imposed in Sunday worship, religious classes, and love feasts.[39] Scenes similar to those played out in Philadelphia spurred the formation of independent black churches. Ezion Church in Wilmington, Delaware, came into being in 1805 after blacks in the Asbury Methodist Episcopal Church were restricted to gallery seating.

In Maryland blacks formed a substantial part of the Methodist movement from the beginning. English missionary Thomas Rankin estimated in 1774 that five hundred blacks belonged to Methodist societies, about 25 per cent of the colony's total. By the 1780s, itinerants were meeting with black classes in Dorchester County, on the Calvert County circuit, and in Prince

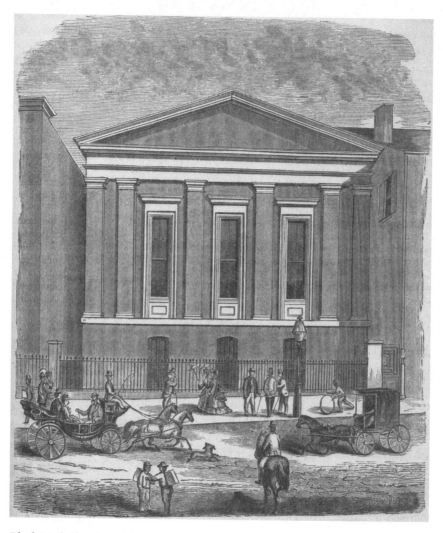

Black Methodists in Baltimore established their own congregation at Sharp Street, near the harbor, in the 1790s and built a church by 1802. Engraving from the 1840s or 1850s. (Maryland Historical Society.)

George's County. There William Colbert encountered a "very numerous and very orderly" black congregation operating its own meetinghouse, near today's Oxon Hill.[40] In Baltimore, Jacob Fortie and Caleb Hyland led a class that met in Hyland's boot-blacking cellar. Repeatedly, white insistence on segregated seating led to black demands for their own churches. In 1793 black Methodists leased a building on Sharp Street near the Baltimore harbor for their own use and two years later sent a delegation to Bishop Francis Asbury, asking to build a church that would be under their own direction, with no white stewards or trustees. Though Asbury rejected this proposal, by 1802 blacks owned the Sharp Street building and lot, and, led by blacksmiths Jacob Gilliard and Richard Russell, had established an independent congregation that retained its formal affiliation with the white-dominated Methodist Episcopal Church.[41] Other black dissidents would join in creating the African Methodist Episcopal Church, from their base at Bethel Church, also active since the 1790s.

Virginia's African Americans chose to affiliate with Baptist congregations. In 1809 the Dover, Ketocton, and Portsmouth associations of Baptist churches reported over nine thousand black members, roughly double the number of black Methodists in the state. Black Baptists actually outnumbered whites in these associations, and the same pattern of rising dissension between the groups prevailed. Racially mixed congregations broke up over seating arrangements, arguments about whether blacks could preach to mixed audiences, and challenges to black participation in church governance. One mark of slavery's dominance in Virginia society was that fewer independent black congregations emerged or survived the strains of separation from whites in the early nineteenth century.[42]

The growth of the black church remains the single most remarkable social phenomenon of African American life in the post-revolutionary era. In the 1770s, Baptist and Methodist itinerants had preached to handfuls of blacks, mostly in isolated rural meetings on the Delmarva peninsula. By 1816 tens of thousands of blacks had formed congregations, built churches, conducted Sunday school classes, and licensed their own exhorters and preachers. As spiritual sanctuaries, social rallying points, and a powerful element in defining African American identity, churches would anchor the effort to create and sustain free black communities in the face of slavery's surprising resurgence in the Chesapeake.

As blacks in the Chesapeake began to abandon hopes of religious fellowship with whites and look to each other for support, allies from outside the region swept in to offer the prospect of freedom. As in the Revolution forty years earlier, British warships patrolled the Chesapeake Bay during the War of 1812, offering enslaved blacks liberty in return for support.

An amalgam of American discontents and desires had created the war. Westerners yearned to conquer Canada, in part to deprive Ohio Valley Indian nations of British support in struggles for control of the region. Others objected to British interference with American shipping and the impressment of sailors on American vessels into the British navy. Taken together, these forces and a bumptious nationalism generated a declaration of war from Congress in June 1812, followed by American invasions of Canada.

For the British, war with America was an unwelcome distraction from the life and death combat with Napoleonic France. At least until Napoleon's defeat and first abdication in 1814, the British kept chiefly on the defensive in America, striving to hang on to Canada. Their naval raids were aimed at preventing the concentration of American forces and thereby diverting thrusts against Canada. The Chesapeake, with its tidal rivers beckoning as avenues of invasion near the new national capital, proved irresistible to British strategists. Once again thousands of slaves bent British tactics to their own purposes, trading their services to the invaders for freedom.[43] And, as in the Revolution, a smaller number of blacks, slave and free, won laurels aiding the United States against the British.

A British fleet and army appeared in the bay in the spring of 1813, commanded by Admiral John Warren and Colonel Sydney Beckwith. Under orders to give no "encouragement to any disposition by the Negroes to rise against their Masters," the expedition was nonetheless "at liberty . . . to take them away with you" and "to enlist them in any of the Black Corps." As before, the British objective was to disrupt American war-making capacity, not destroy plantation society.

Many slaves ignored the ambivalence of British policy and headed for their warships and troops. A British occupation of Point Lookout, at the southern tip of Maryland's Western Shore, soon attracted hundreds of runaways in the summer of 1813. Blacks familiar with the bay volunteered as pilots and helped conduct raids up the rivers that destroyed houses, seized cattle, and provided a path to freedom for opportunistic slaves.[44]

Charles Ball, an ex-slave living near the Patuxent River, noted in his memoirs that blacks often initiated contact with the British, rowing to their ships by night to propose and coordinate mass escapes. In one such incident, nearly one hundred blacks eluded pursuit and gained haven with the British. Ball joined a party of Americans who subsequently came on board under a flag of truce to persuade the runaways to return to their owner, a Mrs. Wilson. Ball's efforts were unavailing. None of the ex-slaves agreed. "Their heads were full of notions of liberty and happiness in some of the West India islands."[45]

Marylanders and Virginians buttressed persuasion with precautions aimed at forestalling slave flight. As in the Revolutionary War, militia companies and watermen tried to interpose themselves between blacks and their British deliverers, with mixed success. A patrol near Lynnhaven Bay attacked an encampment of slaves waiting for a chance to join the British, killing six and dispersing the rest. In Princess Anne County, near Norfolk, a militia company drew a British naval party into an ambush by blackening their faces and pretending to be slaves signaling a desire to come on board.

Slaveholders also tried to discourage blacks by insinuating that the British would resell them into slavery in the West Indies. Slaves, like their fathers and mothers of the revolutionary era, shrugged off such claims. Perhaps they knew that the British abolition of the slave trade in 1807 had made it far more difficult for the King's soldiers and sailors to seize blacks and sell them for private gain. In fact, the "notions of liberty" in the "West India islands" entertained by Mrs. Wilson's ex-slaves were not as visionary as Charles Ball's narrative suggests. The British were indeed eager to settle free blacks in colonies that needed agricultural workers. Ball himself was invited to join the runaways, who would be sent to Trinidad, a recently acquired British possession.[46]

British prosecution of the war in America stepped up in 1814, following Napoleon's exile to Elba. In April, Admiral Sir Alexander Cochrane replaced Warren, and signaled his more aggressive intentions by openly welcoming slaves. "All persons who may be disposed to migrate from the United States, will with their families, be received on board of His Majesty's ships." In anticipation of taking the offensive in the Chesapeake, Cochrane recruited black soldiers from those who rallied to him, using Tangier Island in the lower bay as a base and training camp. By summer, a Corps of Colonial Marines had sprung into life, composed of two hundred ex-slaves and three hundred regulars.

These freedmen fought with the British in several major battles in the Chesapeake, including the campaigns against Washington and Baltimore. When British forces routed superior numbers of American troops at Bladensburg, on August 24, 1814, the black marines performed with "their accustomed zeal and bravery" according to official reports, and took part in the brief British occupation and burning of the national capital. General Robert Ross quickly withdrew his troops, fearing that Americans would organize a counterattack. As his men pulled back on August 26, slaves sought to join the British ranks, promising to serve as soldiers or sailors if freed, offers that Ross rebuffed as he hastened back to the protection of his ships.

In fact, American militia units allowed Ross to retreat unhindered, immobilized by fear of slave uprisings that had also compromised the capital's defense. As Ross was marching east toward the bay, General Tobias Stansbury took his Maryland regiment in the opposite direction to quell a rumored insurrection in Georgetown. Some regiments all but dissolved after the defeat at Bladensburg, as citizen-soldiers dashed to their homes to guard against the apprehension that blacks "would take advantage of the absence of the men to insult the females." Earlier, Virginia militias had been slow to muster in defense of Washington due to concerns about slave rebellion.[47] Though these fears proved baseless, they had played their part in rendering the Chesapeake all but defenseless.[48]

If black responses to British offers of liberty in the War of 1812 matched the patterns of the Revolutionary War, corresponding chances for distinction and freedom by serving in the American cause were smaller. The Militia Act of 1790 had limited service in state militias to white men, evincing slaveholders' objections to people of color acquiring military training and handling guns. Local defenders of the Chesapeake's cities followed suit. In Baltimore, General Samuel Smith used African Americans as laborers to entrench and fortify the city, but he did not arm them.

African Americans still contributed to the defense of the Chesapeake as sailors. Commodore Joshua Barney's fleet of gunboats, destroyed in the course of the Washington campaign, had its share of black seamen and gunners. Some of those men manned batteries at forts that supported Fort McHenry and helped it withstand the British bombardment of September 13–14. Inside McHenry's walls a runaway slave died defending the "Star-Spangled Banner." William Williams, escaped from a tobacco plantation in Prince George's County, enlisted as a volunteer in a U.S. Army infantry regiment that subsequently saw action at Fort McHenry. A cannonball took off his leg and he died at the end of 1814 in a Baltimore hospital.

At about the same time Williams breathed his last, British and American negotiators agreed to the Treaty of Ghent, ending the War of 1812. The British navy honored promises of freedom to black allies by transporting them out of the United States. After a temporary stay in Bermuda, blacks who had fought in the Colonial Marines took ship for Trinidad, where in 1816 they founded a community that still endures, known today as the "Merikens" and esteemed for their hard-working independence.[49] Some two to three thousand black civilians embarked for Nova Scotia, where unlike their predecessors of the revolutionary era, they successfully rooted themselves, forming settlements in places such as Preston and Hammond's Plains.[50]

Peace in 1815 ended a virtual second War of Independence for the United States. The Treaty of Ghent closed an era of major wars with Britain, clashes at sea over American neutral rights, and covert British support of Native American opponents to westward expansion. After 1815 American preoccupation with Britain would diminish, and national energies would concentrate more fully on conquering and settling a western empire beyond the Appalachians. For African Americans, the final departure of British soldiers in 1815 closed one route to freedom, while the opening of the Old Southwest created a new passage to a much expanded world of plantation slavery in the Cotton Kingdom.

CHAPTER 5

A Flickering Candle

S LAVES WHO HOPED FOR A GENERAL emancipation by backing the British in the War of 1812 saw their dreams dashed, and they also judged, correctly, that there was no chance of an across-the-board liberation from within Chesapeake society. By 1815 emancipationists were extinguished as a political force. The view of slavery as a positive good had not yet prevailed, but the content of "antislavery" took on an increasingly anti-black cast. Whites concerned about slavery responded to this harsher environment in three ways. Many who remained committed to gradual emancipation simply left the Chesapeake, or if they were too outspoken, were driven out. Others refocused their activities from antislavery advocacy to missionary work among the slaves or protecting free people of color from kidnapping. A third highly visible group urged the removal of people of color via colonization, with a distant prospect of ending slavery thereby.

Colonizationists dropped denunciations of slaveholding as immoral or anti-republican. Instead they stressed slavery's deleterious impact on economic growth and development for whites in the Chesapeake. Only a handful of Quakers and evangelicals continued to attack slavery head-on. This virtual cessation of debate on slavery as a moral or political evil predated the rise of pressure from immediate abolitionism in the North. Well before the abolitionist attacks of the 1830s, Deep South defenders of slavery denounced Upper South proponents of colonization as closet abolitionists.[1] Writers of the 1830s and thereafter who insisted on slavery's compatibility with Christianity and republicanism were just re-articulating old arguments

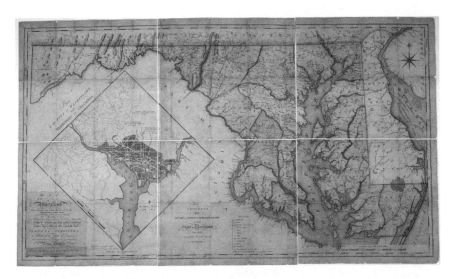

A map of Maryland and its counties, c. 1813. Dennis Griffith, Map of the State of Maryland, 2d. edition, 1813. *(Maryland Historical Society.)*

and directing them against new adversaries. Overall, proslavery advocates tried to draw debate away from economic issues, appealing instead to white fears of free blacks as potential equals in society. Correspondingly, colonizationists' narrow focus on the benefits of their schemes to white people reflected a need to protect their flanks from proslavery sharpshooters.

After 1815 African Americans in the Chesapeake lost their internal allies against slavery. Once-sympathetic whites either departed the region themselves or became colonizationists who demanded that free blacks do so. Blacks and whites could act together to end slavery only when both left the area, as Edward Coles discovered.

Coles exemplified the principled opponents of slavery who chose to free themselves of the "stain" of slaveholding by leaving. A wealthy young man who inherited a substantial number of slaves, Coles was torn between a longing to remain in Virginia and a desire to free his slaves. The revised manumission law of 1806 mandated that newly freed African Americans leave the state within a year of their liberation. Coles shrank from exiling people with few resources and no friends from their homeland. He considered migrating to a free state or territory with those he intended to free and there purchasing land as a stake in life for his ex-chattels. Alternatively, he could stay in Virginia and fight for new laws that would allow manumitted persons to remain.[2]

At first, Coles tried the latter course and in 1814 wrote to Thomas Jefferson seeking to enlist the former president's support. As a onetime aide to James Madison, Coles imagined that he knew enough of politics and Jefferson's nature to move the older man to speak out. His letter castigated slavery as a relic of "British colonial policy," in words that evoked Jefferson's own youthful writings in the *Summary View of the Rights of Virginia* and early drafts of the Declaration of Independence. He assured Jefferson that endorsing the noble cause of antislavery would add luster to his reputation in history even while it swayed contemporary opinion. Jefferson's discouraging reply bespoke both his aversion to African Americans and his lifelong unwillingness to risk public disapproval in the fruitless enterprise of opposing slavery in Virginia. At first, he declined to take up his pen by noting his advanced age and repeating the well worn claim that public opposition to slavery by notable men would only strengthen proslavery sentiment. He buttressed this notion with an avowal that his views had been before the public for thirty years or more. When Coles pressed him, observing that Franklin had taken up the presidency of the Pennsylvania Abolition Society in his eighties, Jefferson firmly rebuffed the younger man. He closed the correspondence by urging Coles not to free his slaves at all, either in Virginia or elsewhere, but to fulfill his moral duty by taking good care of them.

Instead, Coles left Virginia with his slaves in 1819 and freed them while crossing the Ohio River into Illinois. There he purchased 160-acre plots for each black family and went into politics, becoming the new state's second governor in 1822. He subsequently played a prominent role in defeating a referendum seeking to legalize slavery in Illinois. Coles's departure from Virginia may have been influenced by more than the disappointment of Jefferson's refusal to espouse his cause. In 1815, soon after the correspondence with Jefferson, reaction to a proposed mass manumission of Virginia slaves made clear legislators' unbending sentiments on that sensitive subject.

In January 1815, Samuel Gist, a wealthy planter and merchant who had for many years resided in England, died possessing over eight thousand acres in the Virginia Piedmont and some three hundred slaves. Gist's will declared the slaves free and vested them collectively with all his Virginia lands, stock, and tools, under the supervision of white trustees. The trustees were instructed to invest profits from the joint enterprise of the freedmen in capital improvements on the estate as well as "instructing . . . my several Slaves and their Issue in the Christian Religion . . . and Schools for the Education of the Children." This huge bequest anticipated all the objections about turning loose supposedly improvident and thieving blacks on society without the resources to survive. Freedmen would be provided with a means of earning an honest living, religious instruction, and education under white guidance. But Gist, long absent from Virginia, had written the will in ignorance of the 1806 law restricting manumissions.

Accordingly, his daughters had to petition the state legislature for a private law allowing Gist's slaves to remain in Virginia after being freed. In 1816 the assembly approved the manumissions only on condition that the freedmen be relocated outside the state, and added a non-binding recommendation that the trustees consider colonization in Sierra Leone. Under no circumstances were large numbers of newly freed black people welcome to remain in Virginia. Eventually, the trustees manumitted Gist's slaves and settled them in Ohio where some of their descendants still farm today.

When John Randolph of Roanoke willed freedom to several hundred of his slaves in 1833, they too, settled in Ohio. Other groups of freed slaves migrated to towns like York and Columbia in southern Pennsylvania.[3]

In Maryland as in Virginia, a jaundiced view of free people of color hamstrung white efforts to assist them, including those of the Protection Society of Maryland, founded in 1816 in Baltimore. The society sought to protect free black people from being kidnapped and sold for slaves in Savannah, Mobile, or New Orleans, a dreadful business that mushroomed with the onset of the first cotton boom in the Old Southwest. With activists like Elisha Tyson among its leaders, the society proclaimed preventing kidnappings to be its sole objective, a stance that placed it squarely in the tradition of wealthy benevolence to dependent persons.[4]

Eager to avoid the hostility that had dogged the Maryland Abolition Society in the 1790s, the Protection Society stood four-square for the principle of white property rights in black bodies. Its introductory announcement repeatedly disavowed any intent to "interfer[e] with any subsisting legal tie or duty, resulting from the relation between masters and slaves," whether to "lessen the value, impair the obligation, relax the rigor, or shorten the duration of legitimate servitude." Its leaders even denied any desire to "meliorate the condition" of slaves, let alone to seek their emancipation.[5] Indeed, in a memorial to the General Assembly of Maryland, it gave equal billing to the horrors attending "negroes ... entitled to freedom after a term of years ... [being] reduced to perpetual slavery" and on the other hand "masters in many instances [being] deprived of their slaves."[6] The characterization of free blacks as an adjunct to the slave population remained as strong in 1816 as it had been for the past thirty years.

After two turbulent years, the Protection Society reported in 1818 that it had "rescued more than sixty human beings from the grasp of lawless oppression, and restored a number of legal slaves to their proper masters." Still, public reaction was deeply skeptical, as opponents "le[ft] no means untried to paralyze the exertions of the Society," chiefly by allegations about members' abolitionist tendencies. Once again, the society categorically denied any such aims.[7] But the society soon faded from sight, disbanding as the Panic of 1819 temporarily depressed demand for slaves in the Gulf States and kidnapping diminished accordingly.[8] Though scrupulously less threatening to slaveholders than the Abolition Society, the Protection Society fared no better in popular opinion.

The Protection Society fell afoul of a rapidly crystallizing conventional wisdom among whites in the Chesapeake about the pitfalls of a free black population. Central themes in this line of thought characterized blacks as unwilling to work without compulsion, incapable of thrift and accumulation, and prone to theft as a means of subsistence. These habits supposedly led to the "corruption" or "demoralization" of slaves with whom free blacks associated. Such fears also gained ground in northern states as gradual emancipation statutes freed slaves there, and would later typify the atti-

tudes of former masters in post-emancipation societies such as the South
after 1865, or late nineteenth-century Cuba.

Historians of these societies have found that such pejorative perceptions had some small grounding in actual behaviors. When people ceased to
be slaves, crimes they committed became public and thus more visible matters, rather than being settled privately among owners or overseers. Regarding work, freedpeople often did withdraw women and children from field
labor for house work or education after the end of slavery. In urban settings
many preferred self-employment to wage labor for white employers. All
were choices that whites could read as evidence of "laziness."[9]

The workings of manumission by self-purchase or term slavery could
contribute to perceived changes in black work patterns as well. Slaves seeking to buy themselves or family members often performed Herculean labors to scrape together money. Once clear of debts and installment payments surrounding self-purchase, a freedman certainly could subsist on fewer
hours of labor than previously, and doubtless many did.

No matter how hard someone worked, the earnings devoted to self-
purchase generated little or nothing in the way of tangible possessions that
symbolized thrift and industry to whites. Any cutback in wage labor after
being freed, or branching into self-employment could readily be adduced
as "proof" of free black improvidence. Whether or not self-purchase was
involved, a freed African American left behind a realm in which an owner's
interest dictated constant employment, and entered a world in which un-
employment and underemployment of laborers and craftsmen were quite
common. This was especially true in the volatile urban economies of early
nineteenth-century America. Little wonder then that devotees of classical
economics, ready enough to castigate white workingmen for failure to accumulate through steady labor and sober habits, would recoil from the prospects of blacks in freedom.[10] The resulting near-consensus on free black
"failure" drew both on the environmentalism of the late eighteenth century
and a newer view of political economy. Suspicion of all social change as
productive of decay and corruption had begun to recede where white society was concerned but still held the field unchallenged when it came to Af-

rican Americans. This retained skepticism about blacks would now be blended with a new hard-eyed reading of their performances as economic actors. Blacks' status as propertyless laborers became proof of their unfitness for life in a competitive society, making them a threat to stall the engines of destiny propelling American growth. Only elaborate schemes involving the wholesale relocation of thousands of free blacks could purify the environment and nurture habits of freedom and industry.

In this charged atmosphere whites in the Chesapeake began to talk more about removing free blacks. The idea had been in the air since the publication of Jefferson's *Notes on Virginia* in the 1780s. It resurfaced, if only to be dismissed, in St. George Tucker's *Dissertation on Slavery* in 1796, and had been seriously considered in the confidential correspondence between then-Governor Monroe and President Jefferson in the wake of Gabriel's rebellion. In 1816 white dismay over the presence of free blacks, together with renewed fears of slave insurrection stoked by black aid to the recent British invasion, led Marylanders to support the new American Colonization Society.

Prime movers of the colonization campaign in Maryland included attorney Francis Scott Key and former Congressman Robert Goodloe Harper, the latter also a member of the Protection Society. Harper laid out the case for colonization in a lengthy public letter to Elias Caldwell, secretary of the national organization in 1817.[11]

Harper assumed that those weighing the merits of colonization would naturally "be first struck by its tendency to confer a benefit on ourselves, by ridding us of a population for the most part idle and useless, and too often vicious and mischievous." Candidly admitting that white "prejudices" influenced these perceptions, Harper nonetheless saw free blacks as "condemned to a state of hopeless inferiority and degradation" because of their skin color, "an indelible mark of their origin and former condition." Blacks could never attain a state of equality because whites would be unable "to help . . . treating them as our inferiors . . . since we cannot help . . . associating them with the slaves." Specifying the kind of equality that white Americans feared, Harper ruled out black "visits in our houses," marriages with whites, or "public honors and employments."[12] Harper thus combined a view of change as decadence with a perception of public opinion as immutable.

Thirty years earlier in his native South Carolina, Harper, like many in the immediate aftermath of the Revolution, showed more optimism. Then, he asked a crowd, "Can we imagine one being more superior to another than a Franklin, a Witherspoon, or a Jefferson, to a negro just landed from the Coast of Africa? Yet . . . the difference between them, great as it appears, arises wholly from education."[13]

By 1817, Harper thought well-founded white prejudice dictated black colonization rather than education. "The incitement to good conduct . . . which arises from the hope of raising himself . . . is a stranger to his breast." Accordingly, self-discipline and moral restraint had never replaced the master's rule, and "he lives in idleness, and probably in vice." If a free black did "follow some regular course of industry," he would still fail in life because "the habits of thoughtless improvidence which he contracted while a slave" would deny him the prudent economy needed in hard times.

Here, Harper implies that whether the poor were white or black, poverty itself denoted a personal moral flaw rather than a systemic problem. Harper believed that men were naturally averse to labor and free blacks raised in slavery would certainly not overcome its legacy of idleness. If one did shake off that idleness, he would catch it again "from the slaves among whom he is forced to live," leading to the inexorable outcome of "liv[ing] as a pauper, at the expense of the community." People born in slavery could never truly become free men. Imbued with the notion that social change could only occur imperceptibly over long periods, Harper despaired equally of whites accepting blacks in society or of their meriting such acceptance.[14] Unyielding white rejection would retard whatever progress ex-slaves might make, providing fresh fuel for the fires of white prejudice.

Allowing free blacks simply to remain at the bottom of the social ladder, as St. George Tucker had proposed, was unacceptable to Harper. This laissez-faire approach risked "corruption of the slaves . . . by rendering them idle, discontented and disobedient" through bad example. Speaking as a slaveholder, Harper sketched a gloomy picture of free black vice and disorder provoking otherwise hard-working and loyal slaves into flight, theft, and resistance. Untroubled by depicting free blacks as unable to shed the bad habits of slavery and then labeling free persons of color as spreading those same behaviors among slaves, Harper insisted that free blacks would be to blame if future slave misdeeds provoked slaveowners "to a severity, which would not otherwise be thought necessary."[15]

Despite its obvious illogic, Harper's letter distilled genuine and widespread objections to the anomalous status of emancipated African Americans in a society with race-based slavery. Free blacks did not fit satisfactorily in pre-existing social categories. As Harper put it, "You may manumit the slave, but you cannot make him a white man." On the other hand, the presence of black workers, slave or free, also inspired a contempt for hard work among "the class of free whites who ought to labour," and who instead, "saw labour as a badge of slavery." Free blacks, Harper concluded, were "injurious to all."[16]

Colonization would remedy all these ills. Black emigrants would escape white prejudice, and slaves would be secure from corrupting influences and resulting harsher treatment by masters. More whites would migrate into the slave states and all whites would work harder. Harper closed his letter with an adjuration against sending colonists to British-established Sierra Leone, as a committee of the United States Congress had recently recommended.[17] Instead, "our colony . . . ought to be republican from the beginning."[18] This salute to republican institutions was more than a swipe at the British. Rather, Harper's optimism that free blacks could establish a republic in Africa represented another instance of the high value he placed on social homogeneity. While their indeterminate status could disrupt American society, free people removed from interracial struggles and colonized to Africa among their own kind would flourish. They might there erect their own republican society, at the same time contributing by subtraction to the purification of the American republic. As Thomas Jefferson might have put it, blacks were of a separate "nation" and could reach a similar destiny as white Americans, so long as they did not mix with them. Harper's views resonated with the political community of Maryland. In its 1817–18 session, the legislature unanimously endorsed in principle the colonization of free blacks to Africa.[19]

In Virginia, Charles Fenton Mercer likewise supported colonization primarily for its purported benefits to whites, with a nod to the gains blacks would supposedly realize from escaping white prejudice. Neither Mercer nor Harper suggested a general emancipation of slaves. For them, colonization dealt with the issues of ill-considered manumissions and a growing free black population. Slavery itself, while abstractly an evil to them both, lay beyond the reach of human intervention.

For men like Mercer and Harper, colonization of free blacks had little if anything to do with opposition to slavery. To antislavery men like Baltimore editor Hezekiah Niles, however, that made African colonization both impractical and pointless. Niles, a Delaware-born Quaker who edited the nationally circulated *Weekly Register,* ferociously opposed the slave trade. He described the killing of a domestic slave trader in a mutiny at sea as a "just execution," and called for the "Algerine enslavement" of those engaged in the African slave trade.[20] But where emancipation was concerned, he advocated a plan "almost as unpleasant to the very ardent friends of emancipation, as others will prove to the brutal slaveholder."

Niles believed that free people of color regarded labor as an "oppression," and they had no one but themselves to blame for the "slacken[ing] . . . zeal of the friends of emancipation." Echoing Harper, Niles argued that black people, unaided, could not become worthy members of American society. He also saw wisdom in "separating the free negroes" from slaves. Niles nonetheless derided African colonization as too costly to be practical. Instead, he argued for gradual emancipation under a new plan that inculcated self-denial and a love of property among the liberated. Patriarchal guidance was indispensable to fostering the change; in the uncontrolled social atmosphere of the burgeoning city of Baltimore, former slaves were doomed.

Niles proposed annually removing ten to fifteen thousand slave women to northern households, where they would serve a term of years and then become free. His goal was nothing less than to "eradicat[e] the offensive color, and the distinctions in society it causes." First and foremost, removal of female slaves would "[check] the propagation of the slave-species," a first step toward "the final accomplishment of . . . the desire of every man's heart in America—the final abolition of slavery and the extinction of the slave species." Niles assumed that slave women bore an average of ten children, a wildly high figure that underpinned his claim that removal of "only" a few thousand persons a year would cause a decline in a slave population exceeding 1,800,000.[21]

Niles also bluntly advanced "amalgamation" as the only alternative to race war. Disclaiming any veiled approval of race-mixing, Niles argued that skin color was governed by climate and environmental factors, and that "a family of colored people, insulated by white people, and having no communication with others of a darker race . . . would in time lose . . . their darkness." For Niles, the right kind of manumission actually could turn blacks into whites, and changing color was the necessary prelude to enjoying freedom.

Niles extolled the convenience of his proposal for white property-holders. Like Jefferson, Niles thought slaveowners would happily part with female children as having little value, while northern householders would pay part of the slave girls' purchase prices to acquire cheap help. Moral objections to breaking up slave families would not apply; mothers would gladly relinquish daughters to a life of future freedom.

Anticipating criticism, Niles insisted that he favored only the northward emigration of young women, and not that of black men. Because women were "more tractable than men," the "transferred female negro . . . would sooner fit herself for freedom," as exposure to virtuous white women "would daily and hourly impress upon her mind a sense of right and wrong."[22] While the free black man buffeted by the turmoil of society could not hope to improve himself, the black woman, cocooned in a respectable white home, could transform herself into a free person. Niles thus bent the popular image of women as tutors of virtue into a vision of white women, themselves secluded from direct participation in the affairs of the republic, readying black women for a still more circumscribed role.

By reading black men out of his plan, Niles hoped to avoid the charge that a freed black population would demand equal political and social privileges with whites, as well as the visceral fear that black men would hold power over white men and marry white women.[23] Niles underlined the urgency of the situation by reiterating fears of black vengeance unless steps were taken to end slavery by elevating and deracinating blacks through internal colonization.[24]

Niles's remarkable proposal was virtually ignored, as the national debate over Missouri's admission to the Union absorbed all interest in the topic of slavery and emancipation from 1819 to 1821. Still, it indicates the evolution of antislavery thought in the Chesapeake. Niles dwelt little on the morality of slaveholding or its inappropriateness in a liberty-loving people. Instead, he played heavily on the dangers of insurrection, on slavery's drag on economic development, and on the moral desirability of an all-white society. Sharing the world view of proponents of African colonization, Niles merely propounded what seemed to him a cheaper and more practical alternative.

The antislavery behind Niles's advocacy of internal colonization was watery and feeble. Others who combined these views could be more explicit. Jesse Torrey's *A Portraiture of Domestic Slavery in the United States*, drawing on the author's extended stay in the Chesapeake, devoted most of its pages to an unsparing denunciation of the domestic slave trade and the kidnappings that fed it. Torrey concluded that education of slaves, compensated emancipation, and colonization should be undertaken.[25]

Men like Niles and Torrey made the colonization movement suspect to defenders of slavery, particularly in Virginia where only one-tenth of the state's African Americans were free. In the Old Dominion, reception of colonizationist and antislavery sentiments turned in no small measure on who expressed them. Bluebloods like Charles Fenton Mercer or Supreme Court Justice Bushrod Washington could espouse colonization without arousing suspicion, but outsiders and non-slaveholders with less public standing risked their livelihoods and even their lives when they spoke out.

British-born Presbyterian minister George Bourne accepted a pulpit in Lexington, Virginia, around 1815, where he stirred up his parishioners with sermons that condemned slaveholders as "mansteelers" deserving death, and slavery as a modern-day "Golden Calf" to which planters bowed down.

Admonished by his flock for making intemperate remarks, Bourne raised the stakes by publishing *The Book and Slavery Irreconcilable*, one of the first book-length attacks on slavery. This work recalls eighteenth-century religious polemics, with its unrelenting and exclusive focus on the sinfulness of slaveholding to the virtual exclusion of economic or libertarian arguments. At the same time, Bourne's hostile and contemptuous tone and his refusal to concede any legitimacy to defenders of slavery anticipated Garrison and the later abolitionists.[26]

Upon the book's publication, an already simmering controversy between Bourne and his flock boiled over. The congregation tried to expel Bourne. A Presbyterian synod rejected the local church's action and insisted on a retrial, but Bourne declined, having prudently left Virginia and fearing violence should he return. By 1818, Bourne had been removed altogether from the ranks of Presbyterian ministers.

It is not surprising that an uncompromising man with Bourne's gifts for denunciatory prose should be driven from his pulpit. More telling is that less than ten years later, a much milder antislavery Presbyterian, John D. Paxton, was also forced to leave Virginia. Paxton had far more finesse than Bourne, opposing slavery not by confrontation but by admonition and personal example. Stationed in southwestern Virginia near the Cumberland Gap, Paxton became a slaveowner through a bequest to his wife. The Paxtons educated these African Americans and then freed them and sent them to Liberia. Paxton next tried to organize a local chapter of the American Colonization Society, and he attracted some supporters. But public opposition forced cancellation of this project, as well as Paxton's occasional efforts to solicit church collections of funds for the ACS.

Paxton gave up preaching about slavery, since he had some slaves in his congregation and feared offending their masters with any discourse that could be seen as insurrectionary, but he continued to advocate colonization in the church newsletter. His congregation, like Bourne's, moved from opposition to rebellion. Driven out, Paxton could find another ministerial call only outside the Chesapeake.[27]

Jonathan Lankford, minister to a Baptist congregation at Black Creek in Virginia's Southside, met a similar fate when he refused to offer communion to slaveholding members. Though the congregation had a nonslaveholding majority, Lankford was labeled a troublemaker who sought to divide his flock and expelled in 1826. Virginians, never receptive to political challenges to slavery, had by the mid-1820s all but ruled out religiously motivated appeals as well. As the Black Creek congregation said, slaveholding was a matter for the private conscience of each member of the church.[28]

In this atmosphere, the role and presence of Quakers in Virginia steadily diminished. From the 1790s onward, many "made the 'Quaker move' . . . to Ohio." By 1829 such migrations had caused a steep membership decline in the Virginia Yearly Meeting, and continued losses led to its incorporation into the Baltimore Meeting by 1844.[29]

Antislavery faced slightly less obdurate opposition in Maryland and Delaware but eventually came a cropper there, too. In Baltimore, a surge of activism swept into the city when Benjamin Lundy relocated his newspaper, *The Genius of Universal Emancipation,* from Jonesboro, Tennessee. The first Baltimore issue appeared on July 4, 1825. Lundy, a onetime tanner, would expound tirelessly on slavery and freedom until moving on in late 1830. His Baltimore sojourn illuminated the worsening white attitudes toward the city's free black community.

Few aspects of the political economy of African Americans escaped Lundy's attention. He promoted schools and craft training for free blacks, acted as an agent for the colonization of freedpeople to Haiti, and touted plans for gradual emancipation via self-purchase. Combining relentless attacks on the kidnapping of free blacks with ceaseless agitation against the domestic slave trade, Lundy held up to contempt both slave dealers and those who sold to them. He editorialized for Baltimore attorney Daniel Raymond's antislavery candidacies for the Maryland legislature in 1825 and 1826.[30] The *Genius* regularly exhorted against slaveholding as unchristian and immoral, and printed sentimental poetry evoking the sorrows of bondage. On political themes, Lundy never wearied of portraying slavery as a blot on American republicanism and a consequent cause of mockery by Europeans.

But Lundy, like the colonizationists he pilloried, moved beyond the religious and republican arguments of earlier decades and strove to show the bankruptcy of bound labor both at the micro- and macro-economic levels. He claimed that free labor was more productive and hence cheaper than slave labor. On the other hand, both employers and wage workers would find a free labor economy more prosperous because of the consumer demand generated by free men taking the place of slaves.

Like Harper and Niles, this editor concerned himself only tangentially with the fate of ex-slaves once they attained freedom. He, too, focused on whether and under what white-managed plans they could become reliable wage workers. Lundy enthused about slaves buying freedom on an installment plan. Money paid for overtime work would purchase the right to labor for one's own benefit during a portion of the work week. A slave initially allowed to work for himself just one day of the week could become free in seven and a half years. Such a scheme would "ensure the punctual performance" of the slave's tasks while he acquired equity in himself, but more importantly, "he will enter into society with habits of industry and temperance, which are calculated to render him a valued citizen." If the slave failed to amass enough money to buy himself out, "he is scarcely entitled to the enjoyment of civil liberty."[31]

Lundy's progressive and routinized self-purchase plan implicitly denigrated existing manumission practices based on shifting and unenforceable bargains between masters and slaves.[32] He applauded a North Carolina correspondent who advocated statutory protection for slave earnings set aside for self-purchase, as well as for self-purchase agreements themselves.[33] In 1827, Lundy called attention to the *coartacion* laws of the former Spanish colonies, which allowed slaves to request and courts to fix a self-purchase price.[34] Regulated self-purchase, he emphasized, "incite[s] [slaves] to industry and economy, and prevents those from gaining their freedom who are unworthy of it."[35] But for Maryland slaveholders, Lundy's notions smacked of unwarranted intrusion into their own more freewheeling transactions with their slaves.

Slaveholder resentment turned violent when the Quaker editor created

William Lloyd Garrison (1805–1879), editor of The Liberator *from 1831 to 1865, was converted to an abolitionist stance by free blacks William Watkins and Jacob Greener, while serving as assistant editor of Benjamin Lundy's Baltimore-based* Genius of Universal Emancipation, *in 1829–30. Daguerreotype, undated. (Library of Congress.)*

a "black list," a column of diatribe aimed at named slave sellers and slave dealers. Austin Woolfolk attacked Lundy with his fists on a public street for labeling him a "manstealer" in an 1827 column. Lundy charged Woolfolk with assault, but received only one cent in damages. The jury took its cue from Judge Nicholas Brice's charge, in which Brice opined that no man in his memory had a greater provocation to defend his honor than Woolfolk. Two years later, Lundy's assistant editor, twenty-four-year-old William Lloyd Garrison, landed in jail on a libel conviction. Garrison had blacklisted Francis Todd, a merchant from his own home town of Newburyport, Massachusetts, for shipping slaves from Baltimore to New Orleans in his schooner. Garrison admitted the legality of the domestic slave trade, but insisted that "God and good men regard it with abhorrence." Fined fifty dollars, Garrison refused to pay, and spent over two months in the Baltimore jail before abolitionist Arthur Tappan bailed him out. By 1830, Garrison, Lundy, and *The Genius of Universal Emancipation* had left Baltimore.[36]

Like Lundy, Harper, and Niles, Daniel Raymond assessed slavery in the Chesapeake from an outsider's perspective. Born and trained in law in Connecticut, Raymond arrived in Baltimore in 1814 and quickly threw himself into the public sphere. He acted as secretary of the Protection Society in 1816 and organized opposition to the admission of Missouri as a slave state.

In 1820, Raymond published a pamphlet challenging the proposition that diffusing the South's slave population into trans-Mississippi territories would contribute to the gradual withering away of slavery.[37] In it he used census data to advance three claims: (1) That slave population grew at a faster rate than white population in a slaveholding state; (2) That white population grew faster in non-slaveholding states than in slaveholding states; (3) That free black population grew less than half as fast as the white population in non-slaveholding states. For Raymond, these patterns proved that diffusion of slavery would encourage growth in slave numbers while depressing that of whites. In contrast, manumission would reduce the ratio of blacks to whites.[38]

That such an outcome should be desired was axiomatic. "In a political, a moral, an intellectual, and a religious point of view, is not a white population better than a black one?" The key was not to restrain black increase per se, but to ask "whether the increase of one portion of them, ought to be restrained, in order to promote the increase of another."[39] Easing restrictions on manumission would promote this end. If freedpeople did "become a nuisance to society" were they not as slaves, "an infinitely greater nuisance?" Besides, the "mischiefs" of freedmen would gradually dwindle because the "idle, vagabond blacks do not raise families, or comparatively none." Thus, "the character of manumitted slaves [would] materially change in the course of one or two generations." Whites would gain either by promoting extinction of unworthy blacks or by fostering the creation of reliable black citizens.

Raymond in this way adopted to his own ends the suspicion that blacks could not survive without paternal white masters. Instead of insisting that black improvidence justified slavery or colonization, Raymond urged that liberating blacks might produce social good by hastening their extinction and the arrival of an all-white America. To be sure, the pamphlet opposed statutory abolition as wrongful seizure of property. Only voluntary manumission's gradual pace would "open a vein which would let out the polluted blood of slavery from the body politic, silently, constantly, and gradually, without endangering its health." Raymond bluntly concluded that freedmen "would . . . acquire the habits of free men . . . or dwindle to nothing."[40]

Further predictions of manumission's positive impact on the economy appeared in the *Genius* during Raymond's campaigns in 1825 and 1826 for a seat in the General Assembly. He now advocated a *post-nati* emancipation law that would free future male children of slave mothers at thirty and females at twenty-five. "Young slaves, growing up with the knowledge that they were to be free" would follow a "regular course of industry," and whites would find that, "As hirelings they would be more useful and profitable to their employers than as slaves." Moreover, the elimination of slavery would encourage white migration into the state and enliven a stagnant economy. These views garnered Raymond only twelve per cent of the votes cast in 1825; he finished last in a field of seven candidates.[41]

In 1826, Raymond again pitched emancipation as an economic boon for Baltimore and Maryland. He also touched off a new controversy by addressing white presumptions that free blacks and slaves collaborated to steal and resell slaveholders' property. In a statement rarely heard from white lips, Raymond asserted, "we all know many free negroes who are honest, industrious, and worthy citizens." A slave, on the other hand, would readily steal because he could not believe that it was "a crime to enjoy the product of his own labor." Only freeing all blacks and affording them a chance to rise in the world through honest labor could reduce such larceny. Stressing the importance of free birth and the odds against successful mid-life transition to freedom, Raymond repeated his pleas for *post-nati* emancipation.[42] Despite a hail of criticism, Raymond's electoral standing improved. He finished sixth of nine candidates, with about 15 per cent of the vote.[43]

Lundy happily printed a post-election letter from "A Plumper" for Raymond, who stated that with emancipation "there would be a greater demand for all kinds of mechanics." While slaves lived in "small log huts," once freed they would "be dissatisfied with those huts and would endeavor to have houses built," and would likewise crave other modest luxuries such as coffee and sugar. The same issue of the *Genius* announced Raymond's renomination for the 1827 legislative contest and hammered away at the need to emancipate slaves to "exchange the idle worthless slave population for industrious free laborers."[44]

Lundy spied signs of rising antislavery sentiment: the Maryland Anti-Slavery Society he had helped found in 1825 was adding branches. Even the normally hostile legislature took a positive step, repealing laws mandating the banishment and sale for a term of years of free black convicts, in response to criticisms that such sales often led to permanent re-enslavements.[45]

Lundy's hopes were soon dashed by the reshaping of Maryland politics, like those of the rest of the nation, around the figure of Andrew Jackson. By 1827 a crusade to revenge Jackson's defeat in the presidential election of 1824 had reached fever pitch, with candidates for both state and national offices identifying themselves as Jackson or anti-Jackson men. An all out antislavery candidate might split the anti-Jackson vote and unseat incumbents who more mildly opposed slavery. Though Raymond sacrificed his candidacy for the greater good and withdrew just two weeks before the 1827 election, pro-Jackson and proslavery men won anyway. Maryland had seen its last antislavery legislative candidate for decades.[46]

Support for slavery and states' rights, galvanized by the campaigns for Jackson, became the cornerstones of the national Democratic party from the late 1820s onward. Resulting partisan tensions sharpened differences over slavery and heightened suspicions about the ultimate intentions of critics. In the mid-1820s, Benjamin Lundy could advocate gradual emancipation and support someone like Raymond, who in turn could make common cause with a colonizationist like Harper. But by the early 1830s, Raymond and Lundy had left Maryland, and colonization had fallen firmly under the sway of men who wanted to deport free blacks solely to protect and preserve slavery.

Something similar took place in Virginia. There, at least into the 1820s, the few people who hoped that removing free blacks might advance the cause of gradual emancipation worked side by side with conservatives like Mercer. The Virginia General Assembly appropriated funds for colonization societies. Church leaders of the Episcopalians, Methodists, Baptists, and

Presbyterians endorsed the idea and passed the collection plate, and leading citizens like John Marshall and James Madison served as heads of local auxiliary societies.

Colonization attracted evangelical women, who conceptualized it as religious missionary work among blacks rather than as a political matter regarding slavery. Female auxiliaries of the American Colonization Society formed in Falmouth and Fredericksburg in the 1820s, and colonizationist women sewed, baked, and sold their goods at fairs to raise money for the cause. Over the next generation, they selectively manumitted slaves. Anne Rice sent a family of slaves she owned to Liberia, and arranged for the transportation of four other families.[47] Louisa Cocke ran a plantation school in her Fluvanna County home, to prepare slaves for free life in Liberia. Lucy Minor, who had manumitted nine slaves and sent them to Liberia in 1826, became a co-founder of Fredericksburg's branch of the Colonization Society in 1829.[48] At the same time, these women retained or sold other slaves to pay debts and maintain themselves. These were not immediate abolitionists but advocates for what Anne Rice called the "practical abolition of negro slavery."[49]

These self-styled pragmatists often focused on reuniting slave families, coordinating manumissions of husbands, wives, and children with different owners, and then sending the entire family to Liberia. More than two hundred manumitters participated in such "conjunctive emancipations," many of them inspired by black people willing to go to Liberia to gain freedom and reunite family members.[50] Some freedpeople embarked on self-purchase plans with the same end in mind. In one remarkable case, Edmond Brown of Augusta County in Virginia's Shenandoah Valley left for Liberia with nine members of his family, after expending over sixteen hundred dollars to liberate a wife, sons, and daughters-in-law from seven different owners. Much of the money came from donations Brown had solicited from givers as far away as Princeton, New Jersey.[51]

Black and white co-operation in this professedly apolitical, family-oriented colonization would persist in a limited way into the 1850s, but as early as 1828 the American Colonization Society as an organization was in trouble in Virginia. In that year, Richmond men reorganized their auxiliary of the ACS as the Virginia Colonization Society in a bid to win greater financial and political support, and to dispel perceptions of colonization as a stalking horse for abolition. They consciously framed the agenda of the new organization around removing free blacks, while downplaying manumission, let alone legislated emancipation.

The redirection of colonization as a proslavery movement had been under way about three years when a bloody slave insurrection exploded across Virginia's Southside in August 1831. A group of fifteen black men led by the slave preacher, Nat Turner, killed nearly sixty whites, mostly women and children, before local militias suppressed the rebels. In the wake of the Turner Rebellion, panicked whites killed as many as one hundred slaves and free people of color.[52]

Not long after the insurrection, Virginia legislators convened for their 1832 session. They soon faced a wave of impassioned petitions from supporters of emancipation and colonization, including two from women in Fluvanna and Augusta Counties who wanted the "bloody monster" of slavery ended in order to assure domestic security.[53] Governor John Floyd took a different view. His annual message to the legislature denounced free black preachers and northern abolitionists for stirring up "the spirit of insubordination," and urged removal of free blacks and a more stringent slave code to prevent future rebellions.[54]

As they had done in dealing with Gabriel's revolt thirty years earlier, legislators initially leaned toward Floyd's scapegoating approach and denied any fundamental problems with the institution of slavery. A committee appointed to consider how best to secure the safety of the Commonwealth reported that legislation on the subject of slavery was "inexpedient," but a coterie of young members from west of the Blue Ridge disagreed. When William Ballard Preston moved to amend the committee's report to declare consideration of gradual emancipation "expedient," a battle loomed.

On January 21, Thomas Jefferson Randolph, grandson of the Sage of Monticello, rose to offer his plan to remove slaves from Virginia. Carefully disclaiming any direct tie between his ideas and those of his grandfather,

Randolph proposed that all children of slave mothers born after July 3, 1840, become the property of the state upon attaining the age of twenty-one for males and eighteen for females. Until 1861, slaveholders would be free to sell any and all slaves to anyone who would transport them out of Virginia. Thereafter, slaves that became state property would be hired out. Once their earnings had generated enough income to transport them to Africa, they would be deported.

In marshaling his arguments, Randolph echoed political economists like Raymond: "Slavery has the effect of lessening the free population of the country." Citing census data, Randolph noted that blacks outnumbered whites in eastern Virginia, and forecast the growth of that surplus. Should exportation to the southwest cease, "children now living may see 3,000,000 colored persons in Virginia." Facing such numbers, Virginians would have no security against insurrection. Those who imagined that federal help would defeat black revolutionaries must understand the inevitability of "a dissolution of this Union" which would render their hopes illusory. Randolph's gloomy sketch was striking for this insistence that the certainty of secession made state-sponsored diffusion of slavery by sale, emancipation, and colonization imperative.[55]

Randolph and his supporters strove mightily to show that everyone would gain from this deportation plan. Sales would prevent financial loss to owners. Charges that slave prices would be depressed were mistaken: "They would sell as well for exportation as they did before." Indeed, the real danger lay in doing nothing and allowing the natural increase of slaves to glut the market. Gradually reducing slave numbers would allow adequate time for the immigration of white labor replacements. Randolph estimated that slavery would linger for eighty years. The whitening of Virginia would generate rising land values to the benefit of slaveowners and non-slaveowners alike. By comparison, a tax-supported colonization plan would be far more expensive. Hedging a bit, Randolph contended that if his predictions proved unfounded, Virginia could at any point up to 1860 repeal the law and leave things as they had been. In a lone backhanded reference to the welfare of African Americans, Randolph assured his audience that such a repeal would cause no disturbance because slaves would prefer remaining in Virginia with their families to deportation to Africa.

Ultimately, the legislature opted for something far simpler than Randolph's proposal: it voted seventy-three to fifty-eight to table Preston's amendment and end discussion of slavery. Representatives from west of the Blue Ridge, where slaves composed only about a tenth of the population, voted overwhelmingly for consideration of emancipation, while the black majority counties of the Tidewater and Piedmont went solidly for maintaining the status quo. The western Piedmont and Shenandoah Valley swing delegates stuck with slavery.[56]

Some historians interpret Virginia's 1832 debate as Virginians missing a propitious moment to strike down slavery in the wake of Turner's shocking revolt. Others detect no principled opposition to slavery, only a continuation of intra-state power struggles between slaveholding easterners and nonslaveholding westerners. In this latter reading, Randolph's proposal for the exportation of slaves threatened to depopulate the Tidewater and Piedmont, handing more proportional power to western Virginians. Opposition to slavery that focused on the harmful political and economic effects for whites remained respectable west of the Blue Ridge long after 1832, and indeed represented the majority outlook there.[57]

Clearly some contemporaries felt that repairing divisions within the state was at least as important as the future of slavery. Perhaps the most influential commentary, Thomas Dew's *Review of the Debate of the Virginia Assembly*, is often categorized today as a key proslavery essay because of its attack on the impracticality of colonization. Dew did all in his power to show that the natural increase of slaves in Virginia would outpace efforts to purchase and remove them, and he noted that most manumitted slaves would not voluntarily migrate to Africa. He also rehearsed standard moral and philosophical proslavery arguments. Slavery exposed blacks to Christianity and civilized values; Africans were morally and mentally unfit for freedom and needed the protection of a kindly master; and slavery helped preserve republican society by replacing class conflict among whites with racial solidarity.[58]

Dew took pains to point out the benefits of slavery for white women and trans-Allegheny westerners. He insisted that white women benefited from slavery, since black labor replaced that of white women, affording them a social "elevation" denied to northern counterparts. To westerners, Dew extolled slaves as a labor force essential to the road and canal-building they so much desired. Here Dew obliquely acknowledged the complaint that the Tidewater and Piedmont, overrepresented in the Assembly by virtue of counting slaves for apportioning seats, had used their power to block appropriations for the development of the Trans-Allegheny. Dew, a professor at William and Mary in the Tidewater, contended that the westward spread of slavery within Virginia, rather than out of the state as Randolph wished, would give men on the other side of the mountains the development they wanted. He also implied that westerners' hostility to slavery would ebb as their political power increased.

Diehard colonization supporters remained skeptical. Dew's essay elicited a strong rebuttal from westerner Jesse Burton Harrison. James Madison insisted in a letter to Dew that colonization remained a "National object" that should be pursued. All the same, Dew signaled the emergence of something more than what Madison characterized as a "torpid acquiescence" in the perpetuity of slavery, judging by the frequent references to his work by later proslavery Virginia writers such as Edmund Ruffin, Nathaniel Beverley Tucker, and George Fitzhugh.[59]

The 1832 debate represented the virtual end of serious political discussion of emancipation. This suggests a fundamental agreement on slavery had emerged among Virginians. Some see the death of discussion about emancpationist antislavery as a response to the blooming of uncompromising immediate abolitionism in northern states, the so-called Southern Great Reaction of the 1830s. In this scenario, Virginians closed ranks against outside critics and made loyalty to a slaveholding regime a litmus test for participation in public life. But the censuring and ostracizing of emancipationist antislaveryites had begun long before Turner's rebellion, and deportationist opposition to slavery lived on in Virginia even after 1832.

One indisputable outcome of the Turner Rebellion was the further marginalization of antislavery colonizationists in Virginia. Mary Minor

1st Regiment, Montserrado County, Liberia. The ability to bear arms and participate in self-government attracted black migrants to Liberia. (Maryland Historical Society.)

Blackford, who helped found the Fredericksburg and Falmouth auxiliaries of the ACS, and who drafted an antislavery petition in 1832, found it increasingly difficult to pursue her goals. Her "Notes Illustrative of the Wrongs of Slavery," characterized as one of the most "thoroughgoing attack[s] on slavery by a white southern woman," existed only as a private journal. Men like Dew and Virginia governor John Floyd had portrayed colonizationists as abolitionists' catspaws, or worse, covert abolitionists themselves. Colonization societies survived, barely, by proclaiming "Friendship to the SLAVEHOLDER." [60]

A prominent Maryland colonizationist, Francis Scott Key, drew the line between his views and those of abolitionists in a more direct way. Key helped prosecute Reuben Crandall, a New York physician charged with criminal and seditious libel and with inciting insurrection in 1836 for having distributed antislavery pamphlets in the District of Columbia. [61] The indictment against Crandall cited as libelous an article by Arthur Tappan contending that free African Americans had "as good a right to deport us to Europe, under the pretext that we shall there be prosperous and happy, as we have to deport them to Africa." Crandall had to be rescued from a lynch mob of irate citizens before he could stand trial. Crandall's attorneys defended him by pointing out parallels between the language of Crandall's pamphlets and that of such leading lights of the Chesapeake as Thomas Jefferson, George Washington Parke Custis, and Key himself. The author of *The Star-Spangled Banner* indignantly, and a trifle defensively, replied that he and the American Colonization Society had nothing to do with slavery, and only concerned themselves with free negroes. Though Crandall escaped punishment due to a technical deficiency in the indictment, the larger lesson was that colonizationists had to eschew even faint tinges of antislavery sentiment to survive censure as abolitionists.

In Maryland itself, interest in colonization picked up in the wake of Nat Turner's rebellion. Its adherents, registered legislative victories in a state whose lawmakers were dominated by slaveholders from lightly populated but overrepresented counties of the Eastern and Lower Western Shores of the Chesapeake Bay. The unusual combination of slavery's weakening economic base in the countryside, slaves' access to work and money in industrializing Baltimore, and the proximity of free territory, allowed enslaved people to push self-liberation much further in Maryland than in the Old Dominion. The 1830 census counted over fifty thousand free blacks, about one-third of all African Americans in the state and four times the proportion of 1790. These increases alarmed whites who viewed them as job competitors or stigmatized them as thieves. Such stereotyping helped spur interest in colonization plans that focused on deporting freedpeople in order to stabilize slavery. At the same time, the fact that Maryland whites outnumbered blacks two to one dampened fears of black insurrection, and lessened the impulse to consider schemes to remove the black population through a blend of emancipation and colonization.

In this climate, news of the Turner rebellion produced a threefold reaction. Fear of insurrection appeared briefly, with wild stories of a rising by Baltimore blacks, but soon subsided.[62] Then antislaveryites, perhaps joined by those anxious about possible revolt, petitioned the legislature for enactment of a gradual emancipation plan. Finally, legislators channeled these sentiments into assaults on the state's free people of color, fashioning statutes that encouraged publicly funded colonization as well as involuntary deportation of African Americans.

A special committee of the Maryland House of Delegates, chaired by Henry Brawner, quickly brushed aside the abolitionist petitions and concentrated on the question of how to remove black people. "It is not . . . a question of whether the coloured population of this state is injurious to her prosperity," Brawner's report intoned. Maryland's "situation . . . has long since forced this conviction upon the most careless observer." The report extended commonplace comparisons of languishing Maryland and an economically vibrant Pennsylvania to intra-state examples: "The comparison within [Maryland's] limits, between counties largely infected with this evil, and those where it exists in a slight degree . . . bring us to the same result."[63] Counties in northern Maryland, with smaller proportions of black people, fared better economically than the state's southern areas.

The legislature accepted Brawner's package—energetic promotion of colonization, restrictions on future manumissions, and new laws aimed at pushing existing free blacks out of the state in order to reverse longstanding growth in that population. The upshot was a state appropriation of twenty thousand dollars a year for ten years to fund removals of free blacks or slaves emancipated on condition of sailing to Africa. The legislature stopped short of an outright ban on future manumissions but did make it more difficult for free people of color to remain in Maryland, to enter the state from elsewhere, or to re-enter the state if they left to find seasonal employment. By the close of the 1830s, Maryland had also widened the scope of laws that re-enslaved free blacks by condemning debtors, vagrants, and criminals to be sold into servitude.[64]

In Delaware, even more than in Maryland, the politics of slavery and emancipation focused on free people of color. By 1830 some fifteen thousand free blacks outnumbered slaves nearly five to one, and they made up about one-fifth of the state's population. The virtual disappearance of slavery made the institution politically vulnerable throughout the nineteenth century, and gradual emancipation proposals came close to enactment in 1803, 1823, and 1847. But the legislative overrepresentation of rural southern Delaware, where slaveholding planters, loggers, and ironmakers continued to eke out profits from bound labor, allowed proslavery lawmakers to block action each time.[65]

The strength of emancipationist sentiment among northern Delaware whites betokened little tolerance for free blacks, though. Delaware's whites, too, worried about black people attaining political and social equality and sought to preempt this unwanted development through discriminatory statutes and support of colonization. The Wilmington Union Colonization Society, founded in 1823, succeeded in the 1830s by the Delaware State Colonization Society, agitated for the removal of free blacks. These organizations drew on a familiar mix of fears and desires: colonization would ameliorate the condition of free blacks, and eliminate the threat of insurrection that they otherwise posed. As in Maryland, supporters of colonization included morally committed opponents of slavery, such as Thomas Garrett, a sponsor of gradual emancipation proposals and an active participant in the Underground Railroad.[66]

Enthusiasm for colonization was tempered by awareness of whites' reliance on free black agricultural laborers. So while the legislature repeatedly voiced its support for the colonization societies, it never provided them with the financial backing offered in Maryland. Likewise, efforts to control black mobility differed in Delaware. In Virginia and Maryland, black codes unequivocally attempted to propel blacks out of the state and to forbid their entry. In Delaware, migration laws repeatedly sought to forestall blacks from seeking seasonal work in nearby Pennsylvania, with a view to keeping them in Delaware as a pool of dependent low-wage laborers. Dependency could also be sustained by selling black debtors or criminals into temporary servitude, even after these practices were abolished for whites.[67]

Until the Panic of 1837 launched a long depression, slaveholders in the Chesapeake enjoyed unprecedented opportunities to profit by selling slaves to the booming Cotton States. Surges in slave sales to southwestern dealers for a time outpaced natural increase in the African American population, and soothed fears that growing black numbers would some day spark a successful insurrection. But with the return of hard times and a renewed upswing in Virginia's slave population, a few opponents of slavery again spoke up.

Samuel Janney, a Loudoun County Quaker, had published anonymous essays urging gradual emancipation in the *Alexandria Gazette* in 1827, perhaps inspired by the brief flowering of Lundy's *Genius of Universal Emancipation.* Like Baltimore's antislaveryites, Janney also endorsed colonization, and he had been involved in the unsuccessful petition drive of the late 1820s asking Congress to end the slave trade in the District of Columbia. In 1843, Janney broke a long silence on slavery to reply to the proslavery arguments of Thornton Stringfellow, a Baptist clergyman from Culpepper County, Virginia. Not content to rebut Stringfellow's biblical defense of slavery, Janney launched a full-blown moral and economic attack on the institution and defended allowing freed blacks to remain in Virginia. He insisted that African Americans of the Chesapeake were far better prepared for freedom than those in the West Indies, where in 1838 the British had abolished slavery.[68] Janney's review appeared in the *Baltimore Saturday Visiter*, a periodical edited by Joseph Snodgrass.

Over the next two years Janney stepped up his criticism of slavery, emphasizing its economic detriment to the Commonwealth. He downplayed attacks on slaveholders and stressed his lifelong Virginia residency in an effort to get fellow citizens to engage with his views. In 1845 he persuaded John H. Pleasants, editor of the *Richmond Whig* and erstwhile supporter of Randolph's emancipation and colonization proposals of 1832, to publish another series of antislavery essays. Pleasants sidestepped the question of whether emancipated blacks should reside in Virginia but did hold that white interests demanded the end of slavery: "I am not opposed to it because I think it morally wrong, for I know the multitude of slaves to be better off than the whites. I am against it for the *sake of the whites,* my own race."[69] These forthright statements drew taunts from rival editor Thomas Ritchie that Pleasants was an abolitionist. The ensuing exchange of insults led to a duel in which Ritchie killed Pleasants.

By 1849, after the bitter fight over the Wilmot Proviso and the extension of slavery into territories conquered in the Mexican War, not even the mild mannered Janney could speak out safely in Virginia. His critical review of a proslavery speech by William Smith, a Methodist minister and president of Randolph-Macon College, brought a crushing reaction. A grand jury in Loudoun County presented Janney for inciting slaves to insurrection by challenging Smith's claims that slavery was inherently good and sanctioned by scripture. Though acquitted, Janney withdrew from further controversy, turning to works of Quaker history and biography for the remainder of his career. His Baltimore publisher, Snodgrass, had also been driven from the field. He was charged in 1846 by a member of Maryland's House of Delegates with violations of the state's 1836 law banning abolitionist writings. Though never convicted, Snodgrass was damaged by the charges. His subscription list dwindled, and he shut down the paper.[70]

Perhaps the last gasp of open political opposition to slavery in Virginia came from Henry Ruffner, a minister and college president. His *Address to the People of West Virginia,* published in 1847, offered yet another economically focused critique of slavery's impact on land values, white immigration and emigration, and the comparative social development of slave and free regions. Like earlier Virginians, Ruffner envisioned a combination of gradual emancipation, colonization, and slave sales to the southwest to extinguish black presence in the Old Dominion. Sensitive to the animus against both slavery and blacks that permeated western Virginia, Ruffner soothed his readers with pictures of a wealth-creating magic in rising land values that would be realized, "before the emancipation of a single negro."[71]

Ruffner's new idea was an intra-state ban on the importation of slaves into western Virginia, coupled with *post-nati* emancipation at age twenty-five of children born to slave women resident in those counties. Prospective freedpeople would be educated and trained to labor but still would be colonized out of the state when freed. Slaveholders would not be allowed to sell those promised freedom to the Cotton States, except for children too young to appreciate the loss of freedom, defined by Ruffner as age five or under. In such cases parents and children would have to be sold together. Finally, Ruffner suggested that individual counties have the option of ending slavery more quickly through local referenda. Though Ruffner was himself a slaveholder, his scheme was excoriated as that of a "lunatic" abolitionist and received no serious consideration by the legislature. With the requickening of the southern plantation economy soon thereafter, and the heightening of sectional tensions over slavery, not even Virginians like Ruffner and Janney could win a respectful hearing.

Across the Potomac in Maryland, the lean times of the 1840s also briefly resuscitated public discussion of gradual emancipation. Snodgrass's *Baltimore Saturday Visiter*, in addition to publishing Janney, defended free people of color against stereotyping as improvident criminals. Though it is difficult to measure the popularity of this periodical, Snodgrass attracted the attention of the Maryland House of Delegates, which considered denouncing the magazine as "incendiary" in 1846.[72]

A perhaps more typical emancipationist of the 1840s was John L. Carey, an essayist and unsuccessful candidate for the House of Delegates, who urged Marylanders to combine emancipation and colonization of freedpeople.[73] Carey dwelt on themes familiar to residents of the Chesapeake since the 1790s, evoking pictures of blooming free labor areas and blighted slave districts, while viewing with alarm the dangers of civil strife inherent in the presence of free but unequal blacks in a white-led society. For him, emancipation without colonization was a proven failure, as demonstrated by the depressed condition of free blacks in Pennsylvania and points north. Carey's one new contribution to this formula was an attempt to redirect antipathy to free blacks against slavery. Inverting the usual proslavery claim that keeping blacks in bondage was the only alternative to being swamped by freedpeople, Carey argued that "so long as slavery remains a prominent institution ... [it] has the effect of protecting the class of free negroes ... from the competition ... of white labor." Shades of Daniel Raymond—ending slavery might also end the "curse" of a free black population.[74]

Historians have struggled to make sense out of colonization advocates like Carey and the many apparent contradictions in their writings. Can their antislavery claims be taken seriously, coupled as they so often are with virulent anti-black sentiments? Was colonization a plausible program, or were its opponents right to ridicule the impracticality of transporting hundreds of thousands of blacks across the sea? Alternatively, what informed the thinking of proslavery men who abhorred colonization as a deadly threat to their culture?

On the first point, the focus on benefiting whites expressed by all the major colonizationists of the Chesapeake was precisely what appealed to its adherents, and correspondingly, what made it threatening to large slaveholders. Supporters of colonization repeatedly calculated the comparative benefits of slave labor and free labor societies and found slavery disadvantageous for most whites. Slaveholding politicians did not welcome such discussions, fearing that many voters might reach the same conclusions. Accordingly, they looked for ways to stifle all forms of opposition, both before and after the rise of immediatist abolitionism in northern states.

Colonization threatened slaveholders because it could not be dismissed offhandedly as a wildly impractical scheme. In the 1830s, the United States forcibly removed thirty to fifty thousand Cherokees, Creeks, Choctaws, and Chickasaws from southern states to the Indian Territory, today's Oklahoma. Voluntary emigration of Europeans to America surpassed one hundred thousand a year in the 1840s. Backed by a strong political commitment, perhaps colonization of blacks to Africa, Haiti, or somewhere in Central America would be equally achievable.[75] Non-slaveholding whites, and even some slaveholders might rally to its cause. Colonization, therefore, had to be sternly opposed by slavery's defenders.

Opposition to colonization came readily to politicians of the Deep South, where free black populations were very small, and the felt need to remove them was correspondingly weak. In the Chesapeake, in contrast, colonization attracted more adherents, albeit unevenly. In Virginia, questions of whether planters from eastern counties could retain control of the legislature led to strong opposition to colonization from those regions. In Maryland, slaveholders endorsed colonization to defuse outright emancipationist sentiment from the largely free labor counties of the state's northern tier. In Delaware, the virtual disappearance of slavery and white resignation to a free black presence rendered colonization all but irrelevant.[76]

Of course, colonization cannot be comprehended solely in terms of debates among whites about the fate of blacks. One key reason for colonization's apparent impracticality was resolute, organized black opposition to its program of deportation that rendered its legislative victories largely symbolic. For blacks in the Chesapeake, resistance to slavery in the years prior to 1815 had been characterized chiefly by efforts at self-liberation via manumission, flight, or rebellion. Although these challenges to slavery continued after 1815, they were augmented by the creation of self-sustaining communities of free people of color, communities which endured, and even grew, in spite of pressure from those who would expel them from the land.

CHAPTER 6

We Got This Far by Faith

RESISTANCE TO SLAVERY BETWEEN 1815 and 1860 had its moments of drama, including Nat Turner's rebellion and Frederick Douglass's journey to freedom and subsequent fame as an abolitionist. The spirit of Gabriel still lived. Nonetheless, the great majority of African Americans challenged slavery less directly. Wherever possible, they built autonomous communities of free and enslaved people, centered on churches that promoted literacy, respectability, and uplift. Enslaved people who remained within white-led biracial churches also found ways to assert themselves as Christians, and to demand protection for their marriages from abuse by slaveholders. The creation and maintenance of African American institutions, and slaves' claims to respect as fellow Christians, in the face of intensifying white hostility to such enterprises, constituted a visible and sometimes successful challenge to the ideology of black inferiority and pointed to the possibility of a stable multi-racial society, proslavery and colonizationist claims to the contrary.[1]

Religious motivation came to the fore in all black resistance to slavery, peaceful or not. Blacks had opportunistically sought freedom by fighting for both sides in the American Revolution. Gabriel's rebels had hoped to see freedom acknowledged as their natural and political right, but Nat Turner, a nineteenth-century American evangelical, sought freedom because his God told him that he would be the instrument for ending the evils of slavery and bringing on Judgment Day. Turner's uprising in 1831 can be understood as one end of a continuum of African American religious experience. Driven

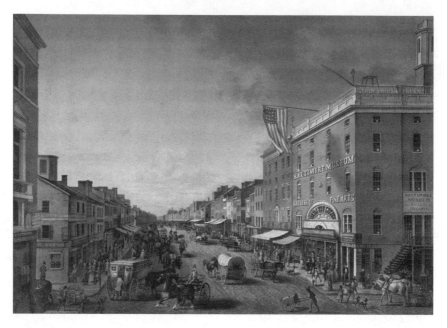

A Baltimore scene, looking west on Baltimore Street from Calvert Street, shows various African Americans, c. 1850. The city then had the United States' largest free black population. Lithograph, E. Sachse and Company, 1850. (Maryland Historical Society.)

metaphorically by the theme of the exodus of a chosen people from slavery, black religion incorporated everything from the quiet practice of faith and the slow building of institutions through millennialist violence inspired by visions and portents.[2] Stopping points along this continuum included trying to lead a free people out of slavery to a promised land across the sea, in the manner of black colonizationists Daniel Coker or Lott Cary. Another approach would be to venture into the Chesapeake to evangelize slaves, as Zilpha Elaw and Jarena Lee did, or to migrate north to preach the gospel and testify against slavery, like J. W. C. Pennington or Henry Highland Garnet. In their variety of responses to and appropriations of evangelical doctrines and perfectionist impulses African Americans resembled the European American society that enveloped but refused to incorporate them. While evangelical whites in the Chesapeake retreated from religious criticism of slavery and refined Biblical defenses of black bondage, black people strove

A loyal servant, "Old Hagar" sets forth to do the marketing for her Baltimore owner. Sentimental images of slavery appealed to antebellum slave owners in the Chesapeake. Print, c. 1835. (Maryland Historical Society.)

for both temporal and spiritual freedom from slavery, turning their daily lives into visible testaments against the peculiar institution.

Notably, free people of color stood up to mounting pressures to colonize them in Africa, pressures generated by resentment of black autonomy and fear of slave insurrection displaced onto free African Americans. Colonizationists failed to persuade, cajole, or coerce many blacks in the Chesapeake to emigrate. The handful of blacks who did embrace migration, whether to West Africa, Haiti, or Canada, sought generally to build independent communities on terms and conditions chosen by themselves, rather than by the colonization societies.[3]

Initial black reactions to the founding of the American Colonization Society in 1816 were mixed. Some opposition rose literally within weeks. In Philadelphia, James Forten and the Reverend Richard Allen, who had been intrigued by black New Englander Paul Cuffe's plans for trade and settlement in West Africa, presided over a public meeting that emphatically rejected white-led colonization.[4] Free people of color in the District of Columbia expressed reservations that colonization might become forced deportation. In Richmond, African Americans sent a memorial to Congress early in 1817 suggesting that the western United States be the locus of black colonization, rather than the "alien land" of Africa.[5] These notable actions aside, black opposition to colonization remained muted until the late 1820s. By then, colonization societies in the Chesapeake had shed early interest in black emancipation and were focusing on the removal of freedpeople. Blacks would adamantly and successfully oppose this evolved version of colonization. Nevertheless, in the years from 1816 to around 1830, resettlement in Africa appealed powerfully to some black leaders in Richmond and Baltimore who combined religious inspiration with the drive for autonomy.

When the colonization movement came to Richmond, in 1817, most black churchgoers belonged to the white-led First Baptist Church. Freedpeople and slaves in the congregation had helped found an African missionary society in 1815, and black elders Lott Cary and Colin Teage volunteered to serve as missionaries. Like many of their generation, Cary and Teage had purchased their freedom with money they had earned working as urban tradesmen, Cary as a tobacco factory foreman, and Teage as a harnessmaker. Each man may have learned to read in church-sponsored Bible schools, and each had become a lay preacher.

For these men, missionary work in Africa represented both a spiritual quest and an opportunity to attain a social status denied to blacks in America. Each was ordained and recognized as a minister by a national Baptist mission organization, but only on the eve of departure for Africa. Cary apparently accepted the analysis of men like Robert Goodloe Harper, saying, "I am an African, and in this country, however meritorious my conduct and respectable my character, I cannot receive the credit due to either. I wish to go to a country where I shall be esteemed by my merits." Cary and Teage led a small group to Liberia; in all about one hundred people from Richmond made this journey in the 1820s. Once in Africa, Cary found that the white agents of the American Colonization Society did little to promote missionary work, and he organized blacks to take greater control of the colony's affairs. Thenceforward, Cary remained an exponent of colonization and even promised to return to America to confront black opponents, a pledge left unredeemed by his death in 1829.[6]

Cary's Baltimore counterpart, Daniel Coker, also endorsed colonization out of a desire to evangelize Africans, a need to leave white prejudice behind, and a drive to fashion an African identity. For Coker, who had a white mother and a black father, unifying a fragmented identity appears to have been a particularly strong motivation. Symptomatic of African American life in the Chesapeake, his struggle played out in the world of religion and the church.[7]

Born out of wedlock to an indentured servant, Coker would normally have been bound to his mother's master until he turned twenty-one. But as a *mulatto* bastard, he was obliged to serve until his thirty-first birthday.[8] Instead, he ran away to New York as a teenager in the 1790s, where he converted to Methodism. Ordained a deacon by Bishop Francis Asbury, Coker yearned to itinerate as a missionary to black people in Maryland. Several black Baltimoreans arranged to purchase his freedom from his Frederick County master, and by 1807 Coker was conducting a school under the aegis of Baltimore's Colored Methodist Society and the African congregation of Methodists on Sharp Sheet, near the harbor. A few years later Coker led a Bible study class of Baltimore Methodists and exhorted as a lay minister, but he had failed to attain ordination.

In 1810, Coker published one of the earliest black-authored antislavery tracts, "A Dialogue between a Virginian and an African Minister." Coker's black minister patiently refutes a series of defenses of slavery, using natural rights arguments bolstered by scripture. He destroys defenses of slavery based on black inferiority, its supposed authorization by scripture, or claims that racial conflict would flare up in the wake of emancipation. The conversation closes when the slaveholding Virginian has been won over by the African's eloquence and promises to manumit his chattels. Produced during the later stages of white Methodists' retreat from antislavery in the Chesapeake, the dialogue bespoke dismay at moral slippage by onetime white allies and called for black solidarity.[9]

By 1815, Coker and other black Methodists had become thoroughly frustrated by the white leadership's insistence on controlling both spiritual and temporal matters affecting blacks. They chafed at the obdurate refusal to ordain black ministers, to allow black congregations to choose the white ministers who preached to them, and at increasing segregation and subordination of black members in white-majority congregations. A further irritant lay in the growing unwillingness of the Baltimore Conference of Methodists to take strong action against slaveholding among its white ministers and elders.[10]

Aware of similar confrontations among Philadelphia's Methodists, and of the legal struggle there to achieve black-led congregations and black-owned and managed chapels, the Baltimoreans formed their own religious society. In May 1815, Coker, Nicholas Gilliard, Stephen Hill, Don Carlos Hall, George Douglass, and David Brister formed the African Methodist Bethel Society and set about the business of creating their own church. Within two years Bethel was six hundred members strong and a mainstay of the African Methodist Episcopal (AME) church, organized in 1816.[11]

Coker proselytized aggressively for the African Methodists in Maryland, organizing camp meetings and preaching to black audiences in Hagerstown, Frederick, and elsewhere. As the leading black church figure in Baltimore, Coker had in fact been a strong contender for the office of bishop in the new church. Delegates to the AME's founding conference in Philadelphia initially named Coker and Richard Allen as co-holders of the episcopate, but a day later, Coker withdrew his acceptance of the title under pressure from delegates who balked at having a light-skinned leader of a self-proclaimed African church.[12]

Coker's writings reveal little about this disappointment, or about its influence on his decision to go to Africa as a colonist and missionary in 1820. The palpable worsening of conditions for free people of color in Baltimore surely played its part. At the outbreak of the War of 1812, a decade before Coker's departure, free blacks were beaten and their homes burned by a mob who thought them to be British sympathizers.[13] Following the war, a wave of kidnappings of free African Americans who were sold as slaves to the Cotton South had been met with indifference by much of the white community.[14]

The status of black worshippers continued to deteriorate. Coker found himself, maddeningly, unable to induce a majority of blacks to leave the white-dominated Methodist church, even as whites enforced stricter segregation. In 1817, Methodist Episcopal elders asked loyal blacks to "retire" from a number of Baltimore's mixed congregations and concentrate themselves in one or two black-dominated churches. In a token concession the Baltimore Conference did name its first black deacon, John Mingo, in 1818 "in consideration of the peculiar situation of the African Society in the city of Baltimore."[15] But later that year they censured a white member for attending a camp meeting sponsored by Coker and Bethel. The camp meeting itself came under attack from suspicious whites who spread rumors that participants were secretly aiding runaway slaves and black convicts. A year later these woes were compounded by hard times, as the Panic of 1819 depressed Baltimore's economy, with particularly grim effects on the city's black community.[16]

By 1820, Coker had had enough and embarked for Liberia. He remained in West Africa for the rest of a long life, preaching, engaging in coastal trade, and finally dying in Sierra Leone in 1846. For him, the path of testimony against slavery led back to the land of his father's ancestors.

But Coker, like Cary in Richmond, found few African Americans willing to follow him, despite his enthusiastic letters from Liberia and a published journal of his experiences. For most free blacks colonization looked more and more like white-imposed deportation. This perception galvanized public meetings and later helped inspire the first national conventions of people of color in the 1830s. While black activism then flourished most notably in Philadelphia, New York, Boston, and later, Buffalo, Pittsburgh, and Cleveland, blacks in the Chesapeake faced a more immediate threat of removal.

Colonization loomed largest in free black life in Maryland, where the state legislature had in 1831 promised to make up to two hundred thousand dollars available to the newly formed Maryland Colonization Society for transporting free blacks to Liberia and later to a Maryland-sponsored colony on the coast of West Africa.[17] The society boasted prestigious leaders like architect John H. B. Latrobe, and attorneys Francis Scott Key and Charles Carroll Harper, son of Robert Goodloe Harper and grandson of Charles

Carroll of Carrollton. Its first agent was another second-generation colonizationist, Robert S. Finley, namesake of an American Colonization Society founder.

Yet as a subsequent agent in Maryland wearily noted, "the society has always had more room for emigrants than was filled in their vessels." When agents went out to "collect" blacks who had been persuaded to emigrate, they "invariably found that . . . the enemies of colonization . . . have led the minds of those who proposed to emigrate, with the doctrines of abolitionists, . . . that by leaving the United States, the colored people impair their chance of 'getting their rights.'"[18] In one dramatic incident in 1832, free blacks boarded a ship about to embark from the Baltimore harbor and persuaded half of the Africa-bound passengers to remain in America.

This episode typified prevalent black reaction to colonization in Maryland. Discriminatory laws and worsening job competition with Irish and German immigrants, combined with white pressure and inducements, could make emigration attractive to some. Countervailing pressures from other African Americans often outweighed such considerations. On the whole, "the overwhelming majority of free Negroes in Maryland . . . remained stridently opposed to relocation efforts."[19]

That opposition can be credited in no small measure to the words and deeds of Baltimore's leading anti-colonization figure, William S. Watkins.[20] Born free around 1800 and educated by Daniel Coker in the African school at Sharp Street, Watkins became a teacher, succeeding Coker as master of the African school when the latter left for Liberia. When Benjamin Lundy arrived in Baltimore in 1825, the two men struck up an acquaintance, and Watkins began writing for the *Genius of Universal Emancipation*. His first piece celebrated formal French recognition of Haitian independence, which Watkins interpreted as proof of black capacity for self-rule. Signing himself as "A Colored Baltimorean," Watkins's passionate denunciations of colonization appeared in *The Genius*, winning the commendation of David Walker in his famous "Appeal to Colored Citizens" in 1829.[21] Later Watkins wrote for William Lloyd Garrison's *Liberator*. Garrison, who met Watkins while serving as Lundy's assistant editor in 1829–30, credited him and another black Baltimorean, Jacob Greener, with opening his eyes to the iniquities of colonization and the desirability of free people of color remaining in the United States.[22]

For Watkins, as later for Garrison, free black departures strengthened the institution of slavery and contributed to the further degradation of those who stayed on. Watkins called for blacks to "die in Maryland under the pressure of unrighteous and cruel laws" rather than be "driven, like cattle . . . to Liberia."[23] Denying that white prejudice made emigration the only hope for black liberty, Watkins asked, "Why should we abandon our firesides and everything associated with the dear name of *home* . . . for the enjoyment of liberty . . . surrounded by circumstances which diminish its intrinsic value?" Blacks who supported colonization, or meekly acquiesced in white denigration of African Americans, became targets for Watkins's tart pen. An apologetic public letter from ministers of black churches during the anti-abolition controversies of 1835 led Watkins to snap that, "It is time enough . . . to make . . . disclaimers . . . when we are charged with some crime other than that of our colour."[24]

Watkins also supported Hezekiah Grice, a Baltimore butcher, in founding the American Society of Free Persons of Color, the sponsoring organization for the black national convention movement.[25] The society held conventions from 1830 to 1835 that brought together delegations from most of the mid-Atlantic and New England states, including Delaware, Maryland, and Virginia. Operating as a sounding board for a variety of black concerns, the conventions repeatedly denounced African colonization, though expressing some openness to black-led schemes for colonies in Canada or Haiti.[26] They also appealed for betterment of black social and political conditions while admonishing African Americans to improve their moral conduct in the hope of dispelling white prejudice. Thus the 1831 convention asserted in one resolution that the U.S. Constitution, correctly interpreted, "guarantees in letter and spirit to every freeman, all the rights and immunities of citizenship," while another measure urged "reflection on the dissolute, intemperate, and ignorant condition of a large portion of the coloured population" and recommended "Education, Temperance, and Economy" to promote the elevation of blacks in white esteem.[27] By 1835 dissension over whether political or moral themes should be emphasized split the movement. William Whipper of Pennsylvania founded the American Moral Reform Society, and Watkins, who saw black uplift as the only possible tool for chipping away at white prejudice, supported the new society and addressed its 1836 convention.[28]

Back in Baltimore, Watkins and other black activists of the 1820s and 1830s promoted the formation of temperance societies. They also petitioned the state legislature for either exemption of blacks from school taxes or allotment of a portion of such taxes for black education, and they supported "free produce" societies that aimed at selling cotton, sugar, and tobacco goods made with free rather than slave labor.[29] Watkins drummed up subscribers for *The Liberator* and in its pages continued to challenge the Maryland Colonization Society in columns charged with religious imagery and rhetoric. Colonization to Liberia would send Maryland blacks to a "heathen" land. Colonizationists, with their insistence on forcing blacks to emigrate, had abandoned the "humble reliance for success upon the goodness of the Divine Being" that became true-hearted Christians. Watkins sharply criticized Quaker supporters of colonization, presumably pacifists because of their faith, as hypocrites for their endorsement of arming African colonists in struggles with indigenous peoples. These sentiments, expressed at the height of the anti-abolitionist frenzy of the 1830s, put Watkins in danger. Writing to Garrison in 1835, Watkins reported a threat to tar and feather him. He wrote little for *The Liberator* thereafter, shifting his activities into the moral reform arena. His last public communication, written in 1838 to *The Colored American*, added Watkins's voice to calls for the creation of a black college, a cause that would not come to fruition in his lifetime.[30]

By the 1840s, Watkins, like Coker before him, grew discouraged with the prospects of improving African American life through uplift and dissolution of white prejudice. He turned to the hope of societal regeneration through religion, and became attracted to William Miller's millennial prophecies predicting the end of the world in 1843, and again in 1844. The derision that attended the failure of these visions compromised Watkins's stand-

ing in the African American community of Baltimore. By 1851, after passage
of the Fugitive Slave Act, the onetime anti-colonizationist reluctantly decided to leave the United States. Still skeptical of Liberia, he emigrated instead to Toronto, where he died in 1858.[31]

The disappointments of Watkins's later days notwithstanding, his earlier militancy symbolized the limited empowerment of African Americans
in Baltimore, the city with the United States' largest free black population.
The importance of Baltimore's free black community in rallying others to
the cause of defending blacks' rights was not lost on colonizationists. White
promoters of the Maryland State Colonization Society (MSCS) bitterly reported the undermining of their persuasive efforts by black counter-agents
from the Chesapeake's chief city. The upshot was that Maryland's colonizationists, like their Virginia counterparts, numbered actual emigrants at less
than one hundred per year on average in the 1830s and 1840s. A substantial
proportion of colonists from both states were slaves manumitted on condition of emigration to Liberia, rather than already free African Americans
making their own choices.[32]

Whether freeborn or freed on condition of their migrating to Africa,
some black Marylanders chose to live in Maryland in Liberia, a colony established in 1834 near Cape Palmas, in the southeastern part of present-day
Liberia. In the 1820s, the Maryland State Colonization Society had sent colonists to Liberia itself, then a colony operated by the American Colonization
Society (ACS). Black Baltimoreans like George McGill and Remus Harvey,
who had taught Sunday school classes at Sharp Street's black Methodist
church, emigrated, in hopes of evangelizing Africans. In 1832, the MSCS
sent 149 colonists to Liberia, chiefly black farmers and their families from
Somerset and Worcester Counties. Their letters back to Maryland, evincing
dissatisfaction with ACS management, helped spur creation of Maryland's
own colony. The 1834 group of emigrants were led by James Hall, a white
physician. When Hall returned to Maryland, leadership of the colony gradually passed to black men. John Russwurm, onetime editor of *Freedom's Journal*, the first African American owned newspaper, governed the colony for
much of the 1840s. After his death in 1851, William Prout played a major role

in the colony's affairs. By the mid-1850s, neighboring Liberia had become a black-led independent nation, and colonists of Maryland in Liberia were struggling to maintain themselves in the face of hostility from the indigenous Grebo peoples. They opted for annexation to Liberia, ending their status as a colony of Maryland, in 1857. During its twenty-three year existence, just over one thousand black people, mostly from Maryland, had migrated to Africa. [33]

When blacks controlled their own migrations they often preferred destinations in the Americas, such as Haiti, Trinidad, and Canada. The vindication of Haitian independence and the appeal of living in a black-governed country particularly attracted black Americans in the mid-1820s, when Haitian President Boyer offered cheap land and financial assistance to emigrants, a scheme promoted by, among others, Benjamin Lundy in *The Genius* in 1824 and 1825. But like so many travelers, African Americans who went to Haiti discovered how very American they were: neither the tropical climate nor immersion in a Francophone, Catholic culture suited most colonists.[34] Indeed, William Watkins's first anti-colonization pieces appeared just as the Boyer-inspired colonization boom for Haiti was dissipating. The disappointments reported by returnees from Haiti may have influenced him.

A second set of colonization possibilities opened up with the British abolition of slavery in 1833. Canada at once became attractive for would-be black migrants, though its heyday as a refuge for those fleeing from slavery would not arrive until after passage of the Fugitive Slave Act of 1850.

In 1840, more than 250 black Baltimoreans opted instead to emigrate to Trinidad, attracted by offers of good wages and living conditions from planters attempting to find new sources of labor after Britain's abolition of slavery there. A transition period in which slaves in the West Indies were held on the plantations as "apprentices" had ended in 1838. The next year a public meeting of black Baltimoreans appointed Nathaniel Peck and Thomas Price to investigate the prospects of settlement in either British Guiana or Trinidad.[35] The travelers' report favored Guiana, but the emigrants chose Trinidad, perhaps influenced by the presence there of the ex-slaves from the

Chesapeake who had been settled on the island by the British following the War of 1812.

Like colonization promotions from the days of Jamestown forward, little turned out as advertised. Promises made by planters were not all kept, and the decision to leave the U.S., taken during the depressed times that followed the Panic of 1837, yielded to second thoughts. By the mid-1840s many of the emigrants had returned to the Chesapeake, and there is no evidence of a second wave of migrants to Trinidad.[36]

Though migration to the West Indies ultimately failed to pan out, the emancipation of slaves there inspired African Americans to commemorate its August 1 anniversary in "Freedom Day" celebrations from 1838 onward. While few if any such celebrations occurred in slave states, black people from Baltimore or Wilmington could and did travel to places like Harrisburg or Philadelphia to join in ceremonies that affirmed their desires for slavery to end in the United States as it had in Jamaica and Barbados.[37]

Black attitudes toward colonization were shaped in part by appeals to African Americans in Maryland or Virginia to fight for their rights. These rights were almost certainly not defined as the fearful white colonization agents depicted them, in terms of voting or holding office. African Americans knew that white hostility to their aspirations was too potent for that. "Getting their rights" simply meant encouraging people of color to stay in the Chesapeake so that they could work, worship, and educate themselves. It certainly meant continuing to assist those still enslaved to shed their chains. With such modest, specific goals, the almost universal black resistance to white-directed colonization becomes easier to comprehend.

The focal point of all these activities was a changing black church. The conversion of African Americans to Christianity predated the colonization controversies, having expanded dramatically from the 1760s when Methodist and Baptist itinerants began preaching to slaves in the Chesapeake. By 1800 black people comprised substantial portions of congregations throughout the region, and some African Americans preached to whites as well as blacks. Jacob Bishop, a onetime slave exhorter, pastored the Court Street Baptist church in Portsmouth, Virginia, from 1792 to 1802. During that time,

Bishop revitalized the congregation and with help from his flock purchased his freedom along with that of his wife and a son. But white evangelicals who had at first welcomed black worshippers began demanding black subordination and segregation in everything from ordination to church governance to seating at services. The experiences of Richard Allen, Daniel Coker, and their co-religionists were typical in this regard. Bishop himself left Portsmouth in 1802, possibly forced from his pulpit in the aftermath of the Gabriel and Easter conspiracies of 1800 and 1802. He relocated first in Baltimore and later in New York City.[38]

The second decade of the nineteenth century saw blacks removing themselves from such humiliation. They sought to conduct their religious affairs autonomously within a white church, or through entirely independent institutions. This happened throughout the Chesapeake, not just in Philadelphia and Baltimore. In Wilmington, Delaware, Peter Spencer and William Anderson erected the African Union Church, "Methodist but not Methodist Episcopal," in 1813. This independent black church would boast more than thirty congregations in the mid-Atlantic states by the 1840s, including five in New Castle County, Delaware. There were also eight all-black congregations within Delaware's white-dominated Methodist Episcopal Church. Black Baptists in Virginia directed the Williamsburg African Church and Elam Church, in Charles City County, and numerically dominated a number of other congregations in the Dover, Ketocton, and Portsmouth Associations of Baptist churches. In 1830, Richmond's First Baptist Church had over eighteen hundred members, most of whom were black. Other mainly black congregations included Pocorone, in King and Queen County, and Zoar, in Middlesex.[39] In Maryland, the AME Church rapidly expanded beyond Baltimore and its environs. For example, black itinerant Thomas Henry preached a circuit in Frederick and Washington County in the late 1830s that included Frederick, Hagerstown, Burkittsville, Petersville, Knoxville, Berlin (today's Brunswick), Crampton's Gap, and Red Hill.[40] In Baltimore by the late 1850s, fifteen black protestant churches ministered to over six thousand members and nearly three thousand Sunday school participants. Black Catholics, though far less numerous, initiated in 1828 and sustained

The congregation of Bethel African Methodist Episcopal Church in Baltimore presents Robert Breckenridge, a Presbyterian minister, with a gold snuff box, in token of his support for black emancipation. Lithograph, 1846. (Maryland Historical Society.)

throughout the antebellum decades a "School for Colored Girls" that provided religious training under the aegis of the Oblate Sisters of Providence, a teaching order whose members were of African descent.[41]

Suspected by whites of being nurseries of slave insurrection, the black churches in the Chesapeake faced many perils. In Virginia, new laws reimposed white supervision in the wake of Turner's Rebellion. Governor John Floyd imagined that all the black preachers east of the Appalachians had known of Turner's plans. Ministers like Moses Pamphlet, in Williamsburg, and Joseph Abrams, in Richmond, were publicly whipped for violating the 1832 ban on black preaching with sermons that described the "freedom of the soul." But African Americans could evade or bend these strictures as well. At least nine congregations of black Baptists in Virginia survived after 1831 as branches of white-led churches, with unofficial arrangements that allowed black deacons to manage finances, control membership and discipline, and officiate at prayer meetings. Joseph Abrams resumed preaching at Richmond's First African Baptist Church, with its two thousand members, as an "assistant" to the officially appointed white pastor, Robert Ryland.[42] By whatever means, African Americans made their churches into centers of community building, education, and communication. The ability of often desperately poor people to maintain so many institutions offers strong evidence that "for most black Christians expenditure on their religion assumed a top financial priority."[43]

Building and supporting churches was only part of a wider effort by many free people of color to pursue "uplift," a comprehensive effort to improve individual and community morality, to attain respectability, and thus to testify against slavery and race prejudice. The twin desires to save one's soul and to debunk the myth of black inferiority through godly living proved a powerful inspiration. Slaves came to Sunday worship clean and neatly dressed, proud of homemade suits and dresses carefully washed and mended. Even the poorest contributed to the church in "penny collections." Black churches demanded regular attendance at services and Sunday schools, and they disciplined backsliders in an effort to encourage the "steady habits" so admired in early national America.

In a few white-led congregations, upstanding slaves could even use the church's disciplinary procedures against miscreant whites. When Charity and Forty, members of a Methodist congregation in Annapolis, found themselves the target of unwanted sexual advances from their white preacher, John Chalmers, they demanded and obtained redress. Chalmers was punished by the quarterly conference.[44]

All of these demonstrations of diligence and discipline won grudging admiration from whites. One old-fashioned Methodist itinerant with fifty years of circuit-riding behind him said of Baltimore's oldest black church: "I never found as large a number of members as plain as Sharp-street. . . . I preferred them . . . above any other congregation in Baltimore." [45]

African Americans pursued their religion beyond the settled churches, as worshippers, itinerant preachers and exhorters in revivals and camp meetings. These outdoor meetings were routinely marked by segregation; blacks sat behind the speakers' platform, with a curtain to divide them from the white audience. Demands for white supervision of all camp meetings went hand-in-hand with heightened sensitivity to any remarks that could be construed as erosive of white superiority: itinerant William Colbert's diary noted complaints from white listeners in Sussex County, Delaware, when he addressed blacks as "brethren" and "sisters."[46]

Any remarks that appeared to endorse black resistance to masters elicited explosive reactions. In 1818, Jacob Gruber criticized harsh treatment of slaves and asked slaveholders at an 1818 camp meeting Washington County, Maryland, whether, "the slaves thus abused [may not] rise up and kill . . . their oppressors." He was indicted and tried for inciting slaves to insurrection, despite his having told the slaves that they should do no such thing. Gruber was defended on free speech grounds by a rising young attorney named Roger B. Taney, who won an acquittal, but Gruber's Methodist superiors thereafter stationed him in Pennsylvania or with black congregations in Baltimore.[47]

If whites disliked mixed-race camp meetings, they feared all-black religious revivals. These were often pictured as incubators for insurrection and were restricted by bans on night-time gatherings. Some municipalities insisted that black camp meetings be held far from towns, ostensibly to minimize noise problems but also to discourage black attendance. Churches and synods required that white pastors preside and give the principal sermons. Nonetheless, both slaves and free people of color flocked to hear inspiring speakers and to join in hymn-singing and group prayer, in the hope of experiencing conversion and the promise of saving grace. More and more African Americans also felt called to preach and to become itinerants themselves. Their ranks included not a few slaves, as well as women who found their paths in life through Christian testimony.[48]

Jarena Lee, born free in New Jersey in 1783, exemplified the hopes, desires, and conflicts that the call to preach could engender. Converted by none other than Richard Allen, Lee sought the AME bishop's approval to itinerate, but he replied that as to women preaching, "our Discipline knew

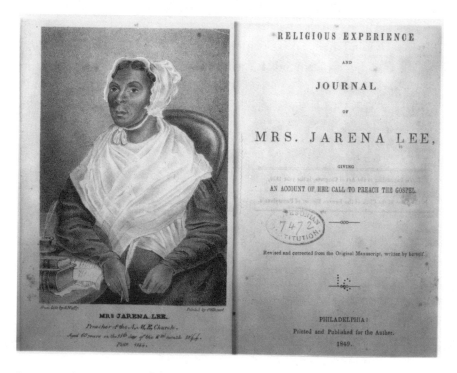

Jarena Lee (1783–post 1849) evangelized and preached against slavery on the Delmarva peninsula in the 1820s and 1830s. Engraved frontispiece, 1849. (Library of Congress.)

nothing at all about it." Eventually, Lee won Allen over by pointing out that the original apostles as "unlearned fishermen" had preached, and that surely God could inspire "a female to preach the simple story of the birth, life, death, and resurrection of our Lord." Allen gave her "liberty" to exhort, and by the 1820s, Lee was touring Delaware and Maryland's Eastern Shore, speaking to packed churches. When white trustees refused to make a chapel available to her in Milford, Delaware, on the grounds that she was not licensed to preach, a mixed black and white audience heard her at the local colored church, and "pride and prejudice were buried" in a successful meeting. At the Denton African Church, "we had everything in good order . . . some of the poor slaves walked from 20 to 30, and even 70 miles to worship God."

Like other black evangelists in the Chesapeake, Lee had to walk a fine line in dealing with slaveholders. Her sermons rarely attacked slavery head-on, at least when slaves were in her audiences. She had to avoid the very real danger of prosecution for inciting slaves to insurrection or legal action against the black churches or preachers that sponsored her. But she seized opportunities to pray with slaveholders anxious about their souls, and noted with pleasure what she saw as heaven-sent discomfitures of those who had harassed her. In Easton, Maryland, she detected a stern providence in the unexpected death of one local official and the bankruptcy of another who had tried to prevent her from speaking.[49]

Lee's contemporary, Zilpha Elaw, had to master inner doubts about her abilities, as well as fears of kidnapping and enslavement before she could embark on a preaching tour in the Chesapeake in 1828. Elaw, like Lee, came to preaching by a circuitous route. Born free in Pennsylvania, she was bound out at age twelve when her mother died. She served her apprenticeship and then married a "respectable" man who "was not a Christian." Awakened to faith at a camp meeting in New Jersey, Elaw strove unsuccessfully to secure her husband's conversion. In the early 1820s she felt a call to preach, but local blacks scorned her and her husband advised her to give up exhorting. Then Joseph Elaw fell ill and died. Penniless, Zilpha bound out her own daughter and resolved to preach after all.

Filled with trepidation, she headed south despite "Satan disturbing my soul" with the idea of being "arrested and sold for a slave . . . on account of my complexion and features." When listeners in Baltimore, Washington, and Alexandria received her well, Elaw moved on to Annapolis and then, overcoming her fear, into the surrounding countryside of Anne Arundel County. Like many free people of color, Elaw sensed an almost palpable change of atmosphere as she left behind the precincts in which freedom was becoming the norm for African Americans and ventured "still further in the interior of the slave States." Invited to stay through Christmas with local evangelicals, Elaw faced her greatest challenge from a young man who mocked one of her sermons. Learning that he was a "slave-driver, a profligate drunkard and habituated to every vice," she took up the challenge and preached a fiery sermon that converted her antagonist, to the joy of black listeners in the church gallery. This episode, presented as a climactic event in Elaw's spiritual biography, led to a twenty-year itinerant career—conducted mainly outside the slave states.[50]

Both Lee and Elaw employed traditional missionary narrative themes to make understated yet potentially devastating critiques of slavery. These black women met Christ's challenge to risk one's life in order to achieve salvation, to jeopardize their freedom in this world to save souls in the next. The implication that slaveholding areas constituted a heathen land, with slaveholders as sinful idolators and persecutors of the righteous, leaps from virtually every page of these accounts. So does the sense that a true Christian should present evildoers with the good news of the gospel, along with a powerful condemnation of those who would practice slaveholding and delude themselves and others with false claims to faith.

Black itinerants in the Chesapeake thus operated within a white-imposed paradigm that spiritual matters be divorced from temporal, and still manged to challenge slavery. Lee and Elaw complied with white insistence that the question of enslavement or freedom in this world be left to the conscience of individual slaveholders, but they also warned slaveholders to fear for their personal salvation. By doing so, they bore witness to the grace that they had received as messengers of the Word.

Oblique attacks on slavery that aimed at achieving spiritual freedom by no means exhausted the possibilities of black testimony. A remarkable case in point is that of the Reverend Noah Davis, a Virginia-born, Baltimore-based Baptist preacher of the 1850s, who used his spiritual gifts to free himself, his wife, and seven children over a thirty-year period. In 1859, Davis published an account of his life that integrated spiritual biography with stories of industry and upward striving.

Davis was born a slave in Madison County, Virginia, in 1804 and witnessed an informal granting of quasi-freedom to his father and mother when they were already in their fifties, too old to receive legal manumission under Virginia's laws. At fourteen, Noah left home to learn shoemaking. The white apprentices and journeymen in his master's shop were "the most intemperate of any class of men in [Fredericks-burg]" and Noah became the "runner" for his workmates. But his white master watched over the impressionable boy, and he was saved from becoming a "confirmed drunkard." After some years at the trade, Davis had a fearful intimation of his mortality and sinfulness at a Methodist prayer meeting. Overcome by doubt, he struggled with his sense of guilt, and eventually joined the Baptists.

Through the good offices of a "colored brother, Armistead Walker," Davis was licensed to preach and exhort by his congregation. Wanting more of his time to pursue this calling, he asked his owner, a doctor Patten, to allow him to purchase his freedom. Patten set a fairly steep price of five hundred dollars, but Davis wangled a pass allowing him to travel and preach to raise his purchase price, thereby falling into the pattern that would govern the next two decades of his life.

Davis toured a series of northern towns, preaching the gospel and soliciting contributions. By the early 1840s he had paid his purchase price. With that goal secured, Davis went back on the road to buy the freedom of his wife and their nine children, seven of whom had been born before Davis could complete the purchase of her freedom. They would accordingly be slaves for life unless redeemed by the contributions of northerners moved by Davis's antislavery message. More than once Davis improvised a purchase of a son or daughter on credit, refinanced old notes, or promised to indenture a child about to be freed to a lender or guarantor, and then took to the preaching circuit again to raise the sums required. Remarkably, he prevented any of his children from being sold to the Deep South during all the years he labored to free them. Funds raised by publishing his memoir purchased the last two held in bondage. Davis's energy, industry, and ever more desperate journeys back and forth across the Mason-Dixon Line ultimately won triumphant liberation for himself and his loved ones.[51]

It might be said that Noah Davis's whole life, and most especially his skills as writer and orator, were a testimony against slavery more powerful than he could give directly in speeches and writings. Those he had to tailor to avoid offending the Virginia slaveholders with whom he dealt for the freedom of his family, and the Baltimoreans among whom he lived.

Not all slaves in the Chesapeake could abide such constraints. Some found their calling by leaving the Chesapeake to challenge slavery. Among

Frederick Douglass's escape from slavery generated intense interest, as this romanticized picture indicates. Engraved sheet music, 1845. (Maryland Historical Society.)

the leading abolitionists of the antebellum period Frederick Douglass, Henry Highland Garnet, Frances Ellen Watkins Harper, and J. W. C. Pennington all began life in Maryland or Delaware but achieved recognition elsewhere.

Garnet and Pennington, born two generations after Richard Allen and Absalom Jones, left slavery in the Chesapeake for lives as ministers. Unlike Allen and Jones, Garnet and Pennington were runaways. Garnet's parents decamped from Kent County, Maryland, to New York City in 1824 when

Henry was nine. Pennington got away from his western Maryland master in 1827 as a teenager. Each would in time become a Presbyterian minister and serve as an antislavery lecturer in the United States and Great Britain.[52]

Garnet took an active role in Liberty Party politics and in the national convention movement of free people of color. His address to the Buffalo convention in 1843 stirred intense controversy when Garnet linked religious and political themes in a call for slaves' resistance to their servitude. Echoing the thoughts of David Walker's "Appeal to the Colored Citizens of the World" of the late 1820s, Garnet insisted that "it is sinful in the Extreme for you to make voluntary Submission." He challenged slaves to see Denmark Vesey and other rebels as their exemplars, and closed with a ringing cry: "Let your motto be resistance! resistance! resistance!"[53] Garnet's call to arms was rejected by many in the black convention movement, including Douglass, then still a devotee of Garrisonian non-resistance, but it portended a shift in abolitionists' attitudes toward a fuller embrace of the idea that slaves could and would assist in achieving their own freedom.

That idea was hardly news to Frederick Douglass, whose moment of awakening to the possibility freedom had come in a fistfight with Edward Covey, an Eastern Shore "slavebreaker" to whom the recalcitrant Douglass had been hired out as a teenager. Douglass's well-known accomplishments and writings resonate with all the themes that black abolitionists used to win white allies in the fight against slavery. As orator, biographer, editor, and novelist, Douglass tapped into every conceivable way of using words, and invoking the Word, to attack slavery.

Douglass's *Narrative of the Life of Frederick Douglass, Written by Himself,* first published in 1845, helped to popularize what would become a new genre in American literature. Douglass recalled his boyhood fascination with literacy, his determination to learn to read, and his treasuring of a tattered copy of *The Columbian Orator,* a popular compendium of spread-eagle speeches about freedom, independence, and duty. Douglass's *Narrative* also registered the classic black indictment of slaveholders as hypocrites claiming but not deserving the name of Christian. Douglass drove home the attack with portrayals of slaveholders as violent, profane, and often drunken men, cloaked in the outward but empty performance of religious duties and rituals. From the time of his escape from Baltimore in 1838, no black American had more visibility than Douglass.[54]

A black Baltimorean from a very different background joined Douglass in winning recognition for her antislavery advocacy. Orphaned at the age of three in 1828, Frances Ellen Watkins was raised and schooled by her uncle, William Watkins, who tutored her in Latin, Greek, philosophy, Bible studies, and mathematics. Above all else, Watkins strove to inculcate the art of eloquence. Frances became his most successful pupil, and his son William J. Watkins became a notable black abolitionist in Boston.[55]

Frances Ellen Watkins, like her uncle, became a teacher, and held a position in Little York, Pennsylvania, in the early 1850s. There she was drawn into the work of aiding fugitive slaves. In 1854, Watkins published a volume of poetry and launched herself onto the abolitionist lecture circuit. She denounced kidnappers of free blacks, urged a boycott of slave-made goods in favor of "free produce," and read her poems. Her most striking work included the "Slave Auction," in which she drew on her own feelings as an orphan to evoke the anxiety and emotional loss of slave children sold apart from their parents. In "The Fugitive's Wife" an enslaved woman laments her husband's absence even as she celebrates his escape from slavery. Finally, Watkins's "Bury Me in a Free Land" took inspiration from her uncle William Watkins, who died in self-imposed exile in Canada rather than remain in America's slavocracy. Like Douglass, she framed her critique of slavery in religious terms and tied it tightly to the temperance movement which combatted the metaphorical "slavery to drink"; much of her oeuvre is temperance poetry. Watkins lived not only to see the end of slavery but re-entered the public sphere after the death of husband. As F. E. W. Harper she battled for women's rights in the late nineteenth century and published a novel about black adjustment to emancipation, *Iola Leroy*.[56]

For Douglass, Harper, and others, leaving the Chesapeake was the the critical step on their journeys to freedom, but Thomas Henry's passage was a long inward pilgrimage leading to legal freedom for self and family, and to spiritual independence as well. Like many of the founding generation of

Frances Ellen Watkins Harper (1825–1911), anti-slavery poet and Underground Railroad operative, was the niece of William Watkins, of Baltimore. (Illustration, William Still, The Underground Railroad *[Philadelphia: Porter & Coates, 1872].)*

MRS. FRANCIS E. W. HARPER.
See p. 753.

the black church, Henry was born into slavery, circa 1798.[57] Raised in St. Mary's County, he was brought to western Maryland and promised prospective freedom under the will of his deceased master, Richard Barnes.[58] A skilled blacksmith, Henry married while still a slave and later used his wages to purchase the freedom of his wife and two children. Here too, Henry's experience was emblematic: African American smiths played prominent roles in establishing the African Methodist Episcopal church. The AME's insignia today still pictures an anvil in front of the Cross.[59]

By 1828, Henry was a Methodist and head of a free black family. Catechized by Jesuit instructors in St. Mary's County, Henry had learned of Methodism during his apprenticeship under Abraham King, "a German Methodist, called United Brethren," and converted during an 1819 camp meeting in Virginia, just across the Potomac from his home. In 1821, Henry felt a call to preach but held back, deterred by his ignorance of scripture and lack of polish as a speaker. Self-study and attendance at Methodist classes developed his confidence, and he won a license from the white leadership, "to lead prayer meetings, bury the dead, and, in an emergency, to baptise children, whenever they were very sick."[60]

Until 1835, Henry labored as a Methodist Episcopal exhorter in western Maryland. Worn down by church elders' persistent efforts to keep him from preaching to audiences that included whites, Henry reached a breaking point when a white steward in his conference sold the child of an enslaved parishioner.[61] Henry promptly left the M.E. church for its African counterpart, which ordained him and made him an elder. Persevering through anti-abolitionist hysteria that targeted AME churchmen, including an unsuccessful attempt to link him to John Brown's 1859 raid on Harper's Ferry, Henry itinerated into the 1860s. His memoir of self-liberation, aptly entitled *From Slavery to Salvation*, appeared after his death in 1872.

These biographies show how the evangelical impulse could lead black people in the Chesapeake down different yet converging paths. The transforming moment of direct communication with God, whether experienced as a vision, voices, or an inward radiation of enlightenment, started thousands of enslaved African Americans on the road to salvation and called not a few of them to spread the good news of the gospel. Blacks' passion to preach and create churches in the early nineteenth century emphasized their belief in equality before God. This created a "crisis of authority in the evangelical community." Offended by such effrontery, whites moved to block black ordinations, restrict or eliminate slave preaching, and, at least in Virginia, to outlaw all black religious meetings not supervised by whites. Although these trends were already emerging by the 1810s and 1820s, they were accelerated by the most shocking of all black responses to evangelical religion, the Nat Turner Rebellion of 1831.[62]

In August 1831, a thirty-year-old slave preacher named Nat Turner and a small band of followers staged what whites regarded as an impromptu uprising in Southampton County, Virginia. With a free black named Billy Artis and a slave known as General Nelson acting as co-leaders with Turner, the rebels seized weapons from the whites they attacked. They killed nearly sixty men, women, and children before hastily organized parties of whites regained control and scattered them. Among the leaders only Turner was captured alive. He successfully hid out for weeks but was taken in late October, convicted of insurrection, and hanged in November. In the interval, eighteen slaves had been tried and executed, and dozens more black people, free and enslaved, had been killed by vengeful whites.

Much of what is known about Turner comes from *The Confessions of Nat Turner*, a pamphlet published by Thomas R. Gray, who had talked with Turner as he awaited execution in a small Virginia town named, ironically enough, Jerusalem. Though some historians see the pamphlet as largely Gray's creation, investigation has shown that most of the material must have come from Turner.[63] As presented by Gray, Turner saw himself as a prophet, marked throughout his life by signs of divine inspiration. At age three or four, he related a story with corroborative detail of events that had occurred before his birth. He learned the alphabet, but without knowing how. Inquiring into the gospel, he reflected on passages about seeking the Kingdom of Heaven. His moment of spiritual awakening came while Turner was "praying at my plough." He heard a spirit speak to him and came to believe he was "ordained" for some great purpose.

Like many another, Turner experienced the power of conversion and redemption through the labors of Methodist itinerants. His owner, Benjamin Turner, frequently invited circuit riders to preach or lead prayer meetings at his house, with his slaves in attendance. There Nat experienced the doubts and despair that often marked conversion experiences for American evangelicals. He ran to the woods to escape a dispute with a new overseer in 1821 and survived there for weeks, but reappeared on his plantation when his spirit told him to return to his as yet undefined, but God-appointed, duty. Soon thereafter, Turner had the first of several prophetic visions. He saw "white and black spirits engaged in the battle" as "the sun darkened" and "blood flowed in streams." A voice interpreted the vision to Turner: "Such is your luck, such you are called to see, and let it come rough or smooth, you must surely bear it."

With this revelation in 1825, Turner withdrew from his slave companions to seek purification and holiness, convinced that the Judgment Day was near at hand. He converted a fellow slave, and the two of them were baptized "by the spirit" in a stream. Turner brought his story of conversion and baptism to a local Baptist congregation, but this group refused to recognize its validity.[64] Further visions now came to Turner; he saw "drops of blood on the corn as though it were dew from Heaven." Turner understood

the drops to be the Blood of the Lamb, symbols of Christ's sacrifice in redeeming mankind.

In May 1828 the spirit revealed that Nat Turner was to take up the "yoke
[Christ] had borne for the sins of men" and "fight against the Serpent." Gabriel
had appropriated the rhetoric of the revolution to cast its heroes as tyrants
and his men and himself as freedom fighters. Now Turner, driven by his visions, saw the pious white evangelicals to be evildoers who must be removed
by black violence in order to consummate God's work on earth. Gray inter-
jected at this point in the narrative, asking "Do you not find yourself mistaken now?" An unshaken Turner replied, "Was not Christ crucified?"

From that moment on, Turner waited for a sign to rise up and "slay my
enemies with their own weapons." Taking a solar eclipse in February 1831 as
his portent, Turner began recruiting associates, and he first named the Fourth
of July as the day for the insurrection until an illness forced a delay to late
August. Once under way, Turner's band killed men, women, and children
but did not move quickly toward the local arsenal at Jerusalem. Had their
chief goal been freedom, the rebels could have covered the ten miles from
their rallying point to Jerusalem in a few hours, seized the weapons there,
and then retired to the depths of the Dismal Swamp to the southeast. The
sacrifice of such efficiency in order to slay their enemies instead is consistent with Turner's own account of his millenarian motivation.[65]

The quick suppression of the uprising demonstrated that whites had
little reason to fear that slave insurrections could overpower them. Few blacks
rallied to Turner, and his men dispersed after one or two brief skirmishes.
But the carefully cultivated confidence that slaves loved and respected their
masters had been seriously challenged. To meet this challenge, Thomas Gray
may have embroidered his account, exaggerating the extent of Turner's religious motivation and overstating Turner's role as the rebellion's primary
leader. Historian Scot French has suggested that Gray's portrait of Turner
as religious psychopath allowed whites to dismiss him as a unique case that
held no lessons or warnings for slaveholders.[66] Nonetheless, older ideas that
all blacks were inveterate enemies of white rule briefly sprang back to life.

The ensuing legislative debates in Virginia over emancipation, colonization, and further restrictions on the lives of free people of color, as well as efforts to enforce greater unity among whites in defense of slavery, all showed how deeply Turner had shaken white certainty about relations between owners and slaves.[67] As with Gabriel's Rebellion thirty years earlier, whites largely ignored a fundamental contradiction between their visions of society and the reality of life under slavery. Both Gabriel and Nat Turner used the whites' most deeply held values as weapons against them.

Turner saw black Americans, not whites, as the chosen people who would enjoy Christ's reign of peace and justice on earth. In 1800, Gabriel and his fellow conspirators had planned to spare Quakers, Frenchmen, and perhaps Methodists because of their antislavery sympathies, and they had some hopes of winning white artisans to their cause. A generation later, with antislavery all but extinct in Virginia, Turner identified no prospective allies or candidates for mercy, nor did he harbor any notions of escape to Haiti. Only God himself, with Turner as his tool, could harrow out slavery in the Old Dominion.

Turner shared the belief held by thousands of enslaved African American Christians that God would deliver them from slavery as He had provided for the Exodus of the Israelites from Egypt. Unlike Cary or Coker, Turner looked to no literal journey to a Promised Land of freedom. Unlike Henry, Davis, and other black preachers and evangelists, he did not see his role as living a sanctified life while awaiting the signs of Judgment Day's arrival. Turner had seen the signs, and he had been chosen to inaugurate the proceedings.

There were, of course, still other ways for African Americans to understand their fate in keeping with the biblical promise of liberation for a chosen people. When AME preachers pleaded for the "Great Deliverer" to "once more awake thine almighty arm, and set thy African captive free," they successfully created a providential identity for slaves as people bound for the land of Canaan. As Frederick Douglass noted, slaves singing of "sweet Canaan" had more than just a "hope of reaching heaven. We meant to reach the *North*, and the *North* was our Canaan." Escape to the North became ever more attractive as a personal fulfillment of Exodus from slavery and as a recruiting ground for allies, white and black, in the fight to abolish slavery altogether.[68]

CHAPTER 7

The Two Underground Railroads

N O ASPECT OF SLAVERY'S HISTORY has attracted so much attention as African Americans' efforts to flee to freedom in the North and the deeds of those, black and white, who helped them. The underground railroad, organized networks of principled men and women who assisted fugitives, is now acknowledged as an important phenomenon.[1] Re-enactments of slave flights along underground railroad routes have generated considerable enthusiasm. Entrepreneurs lead overnight trips that retrace the steps, for example, of fugitives from the Eastern Shore guided by Harriet Tubman. Local historical groups scramble to identify onetime safe houses for presentation to tourists, and a new national museum of the Underground Railroad has opened in Cincinnati.

Scholars now regard slave flight as a major feature of antebellum America. Several works, including Charles Blockson's work on the underground railroad and an exhaustive study of runaway slaves by John Hope Franklin and Loren Schweninger, have refocused attention on the impact of slave flight on both the slave regime and its northern critics. Articles by Paul Finkelman explore the legal and political ramifications that attended North-South disputes on the subject. Stanley Harrold has shown that northern abolitionists took an active interest in slave escapes and even ventured into the slave states to "rescue" enslaved African Americans, in contrast to older accounts which argued that abolitionists discounted such melodramas as distractions from the crusade for legislated emancipation.[2]

The contemporary interest in runaway slaves recapitulates the atmo-

Slaves being sent south after sale. The interstate slave trade separated families, and threat of sale spurred slave flights. Painting by Eyre Crowe, 1853. (Chicago Historical Society.)

sphere of nineteenth-century America. Relatively few people then sustained a deep interest in the philosophical, political, religious, and economic arguments advanced by pro- and anti-slaveryites, but hair-raising tales of escapes to freedom gripped large audiences through the spoken and written word. Indeed, the slave narrative, blending themes of spiritual autobiography, the heroic quest, and what filmgoers might call buddy movies, emerged as a distinctively American literary genre. Frederick Douglass's *Narrative of the Life of Frederick Douglass* (1845) and *My Bondage and My Freedom* (1855), and Solomon Northup's *Twelve Years a Slave* went through multiple reprintings. Harriet Beecher Stowe drew liberally on slave narratives and Underground Railroad themes in her incredibly successful novel, *Uncle Tom's Cabin*, published in 1852. One of the book's climactic moments features a pitched battle in which the fugitive George Harris and his allies drive off slavecatchers, allowing Harris and his family to reach Canada. Josiah Henson,

Josiah Henson, a Maryland slave, escaped to Canada via the Underground Railroad in 1830 and in 1849 wrote his autobiography, which captured the attention of Harriet Beecher Stowe. Stowe met Henson the following year in Boston, and used his experiences as the basis for Uncle Tom's Cabin. (Library of Congress.)

a Maryland-born slave who escaped from Kentucky to Canada, gained celebrity as a supposed model for Stowe's title character.[3]

After the Civil War, former "conductors" and "station masters" of the underground railroad came forward to tell their stories. William Still, a Philadelphian of African American origin, published a mammoth seven hundred page account detailing how he, along with black and white associates, helped hundreds of fugitives, chiefly from Maryland and Virginia, evade pursuit and reach freedom in Ontario. Still's *The Underground Railroad* recounted events from the 1850s, a decade during which the Fugitive Slave Act of 1850 had rendered it unsafe for runaways to move about openly or remain safely anywhere in the United States.

Long before the 1850s, as Franklin and Schweninger point out, flight from slavery was a commonplace act of slave resistance. The number of ultimately successful escapees was not large enough to threaten the existence of slavery, or to diminish significantly the slave population. Nonetheless, the frequency of running away, with associated costs to slaveholders of lost production and expenses of recapture, could influence assessments of profit potential from owning slaves. In non-tobacco growing counties of the Chesapeake, runaways could be troublesome enough to shake slaveowners' very commitment to maintaining the institution.

William Still (1821–1902), assisted hundreds of escapees from slavery who passed through Philadelphia in the 1850s. He published their stories in 1872, in part to aid black people in reuniting separated families. (William Still, Underground Railroad, *1872.)*

Moreover, slaveholders' growing awareness that African Americans were seeking and finding white allies from outside the region, a particularly acute problem in the Chesapeake, inflamed political and cultural relations between North and South. Pennsylvania was an especially turbulent case. There, white assistance to black escapees, coupled with resistance to recapturing those who had taken refuge in the state, dated to the 1780s. For decades, Maryland officials voiced irritation and even outrage over the situation through legislative resolutions and governors' letters to Pennsylvania counterparts.

By the 1830s and 1840s, Chesapeake slaveholders had fended off the British twice, weathered Gabriel's conspiracy with its unrealized appeal to white workers in Richmond, and survived the fright of Turner's bloody apocalypse. They had largely silenced or driven out internal religious antislavery thinkers. In defense, they had articulated a proslavery Christianity that legitimated master-slave relations as a familial or household relationship akin to that of husband and wife or parent and child. They had marginalized those who continued to call for colonization and/or emancipation on political or economic grounds. Yet, no matter how thoroughly the slave regime thwarted all these threats, runaway slaves and the handful of whites who aided them remained a troubling, and unendurable, threat to their hegemony.

Proslaveryites in the Chesapeake would pursue the issue of fugitive slaves and of laws to assure their rendition so relentlessly that they heightened the controversy between North and South. Their provocative actions would help create an atmosphere of crisis that spawned secession and Civil War. Successful in their flight or not, to the extent that they provoked this overreaction fugitive slaves catalyzed the emancipation of their people.

If striking out for freedom in the North, with or without the assistance of the underground railroad, became the dream of untold thousands of African Americans in the Chesapeake, the corresponding nightmare was the ever-present threat to free blacks of being kidnapped and sold as slaves in the Deep South. There existed not one, but two underground railroads. Kidnappers, like their antislavery counterparts, transported black people secretly at night and hid them in safe houses, taking them to a new region where they would assume a new identity, in this case that of an enslaved plantation worker.[4] If many whites in the free states supported the actions of underground railroad agents in defying the fugitive slave laws, many in the Chesapeake winked at the depredations of kidnappers. Some all but endorsed these crimes for their supposed benefit of removing free people of color from the region.[5]

The abolition societies of Maryland and Delaware did oppose kidnappers in the late eighteenth and early nineteenth centuries, sometimes successfully, as in the case of Aaron Cooper. Cooper and his parents had been manumitted by Thomas Hanson of Kent County, Delaware, in the 1790s. Aaron supported his wife and daughters by working as a baker in Duck Creek Hundred. One night in 1811, five armed whites broke into Cooper's house, bound him, and dragged him off. The gang apparently seized both slaves and freedmen, despite laws punishing kidnappers with whipping. Local whites pursued Cooper's captors into Maryland and obtained a writ of *de homine replegiando* from a Dorchester County judge that might have freed Cooper if a sheriff sympathetic to slave dealers had not refused to execute the writ. Cooper ended up in Natchez, Mississippi, where he somehow man-

Kidnappers stage a night raid and capture a free black woman and her child, in order to take them south and sell them as slaves. Alexander Rider, engraving, c. 1820. (Library of Congress.)

aged to gain the attention of an attorney who helped him file a petition of freedom. Backed by correspondence from white Delawareans that testified to his free status, Aaron Cooper was released from bondage and returned to his home after three years of litigation. His captors were never punished.[6]

Cooper's remarkable resurrection from slavery was the exception, not the rule. Kidnappers operated with virtual impunity in many settings. According to grand juries of the early 1800s, night-time assaults on blacks rendered them "unsafe in their own homes" and led to their being "dragged by force" to slave traders' private jails. Kidnappers used trickery as well as force. Baiting the hook by offering a job unloading a ship or clearing brush in an isolated spot was a common ploy, most likely to succeed when another free black person set the snare. Patty Cannon's gang of kidnappers on the Delmarva peninsula relied on John Purnell, a free black, to decoy potential victims. Solomon Northup, a freeborn black man from New York, fell prey in 1840 to white con men who induced him to play the fiddle with them as part of a traveling show. When they reached the District of Columbia,

300 Dollars
REWARD,

For the apprehension of the following Negro Men, and lodging them in any jail, so that I get them again—or in proportion for either.

HANSON,

Who calls himself HANSON MARSHALL, very black, about 40 years of age, 5 feet 5 or 6 inches high, a stout well set fellow, the front of his head bald, teeth remarkably white, nose flat, and eyes small; *he is ruptured, and did wear a truss*; can read, and will occasionally exhort and preach. He left my farm on Elkridge, in Anne Arundel County, Maryland, in May, 1827.

PETER,

Who calls himself PETER SNOWDEN, very black, about 23 years of age, 5 feet 5 or 6 inches high, a stout fellow, with thick projecting lips, and a remarkable *Scar on the left cheek bone*, and a similar one between the thumb and finger of one of his hands, both occasioned by accidents when young. Peter left the same farm on the 22d July last, and has, no doubt, gone to Hanson, and there is reason for believing that both are now in Pennsylvania.

These servants are accustomed to plantation work, and are good hands with the scythe or axe. Their clothing were of the best Oznaburgs and fulled cloth, with strong shoes; but as they are supplied with other apparel, they will no doubt change their dress. Any intelligence of those servants, leading to their apprehension, will be handsomely rewarded, on addressing me at Baltimore.

RICHARD DORSEY.

Baltimore, October 11, 1828.

Printed by SAMUEL SANDS, corner of Gay and Water-Streets—Baltimore.

Slaves in cities like Baltimore, located near free territory, frequently attempted to escape. Some slave owners tried to prevent such costly escapes by offering freedom after a term of faithful service, so-called "term slavery." (Maryland Historical Society.)

Northup was drugged, turned over to a slave dealer, and shipped to Louisiana, where he toiled for twelve years before regaining his freedom. In perhaps the most heinous variation on the confidence game, a Philadelphia man married black women and then sold them into slavery.[7]

More sophisticated methods included taking up free blacks as suspected fugitives and then having confederates come forward to claim them as runaway slaves. Lunsford Lane, a freedman from North Carolina, found himself in this predicament in Baltimore. Able to produce a certificate of freedom, a letter of introduction, and a permit to travel on the railroad, Lane remained free, but not all victims had Lane's forethought, or his good fortune in not having his papers stolen by the kidnappers.[8]

Finally, kidnappers exploited jurisdictional ambiguities to baffle their opponents. Hustling across state and county lines, they invalidated the warrants of pursuing constables. Not for nothing did the notorious Cannon gang of the 1810s and 1820s operate on the Delaware-Maryland border, near present day Reliance. Cannon, her sons, and sons-in-law avoided prosecution for many years by slipping back and forth across the state line to evade the execution of warrants and writs, while kidnapping and selling dozens of people. At last run to earth in 1829, Cannon committed suicide while awaiting trial. Her associates were never tracked down.[9]

Free black people could be re-enslaved through legal process. In 1858, Maryland mandated that free blacks convicted of certain felonies be sold into slavery for a term of years or for life. The state subsequently re-enslaved eighty-nine persons.[10] Free blacks taken up as suspected runaways might be held in jail for months; when no one came forward to claim them, they could then be sold into temporary servitude to pay their jail fees. Insolvent black debtors faced the same fate. Imprisonment and sale into servitude for debt were expunged from statute books in the antebellum period only for whites. Black people were legally being sold for debt into the 1860s.

Fear of kidnapping was only one of the things discouraging African Americans from purchasing freedom and then remaining in the Chesapeake. In Virginia the law had required manumitted slaves to leave the state since 1806. Though seldom enforced in the 1810s and 1820s, that law led to a decline in manumissions, perhaps because slaveholders convinced themselves that freedom accompanied by exile from home and family conferred no boon.[11] Some slaveholders dodged the law and allowed slaves to live and work on their own, virtually free, or sold them to black kinfolk. Either approach could circumvent the banishment requirement, but both loopholes were plugged by further legislation after Turner's uprising. In Loudoun

County, for example, the proportion of free black households in which slaves resided declined from 14 per cent to 4 per cent between 1820 and 1860. In Augusta County, petitions to remain in Virginia met with decreasing success, especially in the 1850s.[12] Over time, law and white opinion made it more difficult to keep black families together through nominal ownership of virtually free children or spouses, or through informal grants of quasi-freedom. Some locales zealously enforced the ban on newly freed persons remaining in Virginia.[13]

Obtaining delayed manumission from masters via term slavery and self-purchase also became more expensive. Demand for slaves in the Southwest drove up slave values and corresponding prices for liberating oneself or kinfolk while decreasing the likelihood that slaveowners would cooperate with the slow payoffs entailed.[14] Slaveholders most likely to manumit on easy terms—those with religious or egalitarian philosophical scruples—had by 1815 largely unloaded their holdings, and few new converts to antislavery joined their ranks.

Slaveholders who did offer self-purchase were increasingly likely to engage in chicanery and fraud to maximize their profit. Martha Scott of Prince George's County allowed Lucy Crawford to hire herself out in Washington, D.C., and to purchase herself on installment payments. But when Crawford had paid all but twenty-one dollars of the agreed upon sum, Scott declared her a runaway slave, had her arrested, and then sold her from the jail. Adam Johnson arranged to buy himself from his mistress and paid the amount in full over several years. In the interval, her death had made him the property of her son. When Johnson came to claim his manumission papers, he was told that he owed an additional 140 dollars for "back wages."[15]

Slave narratives abound with stories of fraudulent slaveholders who violated self-purchase agreements.[16] Josiah Henson struck a bargain with Isaac Riley, in Montgomery County, Maryland, for liberation at the price of 450 dollars. Henson paid 350 dollars in cash and gave a note for the rest, and then returned to Kentucky, where he was to claim his freedom from his owner's brother, with whom he and his family lived. Upon arriving, he discovered that Riley had drawn up his manumission papers contingent on an impossibly high purchase price of one thousand dollars. Henson had been swindled and left in slavery.[17] In 1829, shortly after this incident, Henson and his family fled to Canada.

One of the most famous escapees in the Chesapeake was Henry "Box" Brown, who traveled by rail and express wagon from Richmond to Philadelphia in 1849 in a wooden packing crate into which a confederate had sealed him. Brown's incredible journey won him celebrity on abolitionist lecture tours in New England and later Great Britain. His published narrative, in addition to recounting his trip to freedom, dwelt on self-purchase and its manipulation by slaveholders. Born in 1816 in Louisa County, Virginia, Brown knew that his parents had been able to purchase their freedom, but not his own. In Brown's experience, slaves were "very often" cheated of freedom after producing large sums for their masters. Brown himself had attempted to buy his wife's freedom, to ensure that they could continue to live together. He made a down payment of fifty dollars and then arranged to hire his wife from her owner, so that she could keep money earned as a laundress and apply it toward her purchase price. After a year or two of this arrangement, Nancy Brown and the couple's children were jailed and sold off to a Methodist minister in North Carolina. The disconsolate Henry Brown then began planning his escape.[18]

Occasionally, slaves could turn the tables, dangling the profits of self-purchase before a prospective master as a lure, then running away when opportunity presented itself. Elias Burgess, a Maryland term slave, persuaded William Kriesman of Baltimore to purchase him, despite a record of absconding, claiming a desire to live and work in the city. Once in Baltimore, he ran off repeatedly. Rural slaves might convince a master to allow them to hire their time in the city and then use the master's pass for seeking work as a springboard to an attempted escape. In a variation on this theme, masters saddled with an uncooperative term slave might quickly sell him, with another series of escape attempts as the likely result.[19]

All in all, enslaved African Americans more and more frequently took the long odds of winning freedom through flight. In the most comprehensive work on the subject, John Hope Franklin and Loren Schweninger esti-

Henry Brown had himself shipped in a small crate from Richmond to Philadelphia in 1849. The black man assisting in unpacking him is William Still. Lithograph c. 1850. (Library of Congress.)

mate that by 1860 at least fifty thousand slaves across the entire South ran away annually.[20] If we assume that runaways were distributed evenly across the South, the Chesapeake's share would be about six or seven thousand, though in view of its proximity to free territory, a substantially higher number might be in order. Most of these fugitives, probably over 90 per cent, were arrested or gave themselves up. Still, somewhere between thirty and sixty thousand blacks successfully escaped to freedom between 1830 and 1860. Again, a disproportionate share of these probably came from the Chesapeake, where the recapture rate was undoubtedly lower than in the Deep South.[21]

Certainly, slaveholders grew ever more vehement regarding runaways. Their reactions may signal a real change in blacks' behavior, occasioned in part by desire to avoid slave dealers and kidnappers, in part by declining prospects for wheedling manumission from an owner. At least one local study shows a correlation between runaway levels and slave dealing. In Baltimore the number of runaway advertisements spiked upward during the first cotton boom of 1816–18, just as major interregional slave dealers set up shop in town and kidnappings of free blacks and slaves surged. The number of runaways advertised increased by more than 40 per cent as the number of slave dealers advertising rose from one to seven, then abruptly fell by more than half in 1819–20, as depressed markets arising from a financial panic temporarily drove traders elsewhere, reducing their number to two. The activities of kidnappers in the same period can be documented from the formation of the Protection Society in 1816 to defend free blacks, and the passage of an anti-kidnapping measure in the Maryland legislature. If this episode is typical, slave flight in the Chesapeake would have increased in the relatively prosperous 1830s and 1850s, when slave sales correspondingly rose again.[22]

A profile of the typical runaway slave supports the idea that fear of sale or kidnapping operated as a "push" factor inducing flight. A large majority of those who departed were young adult males, aged fifteen to thirty. Disproportionate numbers of them lived or worked in urban areas and possessed craft skills.[23] In this respect, the characteristics of runaway slaves resembled those of free migrants—young, single males who frequently had fewer familial and social ties to the region they left, and whose skills gave them a greater chance of succeeding economically. These same attributes also identified the slaves most at risk for forced migration to the Southwest by sale, transfer with a migrating slaveowner, or kidnapping. For blacks, then, the same "push" and "pull" factors that historians of immigration have discerned to explain the prevalence of young men as migrants operated to inspire African American runaways.[24]

Anguish over separations from family and loved ones no doubt deterred many from attempting permanent escape to the North. Others reasoned like J. W. C. Pennington, "when I remembered that one of the chief annoyances of slavery, in its mildest form, is the liability of being at any moment sold into its worst form, it seemed that no consideration, not even that of life itself, could tempt me to give up the thought of flight."[25] For Pennington, born a slave in Washington County, Maryland, the precipitating event was seeing his father Bazil beaten by their owner Frisbie Tilghman for having the presumption to contradict him in conversation. The episode left bad blood between Tilghman and Pennington's entire family. Eighteen-year-old James fell under suspicion as "pert" and "impudent" and was caned under his mother's eye. Determined to leave such disgraces behind, and buoyed up by the knowledge that his training as a blacksmith would help him to earn his own bread, Pennington fled on a Sunday in November 1827.

His journey typified that of many fugitives. Traveling alone and at night, without an elaborate plan and with little knowledge of the surrounding countryside, Pennington soon lost his bearings. When he dared to ask if he had arrived in nearby Pennsylvania, he learned that he had strayed east-ward, and that some seventy to eighty miles of walking had left him still in Maryland, only a few miles north of Baltimore. A white wagoner told him of slave catchers in the area, but the warning came too late. Captured, then recaptured after he tried to bolt, Pennington was delivered to a local magis-trate. The next night Pennington managed to steal away and take to the roads once more. Two days later, as Tilghman circulated handbills offering a two hundred dollar reward for him, Pennington found his way into Penn-sylvania, probably in lower York or Lancaster County. There, a local woman sized him up correctly and directed him to a Quaker who sheltered him and helped him find a more secure refuge farther east.[26] Pennington would go on to become a Presbyterian minister, a participant in the black convention movement, and a leader among black abolitionists.

His narrative, "*The Fugitive Blacksmith*," captures many of the arche-typal experiences of those who struck out for freedom. He had no connec-tions to or information about anyone, white or black, who might help him, and only his own intuition to assist him in deciding whether to trust hap-penstance offers of advice or assistance. Plenty of men in Maryland and Pennsylvania eyed every solitary African American as a possible runaway and source of reward money.[27] Still, crossing the state line was an important milestone, because then he came into contact with men like William Wright, who used a network of antislavery colleagues to aid him. Pennington also learned that life in Pennsylvania was not entirely safe. The reluctance of many citizens and local authorities to cooperate with slave hunters did not rule out the chance of a midnight raid and a forced journey southward back to slavery. By 1828, a year after his departure from Maryland, Pennington had relocated to New York State. Although Pennington became a well known speaker and writer, he was still a fugitive slave subject to capture and return. He could only secure legal freedom by emigrating to Canada or England or, as Pennington ultimately did, by arranging a self-purchase with the executor of his master's estate in 1851, twenty-four years after his escape. All of this, it is worth noting, was set in motion by Tilghman's efforts to beat down Pennington psychologically and better fit him for slavery.[28]

Like Pennington, James Watkins decided to flee when his master circumscribed his life and tried to make him accept lifelong slavery. His story also illustrates the corrosive effect of a free black community on master-slave relations. Watkins, who lived near Cockeysville, a dozen miles from Baltimore, sought to marry a free black woman in that city. His owner, Luke Ensor, followed conventional wisdom and forbade the marriage, because slaves married to free women were more likely to yearn for freedom themselves, and more able to find help in securing it. Maryland's most notable fugitive, Frederick Douglass, had been crucially assisted by his free wife, Anna Murray Douglass, for example.[29] Besides, if Watkins married a free woman his children would not be Ensor's chattels. Ensor's wife urged Watkins to take up with any of several "suitable" slave women, seeming "anxious . . . that I should be married, believing that I would then be quite settled for life." Instead, Watkins ran away, in June 1841. Retaken by men with bloodhounds while still in Maryland, he resumed life on Ensor's farm, after enduring a public beating meant to discourage others from emulating him.

Only in 1844 would Watkins reach Pennsylvania on a second attempt, this time defeating the bloodhounds by lacing his tracks with snuff and cayenne pepper. Settling in Hartford, Connecticut, Watkins married, after overcoming the reservations of the bride's father about his fugitive status. Shortly after enactment of the Fugitive Slave Law, Ensor discovered Watkins's whereabouts and offered one thousand dollars to Hartford police for his return to Maryland. Tipped off by a sympathetic constable, Watkins sailed for Great Britain, where he lectured to antislavery groups and published his narrative.[30]

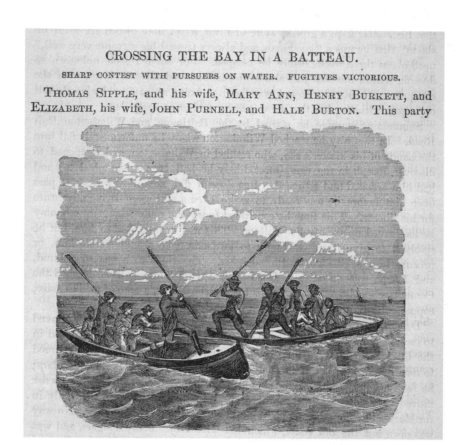

CROSSING THE BAY IN A BATTEAU.

SHARP CONTEST WITH PURSUERS ON WATER. FUGITIVES VICTORIOUS.

THOMAS SIPPLE, and his wife, MARY ANN, HENRY BURKETT, and ELIZABETH, his wife, JOHN PURNELL, and HALE BURTON. This party

Six people crossing the Delaware Bay fend off men who would re-enslave them. These fugitives reached Cape May, and then Philadelphia, where William Still recorded their story, in 1860. (Illustration, Still, Underground Railroad 1872.)

Watkins, like Pennington and most of the escapees described in Still's *Underground Railroad* cases of the 1850s had no help while in Maryland, and secured assistance "providentially" in Pennsylvania rather than through prior arrangement. Those fugitives of the 1840's and 1850s who did find help tapped into a deeper, better organized network of assistance in Pennsylvania. Once he reached a friendly house in York, Pennsylvania, a fugitive might be guided to Columbia, a Susquehanna River town with a black population of nearly one thousand in the 1840s.[31] There, black entrepreneurs like Stephen Smith and William Whipper used their commercial connections to

William Whipper (1804–1876), lumber
merchant and Underground Railroad
conductor, operated out of Columbia,
Pennsylvania, in the 1840s and 1850s.
He also worked with William Watkins
to found the American Moral Reform
Society." (William Still, Underground
Railroad, 1872.)

WILLIAM WHIPPER,
CONDUCTOR AT COLUMBIA.   See p. 735.

move runaways on canal boats, stages, and railroad cars: Whipper even
owned a boxcar with a hidden compartment for transporting fugitives.
Canada-bound travelers could proceed westward toward Pittsburgh or directly north along the Susquehanna Canal as far as Williamsport, and thence
into New York State via a number of routes. Or, as happened to Watkins,
they could be "forwarded" like freight to Lancaster and its environs, also
home to several hundred black people, and then on to the Philadelphia "station" where they passed through the hands of William Still and his associates. As for the volume of runaways leaving Maryland for south central
Pennsylvania, William Whipper estimated that he had helped hundreds of
fugitives who had passed through Columbia in the period 1847–50 alone.[32]

Columbia's thriving black community no doubt drew some refugees to
it, but many also headed that way in order to avoid the zealous policing of
roads from Baltimore to York and Philadelphia in the late antebellum decades. Such vigilance had not always been the case. In the 1790s, Quakers
like Isaac Wilson who lived on the "banks of the Susquehanna" in Maryland, near Rising Sun or Havre de Grace, had been so persistent in hiding
runaways and ferrying them across the river as to earn public denunciation
by Baltimore slaveholders.[33] Frederick Douglass famously made his getaway
from Baltimore to Philadelphia in 1838 by posing as a free black seaman and

Four young men from Delaware row across the Delaware Bay to New Jersey in a gale to gain their freedom, in 1858. (Illustration, Still, Underground Railroad, *1872.)*

riding the aboveground railroad, but authorities all but closed down these options by the 1840s. Thereafter, vigorous enforcement of the laws led to long prison terms for those who supposedly "enticed" or "kidnapped" black runaways. Free people of color who helped fugitives could be sold into term slavery that might all too easily become permanent.[34]

Baltimore itself could not be shut down as a hiding place for runaways. A huge free black population, in excess of twenty thousand by the 1850s, rendered it a permanent magnet for fugitives seeking anonymity or hoping for assistance from free African Americans. One of Harriet Tubman's first rescue journeys took her to Baltimore to lead a sister and her family out of slavery.[35] William and Ellen Craft, an African American couple from the Deep South whose getaway featured the very light-skinned wife passing as a white man accompanied by her husband in the role of black valet, also made their way through the city successfully in 1848. On the whole, though, rural routes proved safer and more attractive, especially on the Eastern Shore, where members of Delaware's large Quaker community, working in concert with free blacks, provided sanctuary to fugitives until the end of slavery in 1865.[36]

Delaware's best known underground railroad station master was Thomas Garrett, a Pennsylvania-born Quaker who moved to the Wilmington area around 1820 and soon thereafter began to help runaways from southern Delaware, Maryland, Virginia, and North Carolina. Most fugitives reached him without prearrangement, for Garrett believed that it was important for slaves to take the first steps toward freedom on their own. The lucky ones made contact, whereupon Garrett undertook to transport them. Some went overland to Chester County and others to the train station at Marcus Hook in Delaware County, either by wagon or carriage. The most perilous moments arose at the closely watched bridges over the Chesapeake and Delaware Canal, Brandywine Creek, and the Christiana River in Wilmington. Still others avoided these checkpoints by being stowed on Delaware Bay schooners that took them to Philadelphia or New York. Over a period of nearly forty years, Garrett helped more than twenty-four hundred men, women, and children reach freedom in Pennsylvania.[37]

Garrett, of course, did not act alone. His coworkers included Quakers like John Hunn, a fellow station master in central Delaware's Kent County who used Quaker meetinghouses in Odessa and Appoquini-mink to conceal runaways. Harry Craig, a black brickmaker, guided blacks along New Castle County's byways, and Patrick Holland, an Irish livery stable keeper, lent his resources to the cause.

The narrative of William Green offers a glimpse of how Garrett and his colleagues worked, and of how freedom-seeking African Americans understood the experience.[38] Born on Maryland's Eastern Shore, Green was entitled to freedom at age twenty-five by the terms of his first owner's will, but he was "handsomely cheated" of his birthright by a scheming heir who sold him as a slave for life. Resolving to strike out for Canada, Green and two friends first hid in the house of a prominent slaveholder in Cambridge and then stole a boat and crossed the Choptank River. Thereafter, they made their way north and east along the river toward Camden, Delaware (a route often traveled later by Harriet Tubman), walking sandy roads at night, holing up in woodlands or marshes by day, and taking shelter with free blacks and at least one white Quaker.[39] One potential ally who had had a previous brush with the law for aiding fugitives declined to help because "he was under heavy bonds to keep the peace." Once in Delaware, Green made contact with a white man who recognized a coded story to the effect that the

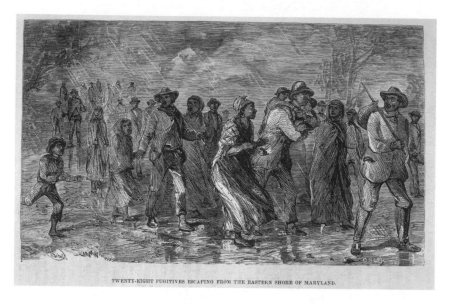

TWENTY-EIGHT FUGITIVES ESCAPING FROM THE EASTERN SHORE OF MARYLAND.

Inspired and given directions by Harriet Tubman, several families of slaves staged a spectacular escape from Dorchester County, Maryland, in 1857. They safely reached Philadelphia, where William Still and the antislavery Vigilance Committee aided them. (William Still, The Underground Railroad, *1872.)*

travelers were "going to visit Aunt Sarah" and steered them away from a tavern frequented by slavecatchers. The men eventually reached "Aunt Sarah's" husband, an African American who placed them as passengers on a boat headed for Philadelphia, vouching for them as his nephews. Green noticed that "the captain seemed to understand all," and silenced "inquisitive" crew members. Green reached Philadelphia without incident and eventually settled in Springfield, Massachusetts.[40]

The men and women of the underground railroad waged a constant battle with proslavery forces. In 1848, Thomas Garrett was convicted of assisting runaways. The fine of five thousand dollars was meant to wipe out his fortune and discourage him from ever helping fugitives again. Undeterred, Garrett assured the presiding judge, none other than Chief Justice Roger B. Taney of the U.S. Supreme Court, that he would "double [his] diligence" and aid blacks "at whatever cost," a promise he kept, as evidenced by his ever-growing tally of slaves forwarded to freedom.[41]

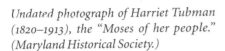

Undated photograph of Harriet Tubman (1820–1913), the "Moses of her people." (Maryland Historical Society.)

If a "station master" like Garrett staked his fortune to free slaves, "conductors" like Harriet Tubman literally risked their lives. Tubman's tale united all the elements of fear, deceit, hope, and determined action that characterized slaves who fled owners and took their freedom.[42] Born enslaved as Araminta Ross in 1820, in Maryland's Dorchester County, she married a freedman named John Tubman in 1844 with the consent of her owner, Edward Brodess. Harriet then hired herself out, perhaps to save money and buy her freedom. Brodess, plagued by debt, had already sold Harriet's sisters, Lina and Soph, to out-of-state buyers, and Harriet, too, faced the threat of separation. When Brodess died in March 1849, the possibility of Harriet's sale as part of an estate settlement dramatically increased.

By then, Tubman had learned that she had a legal claim to freedom. She had employed a lawyer who discovered that Tubman's mother, Rit, and all her children had been prospectively manumitted years ago in the will of Rit's owner Atthow Pattison, with a promise of freedom at the age of forty-five. This pledge had had long been ignored, probably because a technical deficiency in the wording of Pattison's bequest afforded heirs like Brodess the opportunity to claim ownership of the Ross family in perpetuity. Deprived of her chance for manumission, Harriet now learned that Brodess's widow, Eliza, indeed intended to sell one of her sisters, Keziah, and her chil-

DESPERATE CONFLICT IN A BARN.

Slavecatchers recapture three black men fleeing from Martinsburg, Virginia, to Pennsylvania, in 1853. Wesley Harris succeeded in escaping a second time and became free with the help of William Still. (Still, Underground Railroad, *1872.)*

dren, to pay estate debts. With a further loss of kin in prospect, Harriet and two brothers, not yet themselves up for sale, decided to run away.

This first attempt failed, but Harriet tried again in October 1849, this time alone. Tubman, unlike Pennington or Watkins, had help from the outset, from a white woman Tubman thought to be a Quaker. This person gave Tubman directions and the name of another family who would hide her on her way north along the Choptank River and onward into Delaware. Over the next two weeks, Tubman traveled from one safe house to another, always on foot, until she reached Pennsylvania. Over the next ten years, she returned repeatedly, using a network of contacts, black and white, slave and free, to rescue nearly all her family members from slavery.

In one 1854 rescue she conveyed a party of seven, including three of her brothers, to St. Catherine's, Ontario. On that occasion, Garrett helped Tubman evade slavecatchers at the bridge in Wilmington by the subterfuge of hiring a wagon and a party of bricklayers. Posing as workmen on a drunken frolic, the men passed over the bridge unchallenged, with the fugitives in the bed of the straw-covered wagon. Tubman eventually led some seventy to eighty African Americans from bondage in Maryland's Caroline and Dorchester Counties.[43] Dubbed a "Moses" by William Still, her record as a rescuer and guide for runaways in the 1850s was unparalleled in the Chesapeake.

Tubman did have predecessors, including a few white abolitionists, but when white proponents of immediate abolition first organized themselves and began agitating in the 1830s, many in their ranks opposed slave rescues. They felt that individual cases, however dramatic, drew attention and funds away from the larger cause of ending slavery. In addition, rescues might entail the use of force to resist slavecatchers, and this raised a grave moral problem. If the ubiquitous use of violence constituted slavery's great sin, then abolitionists had to foreswear violence themselves according to "non-resistants" like William Lloyd Garrison. Abolitionists also harbored doubts about whether slaves would participate willingly or effectively in potentially violent resistance. Many may have accepted slaveholders' assertions about the docility of black people, claims supported by the infrequency and abject failure of slaves' uprisings.

These perceptions began to change in the wake of two dramatic and successful rebellions aboard slave ships. In 1839 a group of Africans rose and took the *Amistad* from its Spanish masters. The ship subsequently ran aground in American waters. In a case that reached the U.S. Supreme Court, the Africans were recognized as free men.[44] Two years later, as the brig *Creole* sailed from Norfolk to New Orleans with a cargo of 135 slaves, African Americans from Virginia rebelled and took possession of her, killing the slave trader and wounding the captain. Nineteen men carried out the insurrection, led by Madison Washington, a onetime fugitive to Canada who was recaptured when he returned to Virginia to liberate his wife. Washington steered the ship into a British port in the Bahamas, where colonial officials deemed all aboard to be free.[45]

Perhaps inspired by these proofs of black willingness to strike hard for freedom, abolitionists Charles T. Torrey and William L. Chaplin moved to the Chesapeake and devoted themselves to challenging slavery directly. They hoped to encourage more slaves to run away and thereby to destabilize slavery in the border states while also galvanizing opposition to slavery in the North.[46]

Torrey, a Massachusetts clergyman, newspaper editor, and Liberty Party activist, planned and carried out several rescues between 1842 and 1844 while visiting or living in Washington, D.C., and Baltimore. Operating in tandem with a Washington freedman named Thomas Smallwood, his wife Elizabeth, and a Mrs. Padgett, Torrey concentrated on black families about to be broken up by sale and helped steer dozens of people to Canada.[47] Torrey developed a network of contacts who helped him "forward" escapees northward, including the free black man, Jacob Gibbs, in Baltimore, and James J. G. Bias, a black dentist in Philadelphia. Smallwood retreated to Canada in 1843 to avoid prosecution, but Torrey persisted with aid and advice from the likes of Thomas Garrett and the Philadelphia Vigilant Association, an antislavery and anti-kidnapping group. Late in 1844 Baltimore authorities arrested and convicted Torrey for "stealing" the slaves of William Heckrotte and sentenced him to six years in the Maryland Penitentiary. Torrey died there of pulmonary disease in 1846, eulogized as a martyr to freedom and an inspiration to direct action against slavery.[48]

Chaplin, though less extensively involved than Torrey, breathed the same spirit. In August 1850 he was jailed in Maryland for attempting to drive a carriage containing two runaways to Pennsylvania.[49] Both Chaplin and Torrey sought to destabilize slaveholding as a step toward abolition in the Upper South. They opposed purchasing and freeing slaves to avoid their sale south. Such activities, in their view, wrongly acknowledged slavery's legitimacy.

Others felt free to use any and all methods that resulted in liberation. Jacob Bigelow, a Washington lawyer and owner of the city's first gas company, acted as a manumission broker. For much of the 1840s and 1850s he raised money to buy freedom for slaves threatened with sale. But Bigelow also worked with underground railroad operatives to foster escapes. In one dramatic case, Bigelow first tried to arrange the purchase and liberation of

*Dressed as a man, fifteen-year-old Ann
Maria Weems fled from Rockville, Maryland, via Washington, to Philadelphia and
freedom. Jacob Bigelow orchestrated her
escape after failing to purchase her from
her owner in 1855. (Illustration, Still, Underground Railroad, 1872.)*

Ann Maria Weems, a fifteen year-old from nearby Rockville, Maryland.
When negotiations for Weems's purchase broke down, Bigelow orchestrated
her flight to Washington. There, free black families hid her for nearly two
months, until a "Dr. H." journeyed from Philadelphia and spirited Weems
away in a hired carriage, an arrangement co-ordinated by Bigelow and William Still, and paid for by the ransom fund that had been intended for
Weems's purchase.[50]

Bigelow also worked with men like Captain Daniel Drayton, a "soldier
of fortune" rather than a committed abolitionist, whose schooner transported not only grain, timber, and beef, but also smuggled human cargo—
for a price. Drayton had owned and operated bay and coastal schooners for
decades. For him it was a matter of course that slaves in Chesapeake ports
sought out vessels from northern states to make discreet inquiries about the
prospect of buying passage on the return voyage. Drayton at first refused to
engage in such risky business but eventually became convinced "by inter-
course with the negroes, that they had the same desires, wishes, and hopes,
as myself." He knew that slaves were "said to be happy and contented," but
he also knew that no "waterman who ever sailed in the Chesapeake Bay . . .
will not tell you that, so far from the slaves needing any prompting to run
away, the difficulty is, when they ask you to assist them, to make them take
no for an answer." Finally, in 1847, Drayton gave in to these importunities

THE MAYOR AND POLICE OF NORFOLK SEARCHING CAPT. FOUNTAIN'S SCHOONER.
(Twenty-eight fugitives were concealed in this vessel.)

Captain Fountain dissuades the mayor of Norfolk from searching his schooner for run-
away slaves by offering to chop open the deck himself. Fountain had twenty-one escap-
ees aboard, whom he safely delivered to Philadelphia, in 1855. (Illustration, Still, *Under-*
ground Railroad, 1872.)

and agreed to transport a woman in Washington, D.C., whose master had
reneged on a self-purchase agreement. He delivered her and five children to
their already free husband and father in Frenchtown at the head of the bay.[51]

Word of this deed having spread quietly through Washington's black
community, Drayton was approached early in 1848 to effect a rescue of
twelve slaves who feared being sold south as punishment for having filed a
freedom suit. Chartering the *Pearl* for this voyage, Drayton reached Washington to discover a throng of slaves determined to seize the day and flee
their masters. Leaving in the dead of night with seventy-eight runaways,
Drayton was overtaken by a pursuing steamer at the mouth of the Potomac.

Slavecatchers had been tipped off by a free colored hackman who had carried two of Drayton's passengers to the wharf, and who resented not having been sufficiently well paid.

Most of the captured fugitives were sold to Hope Slatter, a slave dealer who sent them to Georgia for resale, and Drayton was tried for assisting slaves to escape and for larceny. His prosecutors, determined to uphold the perception of slaves as contented, tried to prevent the jury from considering the former charge so that the trial record could be interpreted to show that Drayton, and not enslaved African Americans, had initiated the escape plan. Convicted on all counts and fined over ten thousand dollars, Drayton languished in prison until Senator Charles Sumner cajoled President Millard Fillmore into pardoning him in 1853.[52]

Thomas Garrett and William Still also worked with profit-minded sea captains to transport slaves. Their memoirs prominently mention a Captain Fountain, who apparently made several trips from Norfolk and its environs to Philadelphia carrying fugitives in his hold. According to Still, Fountain combined a hatred of slavery with a willingness to be compensated for his services. His customers appear to have been mostly workers in Richmond, Petersburg, or Norfolk whose masters had hired them out to craft shops or tobacco factories. These slaves had opportunities to amass money through "overwork," with which they could buy a "ticket" on Fountain's boat. On one trip, Fountain had twenty-one men, women, and children concealed below decks beneath sacks of wheat when the mayor of Norfolk and a posse armed with spears and axes demanded to search the vessel. Fountain boldly offered to wield the axe himself and chop wherever directed. His nervy bluff worked, and the mayor abandoned the search.[53]

By the mid-1850s, state and municipal laws mandated searches of ships northbound from Chesapeake ports to prevent losses of slave property, which nonetheless exceeded more than seventy-five thousand dollars annually just in the city of Norfolk.[54] Some laws required that ships be "smoked" before departure, to deter slave stowaways. A few African Americans braved even this threat, shrouding themselves in makeshift oil paper cloths, and breathing through dampened towels, in order to make good their escape by sea.[55]

William Still chronicled escapes or rescues by men, women, and children of all ages, by every possible mode of transport, but perhaps no case illustrates the complexities of flight and the fugitive slave law so much as that of Jane Johnson of Virginia. In 1855 her owner, John Wheeler, a U.S. diplomat en route to Nicaragua, came with Johnson to Philadelphia to catch a steamer. There, Johnson passed word to a hotel waiter that she desired freedom. He informed Still, who raced to the wharves on the Delaware with Passmore Williamson, an official of the Pennsylvania Abolition Society. They found Johnson and informed her that she was a free woman under Pennsylvania's personal liberty law, which denied slaveholders the right to bring their slaves into the state, even for the shortest of sojourns. When Johnson declared her willingness to leave Wheeler, he tried to restrain her forcibly, but several black deckhands intervened. In the ensuing fracas Johnson and her two sons walked down the gangplank and sped away in a carriage provided by Still.

Wheeler struck back through the courts. In a bizarre inversion of the processes used by antislavery men to combat slavecatchers and kidnappers, federal district judge John K. Kane issued a writ of *habeas corpus* to Williamson, demanding that he produce Johnson and justify his legal basis for detaining her. Williamson's response to the writ, avowing that he did not hold and had never held Johnson in his custody, infuriated Kane, who clapped Williamson in prison for contempt of court.

Wheeler also charged Still and the black deckhands with riot, and assault and battery, and claimed that Johnson had wished to remain with him. When preliminary testimony at the trial went against the defendants, Johnson herself courageously came forward from hiding to testify to the truth of the matter, defying Wheeler's determination to reclaim her as a fugitive slave. Johnson's appearance provoked a near riot, as state officials and police protecting her right to testify faced off with a U.S. attorney and federal marshals equally determined to apprehend her as a fugitive. Borne into the courtroom within a cordon of Philadelphia constables, Johnson gave the lie to Wheeler's confabulations and got away safely. As Williamson recounted the event, sounding for all the world like a southern champion of

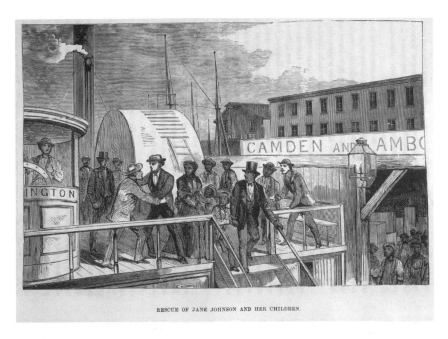

RESCUE OF JANE JOHNSON AND HER CHILDREN.

Jane Johnson and her children walk down the gangplank to freedom in Philadelphia, as deckhands prevent her owner, John Wheeler, from restraining her. (Illustration, Still, Underground Railroad, 1872.)

states' rights, "State sovereignty triumphed over the insolent invasion of usurped authority on the part of Federal officers."[56] The resulting acquittal of Still and his comrades did not move Judge Kane, who resisted all efforts to free Williamson for several months more.

Despite their ingenuity, persistence, and sometime heroism these rescuers gave slavery in the Chesapeake the merest pinpricks. They had no power to harm the institution in numerical terms. The escape of a few hundred slaves a year had little impact measured against the more than half-million enslaved people in Virginia and Maryland. On the other hand, northern reactions to rescuers, and slaveholders' responses to those reactions, elevated the issue into one of consequence. Abolitionists swept aside their reservations about piecemeal action. Garrison, for one, cheered on fugitives and their rescuers who, he wrote, performed "act[s] of mercy worthy of all praise." Antislavery societies generated legal defense funds, and politi-

A BOLD STROKE FOR FREEDOM.

Fugitives from Loudon County, Virginia, repel slavecatchers with pistol fire. William Still recorded this 1855 story to demonstrate the determination of African Americans to use any means possible to obtain freedom. (Still, Underground Railroad, *1872.)*

cians like John Quincy Adams, Salmon P. Chase, and William Seward offered their legal expertise to defendants.[57]

Taken together, slaves' widespread determination to escape bondage, the efforts of a few whites to assist them, and the approval of both groups' actions by a significant sector of the northern public slowly but significantly corroded slaveholders' perceptions of master-slave relations and of the safety of slavery within the Union. Antebellum slaveholders clung to a vision of slavery as a paternal relationship of reciprocal duties and obligations, centered on the idea that slaves accepted their bondage and recognized the virtue of their masters. This world view could withstand the occasional shock of a slave conspiracy or insurrection. Rebels like Gabriel or Nat Turner were crushed militarily, and then written off as aberrations. But a persistent stream of individual runaways from thousands of slaveholders ate away at their self-image as benevolent "fathers" of child-like slaves and called into question their supposedly absolute control as masters.

The deceptions that slaves routinely practiced in order to make good their escapes likewise undercut the myth that they respected and admired their owners. Repeated demonstrations of slaves' deceit while absconding must surely have contributed to the suspicious mindset that characterized late antebellum slaveholders.

Slaveholders' increasingly paranoid outlook applied not only in relations with their chattels but also in assessing the political intentions of northern antislavery men and women.[58] Northern support for the underground railroad and slave rescuers, though uneven, fed into an ever more prevalent southern view that northern society harbored aggressive intentions against the South and slavery. No disclaimers to the contrary by politicians and newspaper editors, or northern acknowledgments of slavery's constitutionally protected status, could assuage southern doubts. Southerners demanded tangible proofs of northern willingness to sustain slavery. For congressmen from Maryland and Virginia, one important test lay in securing and enforcing laws that would compel the co-operation of northern state and municipal authorities in the return of runaways.[59]

Marylanders in particular had long been disgruntled with their neighbors across the Mason-Dixon Line. As early as 1798, only five years after enactment of the first federal fugitive slave law, the state legislature complained in a resolution about the "great loss and inconvenience" that arose from slaves "absconding . . . into Delaware, Pennsylvania, and New-Jersey," where they were "concealed and protected by the citizens thereof."[60] A few years later Eastern Shore congressman Joseph Nicholson demanded a special committee to look into the "harbouring" of slaves, buttressing his case with constituent letters from Chestertown that claimed that neighboring states put "every possible obstruction in [the] way of recovery . . . warrants for a breach of the peace [have been] taken out against the masters, and they have been obliged to give up their property to redeem themselves from jails." One writer estimated that sixty slaves had "made off" in the past month from his part of Kent County.[61]

Most runaways were captured and taken back to slavery. Here, pursuers with dogs have treed a fugitive. Drawing, c. 1860. (Library of Congress.)

Despite these protests, the situation did not improve. The Maryland House of Delegates fired off five more resolutions castigating Pennsylvanians' aid to runaways between 1816 and 1822, and then fell silent after Pennsylvania passed a personal liberty law in 1826 that gave people claimed as fugitives access to legal due process, a right not granted by the federal Fugitive Slave Act of 1793. For Marylanders the personal liberty law was an inappropriate assertion of states' rights and a boldfaced denial of constitutional and congressional authority respecting fugitives. Pennsylvanians, who enacted their law in the wake of an upsurge in violent seizures of free blacks in 1825, saw the issue as one of providing protection to free people of color against kidnappers.[62]

Doubts about the constitutionality of Pennsylvania's law produced a test case in 1842 surrounding the doings of Edward Prigg. This Marylander had forcibly removed Margaret Morgan, a black woman who claimed to be legally free, from her home in York, Pennsylvania, and taken her back to Maryland. The U.S. Supreme Court upheld Prigg's actions and overturned his conviction for kidnapping and assault by a Pennsylvania court. Under the fugitive slave clause of the Constitution slaveholders could act on their own initiative in recapturing runaways and need not rely on state officials, according to Justice Joseph Story's opinion. The Court also struck down Pennsylvania's personal liberty law of 1826 as improperly impeding citizens from reclaiming their slave property.

In an important aside to this proslavery decision, Justice Story declared that while states could not block the rendition of runaways, neither could state officials be compelled to carry out federal fugitive slave legislation. Northern states seized on this part of the opinion and quickly passed laws forbidding magistrates or law enforcement officers from assisting in any way in the capture or return of alleged fugitives.[63]

Removing state and local magistrates from enforcement of the federal fugitive slave law affected escaping slaves in various ways. In communities sympathetic to runaways, or where blacks could form self-defense groups, recaptures of fugitives and kidnapping of free blacks continued to be contested, sometimes violently, often successfully. Slaveholders decided that stricter federal legislation was called for, and demanded a new Fugitive Slave Act as part of the negotiations surrounding the admission of California as a free state in 1850.

Leading the charge for a new law were border South senators like Thomas Pratt of Maryland and James Mason of Virginia. They urged the creation of a network of federal commissioners empowered to assess slaveholders' claims to runaways under rules that virtually guaranteed the rendition of the suspected fugitive. A claimant could introduce evidence to demonstrate ownership, but alleged slaves would have no access to the writ of *habeas corpus* to challenge their being held captive and no opportunity to cross-examine witnesses or produce testimony on their own behalf. Cases would be decided not by juries, but by a commissioner acting alone. If the commissioner ruled in favor of the claimant slaveonwer, his fee was double what it would be if he found for the black defendant. Most gallingly, federal marshals would have the power to deputize citizens as posse members to recover runaways, with fines of up to one thousand dollars for any northerner who refused to cooperate.

Many northern legislators conceded that stronger fugitive slave legislation was needed but balked at denying jury trials, seen as a fundamental right of all Americans. To southerners, long accustomed to trying slaves before juryless magistrates' courts, this demand seemed incomprehensible and suggestive of northern treachery. With free state juries hearing cases, a slaveholder seeking a runaway might as well "go down to the sea, and recover from his native element a fish that has escaped," according to Virginia's Mason. Northerners eventually yielded on this point, as part of the Compromise of 1850, and in September of that year the Fugitive Slave Act became law.[64]

Viewed as a test of northern acceptance of the constitution's protection of slavery, the law received decidedly mixed grades, both in the 1850s and from today's historians. As anticipated by supporters and detractors alike, commissioners ordered the return of most alleged fugitives brought before them. At least two local studies have found that whites only infrequently opposed enforcement, with most resistance offered by free blacks, who understandably read the act as an open invitation to kidnap any person of color.[65] Thousands of African Americans left homes and jobs for refuge in Canada or relocated northward within the United States, away from the Mason-Dixon Line or the Ohio River, where capture and enslavement were easiest. Columbia, Pennsylvania, less than a day's walk from Maryland, lost half of its black population in the 1850s, much of it in 1850 and 1851. Many in Pennsylvania welcomed this black exodus as ridding the state of an "undesirable" element, an unintended benefit of the new law.[66]

The successful taking of fugitives and the removal of many free blacks to Canada tell only part of the story. Far more visible and consequential in shaping public opinion were the handful of clashes between slavecatchers, black people, and their allies. No such incident fed North-South bitterness more than the fatal shooting of Maryland slaveholder Edward Gorsuch in the so-called Christiana Riot of 1851.[67] Gorsuch died when a failed attempt to capture suspected runaways erupted into gunfire as blacks rallied to fend off his party. When local whites also present at the skirmish were acquitted of all charges in connection with Gorsuch's death, Marylanders and the entire South expressed outrage, and sectional antagonism grew.

On closer look, the Christiana incident illustrates the complexities of sustaining slavery—and of challenging it—on the Chesapeake's northern border. Edward Gorsuch, the white protagonist, owned a dozen slaves and operated a substantial farm in Baltimore County, only a few miles from the Pennsylvania boundary. Some of his bondsmen had been inherited from an uncle whose will would free them at age twenty-eight. Perhaps hoping to minimize discontent among the others and thereby forestall flight, Gorsuch committed himself to gradual manumission of all his male slaves at that age. In some cases he subsequently offered seasonal employment at planting and harvest time to the newly freed. A Methodist class leader, reasonable and humane with his slaves by the standards of his time, Gorsuch could have served as a model of the caring, paternal master.

It may be surprising, then, that Noah Buley, Nelson Ford, and George and Joshua Hammond, all prospectively free, bolted from the Gorsuch farm in November 1849. The young men had been implicated in the theft and attempted sale of wheat stolen from Gorsuch. They forsook legitimate freedom some six to nine years in the future over what might have seemed a comparatively minor episode. Yet, the prospect of an undefined punishment might have loomed very large indeed in their considerations. Would Gorsuch withdraw his offer of freedom, or avenge himself by tacking extra time onto their terms? Worse, would he seek to invoke Maryland law and have these term slaves declared "turbulent" and "rebellious," in which case he could legally sell them out of the state, ending any chance of future freedom? Even if Gorsuch did forgive them and continue to hold out the promise of liberation, would this old man live long enough to keep his word? Or would these young men, like William Green, be "put in the pocket" of some finagling heir who would sell them as slaves for life? Buley et al. decided not to wait and see. They made off northward at night, finding their way to York, crossing the Susquehanna at Wrightsville, and heading east into Lancaster County. There they passed as free and found work as farm laborers for the next two seasons.

Meanwhile, Edward Gorsuch bent his efforts to finding the fugitives, pursuing rumors and finally obtaining definite word of their whereabouts

Slaveholder Edward Gorsuch is shot and killed near Christiana, Pennsylvania, in 1851, while trying to recapture four of his slaves. (Still, Underground Railroad, *1872.)*

in late August 1851. Gorsuch was determined to "have his property." Perhaps his sense of honor could not abide his chattels' deception and defiance, as historian Thomas Slaughter suggests, but surely Gorsuch responded to material concerns as well.[68] If he took no action to recover these runaways, how long would his other slaves choose to remain with him? Besides, the recovery of four prime field hands would be well worth the trouble and expense. Once he had the men back in Maryland, Gorsuch could easily have a county court add time to their terms of service as punishment for absconding, or sell them out of the state. In either case, the men's sale value would approach that of slaves for life, a considerable advance on the discounted prices that applied to slaves with short terms of years to serve.[69] Recapture of Buley, Ford, and the Hammonds suited Gorsuch's interests, personal or financial, all the way round. Accordingly, in early September, Gorsuch and some companions set out for Christiana, a village in northeastern Lancaster County, having written ahead to engage the services of federal marshal H. H. Kline.

Waiting for Gorsuch was William Parker, himself a longtime runaway from Maryland, and leader of a loosely organized black self-defense group determined to resist kidnappings and the retaking of fugitives. Parker's memoir, published after the Civil War, portrayed life for rural blacks in southern Pennsylvania as that of a lawless borderland, with self-help and the occasional assistance of antislavery Quakers as the only recourse against kidnappers who operated with the tacit approval of a largely "negro-hating" populace.[70]

Parker had run from an Anne Arundel County planter as a teenager after seeing a series of relatives and friends sold off to raise cash. He had reached Pennsylvania after a sojourn in Baltimore, where he and a companion passed themselves off as brickmakers to avert suspicion about their movements. Settling in Lancaster County, Parker married and joined a "mutual protection" organization. Likening themselves to revolutionary era minute men, these African Americans forcibly liberated several victims of kidnapping before their captors could get them across the state line, and rioted at the Lancaster jail in one unsuccessful rescue attempt. When they detected a free colored man "decoying" fugitives for kidnappers, they burned down his house. A white tavernkeeper who boasted of welcoming slave-catchers met the same fate. Gorsuch's stubborn desire to recover his slaves would collide with Parker's equally unswerving determination to keep them free.

Gorsuch, Kline, and several other men arrived at William Parker's isolated house on a rural road outside Christiana just before dawn on September 11, 1851, hoping to surprise and capture all four of Gorsuch's runaways. Parker and his black allies, including two of those sought by the posse, were ready for them. They had been alerted by Samuel Williams, a black man who had shadowed Kline and his men when they left their Philadelphia headquarters, and then spread the word of a prospective fugitive raid to Lancaster County. When Kline produced his warrant for the fugitives and tried to cow the men into surrendering peaceably, Parker rebuffed him. Then Parker's wife blew a horn, a signal that summoned more than thirty black and white onlookers to the scene. Now outgunned, Kline advocated withdrawal, but Gorsuch would not relent, and declared, "My property I will have, or I'll breakfast in hell. I'll go up and get it." Gorsuch advanced toward the house, and died in the ensuing exchange of gunfire.[71]

Parker and others who had resisted Gorsuch fled to Canada and quickly faded from public view. Attention turned to prosecution of those who had flocked to the scene that September morning. A public meeting of five thousand Baltimoreans demanded that southerners cut off trade with the North and that college students withdraw from northern schools so long as "abolitionists and traitors are permitted to influence public opinion." Maryland governor Louis Lowe picked up on the theme, urging President Millard Fillmore to take severe action against the "treason" that had occurred, and grimly predicting secession in the absence of such retribution.[72]

Bowing to southern pressure, Fillmore's administration sought and obtained more than a hundred indictments for treason, not only for men who had resisted Kline at Christiana but also for "treason by words," consisting of writing or distributing abolitionist tracts. Topping the list was Castner Hanway, a Quaker and local miller who had taken no part in the violence but who had refused to be deputized as part of the slavecatching posse.

Southerners and their friends wanted abolitionist sentiment itself to be outlawed but overreached themselves in characterizing speech alone as treasonous. Hanway's trial on charges of having orchestrated the resistance soon turned into political theatre. Proslavery district judge John Kane and U.S. Supreme Court Associate Justice Robert Grier, presiding for the Philadelphia circuit, proclaimed their determination to uphold the Fugitive Slave Law. Defense attorneys Thaddeus Stevens, antislavery congressman from Lancaster County, and his colleague Theodore Cuyler denounced them as tools of tyrants, like legendary hanging judge "Bloody" Jeffries of seventeenth-century England. Cuyler summarized the mixture of contempt and dismay that many northerners felt at the misuse of the treason statute when he sarcastically asked jurors if they knew that "three harmless, non-resisting Quakers, and eight-and-thirty wretched, miserable, penniless negroes . . . levied war against the United States."

After tumultuous proceedings, the jury deliberated less than twenty minutes before finding Castner Hanway not guilty. Judge Grier's charge to the jury virtually directed an acquittal, pointing out that a treason conviction required proof of a conspiracy to make "general and public resistance" to the laws, a far cry from the impromptu rioting that had actually occurred. Within a few weeks, local grand juries refused to indict the same defendants on state charges of riot and murder—Kline's reputation as a slavecatcher made him an untrustworthy accuser.[73] Denunciations of the acquittals by slave state newspapers virtually ended public discussion of the Christiana incident, but the bitterness lingered. In 1852, Marylanders exacted revenge for Gorsuch when they mobbed and lynched a Lancaster County man who had come to Baltimore County to seek the release of a free black woman who had been kidnapped.[74]

The Christiana episode gained importance as part of a series of confrontations over fugitives from the Chesapeake, such as the celebrated Anthony Burns case in Boston in 1854.[75] More and more, slaveholders became convinced that slavery could not be protected within the Union. They believed that northerners simply would not respect the Constitution and instruments for the protection of slave property like the Fugitive Slave Law. In the North, abolitionists and antislavery men took heart from the popularity of the treason acquittals and from ever more visible runaways and resisters of slavery. They redoubled their efforts to combat slavery and slavecatchers, sparking further rescue-related controversies. By 1854, Frederick Douglass publicly advocated violence to prevent enforcement of the Fugitive Slave Act, insisting that federal marshals be regarded as kidnappers who had "forfeited their right to live."[76]

If William Parker and other blacks who escaped from slavery in the Chesapeake did not cause the Civil War, reactions to their resistance surely diminished prospects for peaceful resolution of intersectional disputes, and prodded slaveholders toward secession. So too did the increasing militance of both free and enslaved African Americans in the Chesapeake.

CHAPTER 8

Civil War and the Destruction of Slavery

B Y THE LATE 1840S, CHESAPEAKE SLAVEHOLDERS had come to fear and detest antislavery agitation and outside assistance to runaways. They also sensed an important internal threat. Slaves were growing assertive, resisting white authority more boldly, and free blacks were making demands for political rights, especially in cities like Baltimore or Richmond. Some whites responded to these challenges by relaxing restraints on their chattels, thereby rendering escape from slavery easier and accelerating a spiral of deteriorating control. Another vexation lay in northern immigrants who wished to "colonize" Virginia for the cause of antislavery. Defenders of slavery, their backs to the wall, lashed out at their favorite bogeymen, free blacks, ratcheting up efforts to exorcise these supposed demons with proposals for their expulsion or re-enslavement. African Americans, especially in Maryland, rallied to blunt or defeat the most repressive measures.

In the end, despairing of sustaining slavery in this climate, secessionists, whose outward bravado perhaps masked inner desperation, took Virginia out of the Union—but only Virginia, and only part of Virginia at that. Maryland, Delaware, and the western third of Virginia, perhaps in part because they were already resigned to slavery's doom, stayed with the Union. A deeply divided Chesapeake would become a prime battleground of the resulting Civil War, one that a fragmented South had only a slim chance to win. Blacks and their allies had done much to dissuade the northern Chesapeake from casting its lot with the South; once the war began they would do more still to ensure Union victory and the destruction of slavery.[1]

202

The pivotal 1850s opened with the passage of the Fugitive Slave Act and the Christiana tragedy, events that intensified intersectional antagonisms. As tensions over slavery escalated, slave escapes to free states assumed a symbolic importance far beyond their effect on the institution: "An organized Underground Railroad" betokened "a uniform spirit of . . . lawlessness," according to one observer. Resistance to slavery within the South became more disruptive to slaveholders' sense of security, too.[2]

Virginia had its counterpart to the Christiana riot only a few months after Edward Gorsuch was killed in Pennsylvania. Jordan Hatcher, a slave hired out to a tobacco factory, killed his overseer while defending himself from a beating. When Virginia's governor commuted Hatcher's death sentence, a riot nearly erupted in Richmond over his perceived failure to check a rising tide of black insubordination. The fact that Governor Joseph Johnson hailed from western Virginia, a region long suspected of insufficient zeal in protecting slavery, only deepened forebodings. Threats seemed to be multiplying. Black insolence had flared into violence, sparked by northern approval of slave resistance. Now both were magnified by a weak response from a Virginian careless of the consequences of tolerating challenges to white supremacy. All of this contributed to an uneasy sense that slaves, especially in Richmond, were virtually out of control.[3]

When Virginia's legislature convened the following winter, Richmond Democrat John Rutherfoord stepped forward to provide a solution to black impudence: the forcible expulsion of free people of color, with re-enslavement for those who refused to leave. Rutherfoord's rhetoric resounded with colonizationist logic that harkened back to Charles Fenton Mercer, Robert Goodloe Harper, and Francis Scott Key—blacks were "unfit for freedom among whites" but could succeed in Liberia. He endorsed re-enslavement only as an instrument to overcome black resistance to emigration. Despite the legislature's rejection of the plan in 1853, its advocacy of compulsory migration was a new departure.[4]

In neighboring Maryland, colonizationists in 1852 also succeeded in securing continued public funding for their efforts despite the adamant refusal of nearly all blacks to migrate. Rising white hostility had propelled some free people of color to take a fresh look at colonization, as white immigrants violently displaced black workers from traditionally black occupations such as stevedoring and ship caulking. Dismayed by these developments, black Baltimoreans James Handy, minister at the AME's Bethel church, and John Walker, a schoolteacher, called for a convention of free people of color to consider the merits of emigration to Canada, Haiti, or West Africa. Though some delegates supported the idea of removal, a vocal group of Baltimoreans carried the convention in opposing any such resolutions, urging blacks instead to stay and fight for their homes, their churches, and their rights as Americans.[5] As of 1853, Maryland's status quo prevailed; whites supported colonization and blacks resisted it firmly

Pressure on free people of color continued to mount. In 1854 a new law in Maryland required free people of color to enter into written labor contracts and forfeit wages and court costs if they quit before serving the full term.[6] White workers petitioned the legislature to exclude blacks from huckstering, from renting market stalls, and from participation in any mechanical trade.[7] By 1858 "job busting" reached new heights, as white gangs destroyed property in Baltimore shipyards and attacked black ship caulkers in largely successful efforts to drive them out of the caulking trade.[8] Delaware followed suit, writing new laws restricting seasonal black migration across state lines to find work, and, like Maryland, threatening to jail or sell into term slavery free black workers who had no employment contracts.[9]

None of these measures reassured nervous slaveholders, who repeatedly confronted new evidence that free people of color were challenging the proscriptions under which they were forced to live. Black Baltimoreans petitioned to have the school taxes they paid dedicated to educating black children, and Richmond's free people of color went even further, asking the city council to repeal the entire black code. During the presidential campaign of 1856, a fight between a party of Irishmen and free blacks near Baltimore took on political overtones. After defeating their antagonists, the black men raised three cheers for Frémont, candidate of the new Republican Party, and attempted to tear down a Democratic Party liberty pole that had been erected nearby.[10]

The Republican Party found at least some white support, too. John C. Underwood, a transplanted New Yorker who lived in Clarke County, Virginia, attended the first Republican national convention where he spoke critcally of Virginia's attachment to slavery. Underwood's indignant neighbors met to adopt resolutions urging him to leave the state. Instead, Underwood toured New York and New England as a Republican stump speaker, capitalizing on his status as an "exile." Meanwhile, a handful of sympathizers held a Republican convention in Wheeling, Virginia.

After Frémont's defeat, Underwood joined forces with Eli Thayer, founder of the New England Emigrant Aid Company, which had sponsored free-state migrants to Kansas. Together, Thayer and Underwood sought to plant a free labor, pro-Republican colony of northern migrants at a site named Ceredo, near present-day Huntington, West Virginia. Underwood had been encouraging northern farmers to come to Virginia since the 1840s to demonstrate the superiority of cultivating with free labor. These schemes had not come to much. Dairymen who emigrated from the Finger Lakes discovered that their cheeses did not fare well in Virginia's summers. Besides, as one black farmer noted, it was not long before some northerners "learn[ed] Virginny's tricks" and began buying slaves. Ceredo attracted no more than a few hundred residents in its first few years of existence, and they were all but hounded from Virginia after John Brown's raid in 1859. Nonetheless, the whiff of free state settlers and politics alarmed proslavery men, as did the founding of several Republican newspapers in Wheeling and other trans-Appalachian towns.[11]

Frémont's campaign and activities like Underwood's supercharged southern suspicions. Northerners and free people of color were targeted as conspirators seeking to foment slave insurrections.[12] In this climate fugitive slave controversies flared into political prominence in the Chesapeake. In 1855, James Parsons of Virginia journeyed to central Pennsylvania's Blair County in pursuit of his escaped slave, Jake Green. Parsons captured Green, who was then rescued from re-enslavement by armed local citizens. To the outrage of Virginians, the authorities came down on Parsons, charging him with kidnapping. The incident ended in 1856 when Pennsylvania prosecutors dropped the charges. In itself, southerners could have dismissed the episode as merely one more case of northerners' occasional ignoring of their constitutional responsibility to render up fugitive slaves. The Virginia House of Delegates thought otherwise and passed a bill that would recoup Parson's losses by the public seizure of property in Virginia owned by Pennsylvania citizens. The Virginia Senate killed the bill, but the explosive tensions that prompted it remained.[13]

The election of proslavery Democrat James Buchanan to the presidency and Chief Justice Taney's resoundingly proslavery opinion in the Dred Scott case in 1857 did little to allay southern fears. Political controversy over slavery's status in Kansas and the continued rise of Republicans in the Northeast and Midwest kept slaveholders feverish with anxiety.[14] By 1858 proslaveryites in the Chesapeake, in addition to worries on the national scene, felt a growing need to arrest the erosion of slavery in counties bordering free states. Escapes, aided by the Underground Railroad or otherwise, were most frequent there, and many slaveholders had prudently moved slaves to the south and east. According to Virginia governor Henry Wise, only the extreme lenience of slaveholders in the slave/free boundary areas kept slavery alive at all. How long would it be before this slow wasting crept farther south and affected tobacco counties in Maryland and Virginia's tidewater and piedmont? Would the whole Upper South see slavery peeled away from its edges?[15]

In response, proposals for expulsion or re-enslavement of free people of color resurfaced, often promoted as the excision of a cancer that "demoralized" otherwise contented slaves. Virginia's legislature, urged on by Edmund Ruffin and John Rutherfoord, debated re-enslaving free blacks in 1858 and 1859. The measures were again defeated, but so were proposals to continue supporting colonization with state appropriations. Public opinion was shifting toward the idea of compulsion against free blacks.[16] In Maryland, with its far larger number and proportion of free blacks, proposals to re-enslave them attracted the most attention and found their greatest champion in the person of Curtis Jacobs, a Worcester County slaveholder and chair of the legislature's Committee on the Colored Population.

By 1859, Jacobs had a decade of anti-free black agitation behind him.

He had lobbied the Maryland constitutional convention of 1850–51 for an outright ban on manumission and for provisions allowing the legislature to banish or re-enslave free people of color. Jacobs thought that "the negro knows what slavery means, because it is natural to him" but that Maryland's laws allowing black freedom with discriminatory restrictions were "jargon and moonshine" to blacks. Turned aside at the constitutional convention, Jacobs regrouped, promoting slave-holders' conventions in 1858 and 1859 that endorsed his proposals: All manumissions would be forbidden in the future, and all free blacks would be declared slaves and compulsorily hired out for terms of ten years. Children would be bound out for longer terms. The offspring of re-enslaved women would become the property of the master to whom they were bound.

Jacobs's speeches for re-enslavement encapsulated in one package two contradictory reactions to free blacks. On the one hand, he denounced them as lazy, thievish people who weakened Maryland's social fabric. On the other, he decried the fact that some free blacks appeared to be succeeding, complaining that "free negroes in Annapolis were building more houses, and owned as much property as any other persons." The incongruity of claiming that "idle" and "worthless" free blacks rivaled whites for jobs and amassing property did not trouble Jacobs and his allies. For them, the "problem" of black labor lay precisely in the fact that free people of color were taking advantage of the need for their services by negotiating for wages higher than rural planters cared to pay, hence the need to curb black independence through re-enslavement.[17]

The Maryland legislature enacted some of Jacobs's proposals. Future manumissions were banned, and free black persons were given the right to enslave themselves to the master of their choice. The legislators chose to send the more controversial mandatory re-enslavement proposals to the citizens of eleven counties, principally those of the lower Eastern and Western Shore.[18] Jacobs soon discovered that black Baltimoreans were raising money to wage a counter-campaign against re-enslavement. Barbers obtained more than a thousand black signatures on petitions opposing the measure. Churches organized days of fasting and prayer, and leading black ministers, including Henry McNeil Turrner and Noah Davis spoke against re-enslavement. In a moment of crisis, disfranchised free blacks in Maryland demonstrated their political acumen and courage by rallying white supporters, too. Opponents of the bill ignored venomous criticism that they were covert abolitionists and fomenters of class warfare among whites and played heavily on how re-enslavement would depress wage levels to the detriment of most non-slaveholders. White voters sent Jacobs's bill down to a shattering defeat, with over 70 per cent rejecting it in November, 1860. Black ministers and churches, serving as nodal points for a statewide effort, had defended black freedom successfully, a major achievement made even more stunning by its timing in the wake of a jarring antislavery incident.[19]

In October 1859, John Brown led nineteen men in an assault on the federal armory at Harper's Ferry, Virginia. A longtime abolitionist who had helped found a would-be model community for ex-slaves in upstate New York and who had fought against proslaveryites in Kansas in the mid-1850s, Brown had come to believe that only bloodshed would end slavery. Others agreed. Dangerfield Newby, a free black Virginian, joined Brown after his wife's owner rejected Newby's attempts to purchase her freedom and that of one of their children. By the late 1850s, high slave prices in the Cotton South were undermining manumission and self-purchase, closing a safety valve for the maintenance of slavery in the Old Dominion.

Brown envisioned that seizing arms at Harper's Ferry would spark a slave rebellion that would "purge this guilty land" of the accumulated sins of slaveholding. Judged in these terms, the raid failed miserably. Enslaved blacks in the upper Shenandoah Valley were far too wise to throw their lives away with no chance of victory. Brown and his men struggled alone and were quickly overwhelmed by federal troops led by Colonel Robert E. Lee and hastily assembled local militia. Brown was turned over to Virginia authorities, who tried him for treason and insurrection and hanged him on December 2, 1859.[20]

While Brown's raid was easily suppressed, northern and southern reactions to it took on a dynamic of their own, deepening intersectional tensions and leading proslavery men in the Chesapeake further down the path to secession. Brown's trial revealed that he had secured financial backing from New England abolitionists, dubbed the "Secret Six," feeding fears of a widespread conspiracy that aimed to bathe the entire South in the blood of a race war. Dread of slaves and abolitionists allying to destroy slaveholders had been deeply inscribed in the consciousness of Chesapeake whites by eight decades of its rhetorical invocation as the inevitable product of emancipation. Now this specter took on flesh.

According to James Redpath, a northerner who traveled extensively in Virginia talking to slaves and free people of color, slaves were not loyal servants; rather, they secretly loathed slavery. "Not more than a tenth" did not want freedom, and "those with good masters are as little contented as those who have bad masters."[21] Free blacks, too, with their growing political awareness, and their growing numbers confirmed by each successive census, posed an ever greater danger. It was not reassuring to learn that black caulkers in Baltimore had decorated the site of their annual ball with pictures that celebrated John Brown as a martyr and slogans that denounced his executioner, Virginia governor Henry Wise.[22]

In 1860 and early 1861 blacks watched and waited as white voters chose among four presidential candidates. John C. Breckinridge, the Southern Democrat, carried Delaware and Maryland, where he narrowly defeated John Bell, the Constitutional Union candidate. Bell barely topped Breckinridge in Virginia. Abraham Lincoln, the newly elected sixteenth president, polled only 3 per cent of the votes regionally and finished last in all three states.[23] In December 1860, South Carolina and the Gulf States seceded. In the Chesapeake, enthusiasm for secession was tepid at best. Only Virginia called a special convention to debate the issue, and in February 1861 that body rebuffed calls for separation from the Union. Events in Charleston, though, forced the hand of "reluctant Confederates" throughout the Middle and Upper South. The attack on Fort Sumter on April 12, 1861, with Virginia secessionist Edmund Ruffin on hand to help fire the first gun, led to Lincoln's call for troops to suppress rebellion. Within weeks four more states, including Virginia, had joined the Confederacy. The remaining four slave states, including Maryland and Delaware, remained in the Union.

At the outbreak of the Civil War, approximately 750,000 African Americans lived in the Chesapeake, of whom nearly 600,000 were enslaved. Virginia contained some 490,000 slaves, Maryland 87,000, the District of Columbia about 3,000, and Delaware only 1,800. Maryland's 83,000 free people of color virtually equaled its slave population, while the District's 11,000 free blacks and Delaware's 20,000 freedpeople far outnumbered their still enslaved kinfolk and neighbors. Virginia's more than 50,000 free blacks made up about one-tenth of the Old Dominion's blacks.

The war confronted white politicians and voters with a host of issues concerning the black population, slave and free. Was slavery economically viable, and should efforts be made to preserve it? Could blacks' workplace resistance, sabotage, and flight render retention of slavery impractical and unprofitable? If slavery were to end, should slaveholders be compensated, and how would compensation be paid? To what extent could federal intervention in the process be tolerated? How would the conduct of the war affect state politics, e.g., would the absence or disqualification from voting of Confederate sympathizers allow opponents of slavery to assume political control of a state? Lastly, but perhaps of paramount importance at least through the end of 1863, what impact would emancipation have on the conduct of the Civil War, and on the prospects for reunifying the nation?

Between 1861 and 1865, Union governments in the Chesapeake confronted these issues, and all witnessed similar evolutions of white public opinion. In the northern Chesapeake, unionists won the upper hand. Maryland's Governor Thomas Hicks, along with legislators from Baltimore and the northern counties, used an influx of Union regiments en route to Washington to quell secessionist sentiment welling up from the tobacco counties and the Eastern Shore. Delawareans saw no serious effort to take their state out of the Union. In western Virginia, loyalists rallied against the state's secession and created their own government, eventually designated as the new state of West Virginia.

At first most unionists offered only "conditional" loyalty, tied to the idea that both the union and slavery should be preserved. "Unconditional" unionists, i.e., men willing to abolish slavery in order to win the war, were in 1861 a distinct minority. They were perhaps outnumbered in all three areas by proslavery Democrats, many of whom opposed the war altogether, perhaps sensing that slavery would be a casualty, whether or not the federal government attacked it. They realized that, as their arch-foe Lincoln put it, "mere friction and abrasion" would shake slavery to pieces in rebel and loyal slave states alike. Lincoln's observation, offered to border state congressmen in the summer of 1862 in support of his plan for compensated emancipation, proved prophetic.[24]

Thousands of blacks in every part of the Chesapeake liberated themselves by fleeing to Union lines, where they worked for the army or, from 1863 onward, signed up as soldiers and fought for the destruction of slavery. Others took advantage of the chaos of war to run away to Baltimore, Washington, or cities farther north, where they lived as free blacks until wartime legislation formally emancipated them. Most only gained freedom with the passage of emancipation legislation.

Lincoln's Emancipation Proclamation, announced in September 1862 in the wake of the battle at Antietam and effective January 1, 1863, was limited to states or portions of states outside Union control and in rebellion. Maryland and Delaware were not affected; emancipation there would await state constitutional change or ratification of the Thirteenth Amendment in December 1865. Throughout the war years came a welter of federal laws that struck at the Confederacy by offering liberty to slaves who fled disloyal masters, or who joined the U.S Army, regardless of their master's politics. African Americans in loyal areas of the Chesapeake refused to be left in slavery as contemplated by the Emancipation Proclamation, and new state constitutions bowed to this reality by acknowledging black freedom in Maryland and portions of Virginia. The Emancipation Proclamation conveyed *de jure* freedom to slaves in Confederate-controlled counties of Virginia, with victory in the war and the amendment finally abolishing slavery and making good on the proclamation's promise. In the upshot, emancipation arrived through state action, congressional legislation, or constitutional amendment at no fewer than six different dates in Maryland, Delaware, the District of Columbia, the new state of West Virginia, and Virginia itself.

During the Civil War, slaves seized opportunities to flee owners and seek freedom in Union-held territory. This postwar illustration of freed black people arriving in Baltimore typifies what occurred throughout the conflict. (Engraving, Frank Leslie's Illustrated Newspaper, *1865.)*

The District, a hotbed of proslavery sentiment in its prewar local politics, saw the end of slavery, with federal legislation mandating compensated emancipation, enacted on April 16, 1862, five months before Lincoln's preliminary Emancipation Proclamation. (The Compromise of 1850 had banned the slave trade in the District but not slavery itself.) Since the outbreak of the war, blacks had been pouring into Washington, from both Virginia and Maryland, hoping to escape masters. Slaveholders placed captured runaways, along with slaves suspected of plotting escape, in the District jail for safekeeping. Union troops, few of whom were out-and-out abolitionists, nonetheless balked at assisting masters and their slavecatchers in recovering fugitives. Meanwhile northern citizens fired off petitions to congressmen, protesting the use of federal troops and facilities to take and hold fugitive slaves in the midst of a war to suppress a rebellion by those slaves' owners.

By early 1862, Lincoln and antislavery Republicans in Congress, citing constitutional authority for the Congress to govern the District, seized an opportunity to end slavery through compensation. They hoped to achieve several goals. As a war measure, the law sent a clear signal to slaves in Virginia, encouraging them to cease aiding the Confederacy through their labor and flee if they could to Washington. For abolitionists, the new law represented an important symbolic victory, wherein Congress for the first time freed slaves. The law ended a decades-long debate over the presence of slavery in the capital of a free country and created momentum for further action. Finally, by promising compensation only to loyal slave owners, the law sought to shore up support for the Union and curb covert aid to the Confederacy amongst border state slaveholders.

District of Columbia Slaveholders tried to evade the new law by removing blacks to Maryland. Several hundred slaves from the District were placed in the Baltimore jail in 1862, for example, but by mid-1863 the process of liberation and compensation of owners had been largely completed. In the meantime, Lincoln had tried unsuccessfully to attract support in Maryland and Delaware for compensated emancipation.[25] Only in the District, where residents could not resist the mandates of Congress, were ex-slaveholders paid for their loss of human property.

Resourceful Republicans found other ways to force the pace of emancipation, notably in the creation of West Virginia. In early 1861, Virginia was deeply torn on whether to remain in the Union or join the new Confederacy. Delegates to a statewide convention rejected secession in February 1861, but on April 17, in the wake of South Carolina's attack on Fort Sumter and Lincoln's call for troops to suppress rebellion there, they reversed themselves and called for a statewide referendum on secession. Most delegates from the northwestern counties of the state opposed secession, as did the region's voters in the ensuing referendum. When secession carried the day, westerners met in a series of conventions at Wheeling in the spring and summer of 1861 and formed what came to be known as the Restored or Reorganized Government of Virginia.

Recognized as the legitimate interim government of Virginia by Lincoln and the Congress, political leaders of the Reorganized Government next contemplated admission to the Union as a new state in order to resolve constitutional questions surrounding the Reorganized Government's status. Accordingly, still another group of delegates convened in late 1861 and early 1862 to draft a state constitution. Despite a long history of regional opposition to the growth of slavery west of the Blue Ridge, many hoped to sidestep the question as a divisive issue. Thus, even though the prospective state's sixteen thousand slaves made up only 4 per cent of the total population, there was at first little prospect of emancipation.

Then Gordon Batelle, a Methodist minister and delegate, introduced resolutions proposing *post nati* emancipation of the children of slave mothers born after July 4, 1863, along with a ban on the immigration of Negroes, free or enslaved, to the new state. The convention adopted Battelle's ban on black immigration but defeated the gradual emancipation scheme. Antislavery forces pursued the issue, predicting correctly that the Republican Congress would not admit any new slave states. When the petition for West Virginia's admission was presented to the Congress with a draft constitution that preserved slavery, it was swiftly returned to the people of the state with conditions. West Virginia would be admitted only if gradual emancipation was incorporated. Conservatives bristled and opposed "congressional dictation" of the constitution, but voters overwhelmingly approved a revised constitution that freed black children while banning immigration of blacks, free or enslaved. West Virginia was duly admitted to the Union on this basis on June 20, 1863; slaves in the state eventually became free either by joining the army, fleeing masters, or with the enactment of the Thirteenth Amendment.[26]

The admission of West Virginia left in place a much diminished Restored Government of Virginia, still led by Governor Francis Pierpont, consisting of about a dozen Union-occupied counties along the Potomac, in and around Norfolk, and across the bay on the Eastern Shore. Like most southern unionists, Pierpont spent the early years of the war lobbying against emancipation, and he persuaded Lincoln to exempt his scattered territories from the Emancipation Proclamation. During 1863, Pierpont acquiesced to antislavery. Hoping to have Virginia formally restored to the Union under the terms of Lincoln's Proclamation of Amnesty and Reconstruction (December 8, 1863), Pierpont co-ordinated efforts to produce a new state constitution that abolished slavery. Adoption of that constitution on March 10, 1864, formally ended slavery in Alexandria, Norfolk, and the Eastern Shore, though again only after the determination of slaves to shed their chains had rendered the institution all but dead anyway.[27]

Delaware contained fewer than five hundred slaveholders by 1860. Paying them to free their eighteen hundred chattels would have cost less than a million dollars, even at a fairly high average valuation of five hundred dollars a slave. Yet Delaware resisted all entreaties from Lincoln on the subject of compensated emancipation. The last slaves in the First State would only go free in December 1865 with ratification of the Thirteenth Amendment, and the slaveowners were left with nothing. Why this unlikely outcome?

The first effort to end slavery in a Chesapeake state came in Delaware in late 1861, when President Lincoln met with Congressman George Fisher to urge consideration of gradual and compensated emancipation. For Lincoln, compensating loyal border state slaveholders promised to end any prospect of those states joining the Confederacy. If successful in the border states, the compensation idea might even draw the seceded states back into the Union and avert the long, bloody war that seemed in prospect after the Confederate victory at Bull Run. Delaware, with its tiny slave population, looked like a good test ground for the scheme.

Fisher drew up a bill that asked the Delaware General Assembly to free all slaves over the age of thirty-five at once and all slaves by 1872, with slaveholders to be paid from a pool of $900,000 in federal funds. Political reactions to the plan presaged those of whites elsewhere in the region. Most observers readily agreed that slavery generated few if any profits in Delaware, but they still balked at emancipation. Opponents dwelt on the theme that the end of slavery would inevitably spur black ambition for equality, leading to a race war. These were not new arguments; they had been heard in every debate on emancipation in Dover, Annapolis, or Richmond since the 1780s. Perhaps age lent respect to these threadbare claims.

The slender roll of slaves in Delaware made the stakes seem small. Proponents of emancipation who rehearsed the equally well-worn argument that ending slavery would cut a canker from the body economic of the state, and render it prosperous á là Massachusetts or Pennsylvania, had a tough sell. How much difference could the status of a handful of blacks in sleepy Sussex County make? Furthermore, buying freedom for slaves in Delaware might cost little, but it could set a precedent for paying off the owners of four million slaves throughout the South. The resulting tax burden would be unsupportable.

In the upshot, a canvass of the Delaware General Assembly in 1862 revealed that as in 1803, 1823, and 1847, the scales tipped slightly against ending slavery. Compensated emancipation would narrowly pass the state's Senate, but would fail by a single vote in the House. Supporters of the concept withdrew the bill without a vote. Thereafter, Delaware refused to budge. Slavery eroded as blacks ran off to Baltimore or Philadelphia. Decay accelerated after October 1863, when recruitment of slaves for the army was extended to the loyal border states.[28] A year later, Maryland abolished slavery, leaving tiny Delaware surrounded by free territory, with perhaps no more than a few hundred African Americans in slavery. Still, in early 1865 the General Assembly rejected Governor William Cannon's call for emancipation legislation and voted not to ratify the Thirteenth Amendment, seeing it as violating states' rights. Continuation of slavery, however vestigial, had come to be synonymous with maintenance of white supremacy and dominance by Delaware's Democrats. Only the Thirteenth Amendment would free Delaware's last slaves.[29]

Early in the war, Maryland's unionist leaders, like those in Delaware and West Virginia, hoped to trade conditional loyalty to the Union for protection of their slave property. As the conflict widened and deepened in the summer of 1861, slaveholders demanded co-operation from federal troops in returning runaways, who from the first sensed that freedom might be found within the army's lines. Ironically, the Army of the Potomac's inability to advance deep into slave-filled Virginia soon spelled disaster for reluctant loyalist slaveholders in Maryland, as the long term presence of troop encampments attracted more and more freedom-bound African Americans.

Little by little, insistent blacks and the necessities of war forced a cautious Lincoln administration to grasp the nettle of what Governor Hicks called the "devilish Nigger difficulty." Some northern soldiers taunted and forcibly blocked slavecatchers who pursued fugitives into army camps. By early 1862, Congress responded, amending the Fugitive Slave Act of 1850 to bar soldiers from aiding in the recapture of fugitives from disloyal masters. In addition, the First Confiscation Act allowed commanders to employ fugitives whose masters had used them to support the Confederacy. By July of that year, a second Confiscation Act declared outright that fugitives of persons supporting the rebellion were free regardless of the ex-slave's employment.[30] Slaves quickly learned that claiming they had run from a disloyal slaveholder could be a pass to freedom within the Army of the Potomac's lines. A bitterly worded protest from the Maryland General Assembly fell on deaf ears.[31]

As Maryland legislators had feared, the abolition of slavery in the District of Columbia in April 1862 further "disturb[ed] the relation of master and slave" in their state. Tobacco-growing counties like Prince George's, Charles, Calvert, and Anne Arundel, were especially hard hit. Only two months later, W. H. Mitchell of Charles County reported that no fewer than thirty-seven of his slaves had taken leave of him, heading for the District.[32] Wherever Union troops were stationed, even at remote Point Lookout, a prison for captured Confederates at the southern tip of St. Mary's County, so-called "contraband" camps sprang up as blacks left slavery behind and tried to eke out a living working for the army.

The rising tide of freedom-seeking blacks impelled whites to contemplate state action on emancipation. As a correspondent to the *New York World* noted, "the rebellion has at least secured to people of the border states what they never had before: The power to discuss the subject of slavery and emancipation in their public journals and on the hustings."[33] Henry Winter Davis and Hugh Lennox Bond, who led the unconditional Unionists in the state, had long argued that ending slavery and recruiting black troops would

By 1862 more than a thousand "contrabands"—slaves escaped from Confederate owners—were working and earning wages at Fortress Monroe, Virginia. Engraving, c. 1862.
(Library of Congress.)

help shorten the war. They had agitated unsuccessfully for acceptance of
Lincoln's compensated emancipation plan in 1862. By early 1863 they sensed
that slavery was dissolving and began advocating immediate, uncompen-
sated emancipation.

These same men even urged the recruitment of slaves into the army
pending emancipation. As Judge Bond complained to Secretary of War
Edwin Stanton, the recruitment of free blacks into the army, which had
begun in Maryland in July 1863, deprived loyal non-slaveholders of laborers
while leaving slaveholders, most of whom were disloyal, untouched. Indeed,
the resulting labor shortage allowed these same slaveholders to rake in ex-
cessive profits at non-slaveholders' expense, due to rising hiring prices for
slaves. These evils could be remedied by enlisting slaves.[34]

Recruitment of slaves from October 1863 onward sounded the death
knell of slavery. Some ten thousand Afro-Marylanders joined the U.S. Colored Troops.[35] Even conservatives like Reverdy Johnson and John Pendleton

Kennedy became emancipationists. By February 1864 the Cecil County *Whig* proclaimed that only immediate emancipation would be acceptable. "If a partial act of emancipation be fastened on Maryland . . . she . . . will . . . meet with the reception, a man would with a dead body strapped to him."[36] The corpse of slavery was unstrapped by an 1864 state constitutional convention that mandated abolition immediately upon its adoption, secured by a razor-thin margin of less than four hundred votes out of more than sixty thousand cast in the October elections.[37] Recalcitrant ex-slaveholders in a few counties fought back, using the apprenticeship laws to bind some three thousand newly freed children as servants, in defiance of the fact that the convention had rejected an apprenticeship period for ex-slaves. Blacks filed lawsuits or sought help from the Freedman's Bureau, and this flickering remnant of slavery was finally extinguished in 1868.[38]

By seizing opportunities provided by the needs of wartime, Maryland's African Americans slowly gained the upper hand against slaveholders. Oases of free territory in the District and within Union lines facilitated the successful transfer of their labor to the Union armies, including military service, drained slavery of its vitality, and ultimately wrung a reluctant acknowledgment of black freedom, if not black political rights, from white voters.

For blacks in the northern Chesapeake, wartime liberation vastly expanded an already familiar process, whereby slaves fled to free territory in relative proximity to their homes, assisted by a substantial free black population and by white allies from outside the state. In Confederate Virginia, on the other hand, the Civil War distantly recalled the slave experience of the American Revolution.[39]

In 1861, as in 1775, white Virginians withdrew their allegiance to an existing government in order to preserve their liberties, paramount among which was the sanctity of property, including slaves. Neither Great Britain nor the Union avowed a desire to abolish slavery, but their military commanders in Virginia found irresistible the temptation to cow rebels into submission by drawing slaves to their banner with offers of freedom. For Virginia's blacks, cramped lives suddenly teemed with threats and opportunities. War brought danger to one's door, but also the promise of freedom. At the outset of the Civil War, as in the Revolutionary War before it, many blacks risked their all to pursue the most promising path. As Betsie Walker later remembered, "We colored people didn't understand exactly what the war was about, but we . . . believed the Yankees to be on our side & we were on theirs."[40] Accordingly, slaves began flocking from northern Virginia to Washington, D.C., and fleeing to Union outposts and ships even before hostilities began.[41]

This time, the role of Governor Dunmore would be played by Benjamin F. Butler, a Massachusetts politician and general in charge of Fortress Monroe. One of the first southern coastal fortifications in Union hands in the spring of 1861, the fort sat at the tip of the peninsula between the James and York Rivers and dominated the waters around Norfolk and Hampton. On May 23, 1861, slaves Shepherd Mallory, Frank Baker, and James Townshend "delivered themselves up" to Butler's men, explaining that they had fled their master, a local Confederate commander, because they feared being shipped to North Carolina to build fortifications there. Hot on the men's heels came their owner, arriving under a flag of truce to demand their return under the provisions of the Fugitive Slave Act. Butler rejected claims of "constitutional obligations to a foreign country, which Virginia now claims to be," and allowed the men to work at the fort. He justified his action to the War Department by pointing out that harboring Mallory, Baker, and Townshend could be thought of as confiscating property to prevent its use as war materiel, labor in this case, by the enemy. The men were thus "contraband" of war, a phrase that would stick to runaways despite efforts to dignify them with the name of "Colored Refugees." By July 1861, nearly a thousand refugees had reached what they called "Freedom Fort"; by May 1863 over 26,000 blacks lived within Union lines in tidewater Virginia.[42]

Like their revolutionary-era predecessors, slaves did everything humanly possible to strike the blow that would free them. "They come here from all about, from Richmond and from 200 miles off in North Carolina," noted Captain C. B. Wilder, supervisor of contrabands, in 1863. Fifty or sixty blacks had reached the Union camp by following General Stoneman's cavalry as they returned from a raid deep into Confederate territory. One woman had walked over two hundred miles, disguised in men's clothing. Successful escapees banded together to go back to their old homes and retrieve wives and children, or guided Union raiding parties to their old plantations to free their kinfolk in another echo of British collaborations with blacks in the Revolutionary War. Wilder observed that "rebel guards have been doubled" to thwart runaways, and that some northern soldiers were clandestinely acting as slavecatchers, "smuggl[ing fugitives] across the lines and the soldier will get his $20 or $50." Despite these hardships, slaves decamped in unprecedented numbers. By mid-1863, when Confederates still held most of Virginia, state officials tallied nearly 38,000 runaways. This amounted to more than 10 per cent of a slave population already much diminished by the "refugeeing" of slaves, i.e., their removal by owners to locations in the Carolinas far removed from the battle lines and the possibility of escape.[43]

In 1863, as northern white resistance to arming blacks melted away in the face of rising casualties and dwindling enlistments, General Butler began recruiting among African Americans within his lines. Eventually the military department that covered tidewater Virginia and North Carolina would raise more than 11,000 black soldiers, including a cavalry unit.[44] By July 1864, the Lincoln administration authorized recruiters trying to fill northern state enlistment quotas to work in the occupied South and sign up blacks for the army. Black Virginians wound up fighting in New York and New Jersey regiments. The business of finding paid substitutes for white draftees unwilling to serve also spread south, where corrupt "bounty hunters" generated a cruel and bizarre variation on antebellum kidnapping practices. General Butler reported in 1864 that Union soldiers were capturing Afro-Virginian slaves or runaways and selling them to northern recruitment agents. These men then smuggled the unfortunate blacks back to the Union for forcible enrollment as soldiers in New York or New England regiments. This is perhaps the only known instance of kidnappers realizing their ill-gotten gains by sending a slave *north*.[45]

The Civil War in the lower Chesapeake, like the American Revolution, thus featured the same triangular conflict between rebel masters, disaffected

Contrabands coming into an army camp. Alfred R. Waud. Pencil, wash, and Chinese white, c. 1863. (Library of Congress.)

slaves, and armies of outsiders trying to crush the revolt. The rhythm of strategic moves and countermoves, thrusts and parries, was also recognizably similar.[46] In each war, slaves initiated contact with outsiders before conflict even began and offered to ally with them to win freedom. In each war, slaveholders countered flight and raids to free slaves by withdrawing slaves to the interior. And in each war, the outsiders would almost from the beginning generate a selective policy of emancipating and arming slaves to put more pressure on white Virginians.

But many things were different in the 1860s, too. The British had maintained their war from a home base three thousand miles away, rather than three hundred, and they had accordingly hugged close to their seaborne supply lines. Rarely, before Cornwallis's fateful Yorktown campaign, had the guns of war been heard by Virginians who could not see blue water. In the Civil War, Union armies were pressing up the James from Norfolk, or down the Shenandoah Valley, or south from Washington toward Richmond.

Slaveholders needed far more help from their slaves in defending Virginia in this conflict.

Strikingly, the men who led Virginia out of the Union in 1861 outwardly evinced far more confidence in their ability to command their slaves' loyalty and labor than did their Revolutionary forefathers. Moreover, forty-eight years had passed since the British had organized a black battalion on Tangier Island, years marked by increasing white insistence on the benevolence of slavery and a perception of a widespread black acquiescence in servitude. The tremors caused by Nat Turner had long faded, and the near hysteria attending the Harper's Ferry raid gradually gave way to public assertions that slaves' failure to rise to John Brown's support proved their devotion to their masters. With the uncertainty of the late 1850's replaced by the bracing call to arms, Southern confidence spiked and with it a renewed faith in their slave system and its bondsmen. While delegates at the state secession convention debated hotly whether slavery would be safer with Virginia inside or outside the Union, their concerns centered more on fending off northern abolitionists than on how slaves might take advantage of secession and war.

When the war began, Virginians expected to employ their slaves as all-purpose workers whose labors would release virtually all able-bodied white men for army service. Whites would fight while blacks grew crops, made iron, and transported goods to market. Blacks, both free and enslaved, would also erect defensive fortifications, build and repair roads, and act as teamsters, cooks, body servants, and nurses for Confederate armies. In short, the much-criticized slave system would prove more than a match for the North's advantage in manpower.

For a time, this optimistic view of black attitudes appeared to be well justified, fostered as it was by paternalist proslavery literature and reinforced by each new enactment of loyalty by slaves in dealings with the master class. Virginia regiments fought with the logistical support of thousands of slaves, ranging from front line stretcher-bearers to forgemen and founders producing cannon at Richmond's Tredegar Iron Works.[47] Ulysses S. Grant concurred in ascribing high value to slave labor: "colored non-combatants

were equal to more than three times their number in the North . . . in supplying food from the soil to support armies. Women did not work in the
fields in the North, and children attended school."[48]

But Afro-Virginians took advantage of the state's heavy reliance on slave
labor for their own ends. They ran away, resisted labor, and spread news
about the advance of northern forces and the approach of emancipation.
Ultimately, slaveholders withdrew most slaves from the front lines, ham-
stringing the Confederate war effort and speeding the destruction of slavery itself. As the trickle of "contrabands" like Mallory, Baker, and Townshend
at Fortress Monroe became a flood, Virginia slaveholders showed increasing reluctance to allow slaves to be hired out or impressed for military labor. Masters quickly learned that sending a slave to work on fortifications
or anywhere near the front lines dangerously shortened the distance between that slave and freedom. Joseph Anderson, the owner of Tredegar Iron
Works, complained in 1863 of the "demoralization" of his enslaved workers,
while his correspondents at upcountry iron furnaces deplored a "stampede"
of runaways occasioned by Union raids in the Valley of Virginia. Once Grant
reached the environs of Richmond in 1864, slaveholders were leery of placing their chattels there for any reason, "so many [slaves] having run off to
the Yankees, a large portion from within the fortifications."[49]

Blacks who did return to their home plantations from service at the
front posed problems as well. Slaveholders objected to the wounds and in-
juries their slaves had sustained, as well as signs of malnutrition or neglect.
Worse, the slaves brought home news of the war, undercutting planters'
propaganda about Confederate triumphs with news of Union advances and
the possibility of emancipating oneself through flight. Lucy Buck of Front
Royal learned this lesson in 1862 when the family slaves informed her father
of their plans to protect the Bucks after Lincoln won the war.[50] More and
more planters reacted to these developments by withdrawing their slaves
from the hiring market, exacerbating a labor shortage in the mines, mills,
railroads, and canals so critical to supplying and transporting Lee's armies.

When the Confederate and Virginia state governments tried to remedy
this problem by drafting free blacks into military labor and requiring coun-

ties to produce quotas of slave workers at fixed prices, local authorities exploited the exemption provisions. As early as 1862, soon after the passage of the first exemption statute, Governor John Letcher complained that exemptions were gutting the intent of the state's impressment laws. Slaveholders withheld their slaves because impressment was "a delicate task," likely to spur runaways. If Union forces were nearby, the appearance of labor agents might "drive as many slaves to the enemy as it will secure to the Confederate Government." The fact that owners of impressed slaves were paid in increasingly devalued Confederate currency also undercut the program. The Confederate govern-ment's efforts to requisition slaves voluntarily fared no better. In a typical example, Lynchburg officials responded to a requisition request late in 1861 with a declaration that their town contained only thirty slaves capable of labor. One exasperated impressment officer commented that "wives and daughters and the negroes are the only elements left us to recruit from, and it does seem that our people would rather send the former even to face death and danger than give up the latter."[51]

If Confederate Virginia found it difficult to exploit slaves' labor, the idea of using them as soldiers raised the stakes dramatically. As war began, both free blacks and slaves volunteered their services for Virginia, just as their northern counterparts tried to help the Union. Slaves could hope to better their lot and even gain freedom by following their masters to the battlefield. Many free people of color no doubt deemed it judicious to exhibit loyalty to the cause of secession. But white southern honor, reinforced by doubts about black loyalty and about the safety of arming a subordinate colored population, ruled out raising black troops. They would serve the cause as teamsters, cooks, and builders of fortifications, but no more.

A few free blacks nonetheless experienced combat on the Confederate side, typically as members of local militia units or volunteer regiments for the army whose enlistment officers winked at the color bar in order to fill their muster rolls. George and Stafford Grimes passed as white to serve in the Fredericksburg Artillery, but both deserted to the Union in the Peninsular Campaign of 1862. Union soldiers' diaries occasionally noted the presence of black Confederates, and *Harper's Weekly* carried a sketch of two black pickets in a Fredericksburg camp in an 1862 issue. These men appear to have been either black military laborers pressed into combat service or members of hastily assembled irregular militias called out to ambush northern supply trains or raiding parties.[52]

Formal enlistment of black troops met stiff resistance from Virginia authorities. As Senator Robert M. T. Hunter saw the matter, arming slaves would undermine the Confederacy's whole reason for being. In the course of opposing a measure to arm slaves and free them after the war, Hunter claimed that "If we offer slaves their freedom . . . we confess that we were . . . hypocritical, in asserting that slavery was the best state for the negroes themselves." Until the very end of the war, Hunter's views prevailed, despite the urgings of Robert E. Lee, who by late 1864 had begun to advocate arming slaves to keep Grant and Sherman at bay.

Only in March 1865 would the Confederacy authorize raising black troops, far too late to affect the war's outcome. Even at that desperate juncture, white Virginians insisted that slaves join the army only with their masters' permission, and that manumission of slave soldiers required the state's consent.[53] A few companies of black soldiers were created in and around Richmond, composed mainly of slaves along with a few free black volunteers. They took part in combat against would-be liberators in several skirmishes in March and April 1865. As in the American Revolution, the path to freedom might be trodden on either side of the battle lines.

The African Americans in the Chesapeake who allied with outsiders in the Civil War won not only personal freedom but also the total destruction of chattel slavery. Regiments of U.S. Colored Troops helped to overwhelm the Confederacy in the war's final two years. Maryland gave the Union about ten thousand black troops, and Virginia supplied more than five thousand. If we add in soldiers from Delaware and the District of Columbia, members of northern black regiments who were ex-fugitives or free migrants from Maryland or Virginia, and sailors from the shores of the bay, the total number of black freedom fighters from the Chesapeake in all likelihood exceeded 20,000, a respectable contribution to the almost 200,000 African Americans who served the Union nationwide.[54]

A crowd of black Baltimoreans celebrates the adoption in 1870 of the Fifteenth Amendment, securing black men's right to vote. Stereoscopic photograph, 1870. (Maryland Historical Society.)

Union victory led to constitutional amendments that forever ended slavery, made African Americans citizens, assured them of equal protection under the laws, and gave black men the right to vote. It did not mean that the majority of whites in the Chesapeake, Confederate or Union, would immediately give their assent to these principles. If chattel slavery per se died in 1865, another century would pass before most African Americans in the Chesapeake could begin to enjoy anything approaching equal legal and political rights.

The troubled history of Reconstruction and the ensuing era of racism and segregation should not cause us to lose sight of the remarkable developments that led to emancipation. In 1770 slavery thrived throughout Britain's mainland American colonies, nowhere more so than in its cradle, the Chesapeake. Slaves' chances of gaining liberty were few or none, and white opposition to slaveholding was confined to a handful of Quakers. The ensuing Revolutionary War showed just how robust and resilient the slave regime could be, as slaveholding patriots withstood the combined onslaughts of British military might and an array of opportunistic attempts by enslaved people to shed their chains.

But the Revolution represented more than just a momentary surge in long-abiding black resistance to slavery. The creation of the American republic also provoked an across-the-board reexamination of slavery's morality, profitability, and appropriateness in a country that cherished freedom. Although whites in the Chesapeake largely resolved these questions with a conservative reaffirmation of the status quo, slaves redoubled their efforts to liberate themselves through manumission, self-purchase, and flight to free northern states. They also resorted occasionally to open rebellion, with or without the assistance of external allies. In the process, new, genuinely African American communities of freedpeople arose. Their unwavering determination to live as free people, however cramped by discriminatory laws and customs, challenged slavery in the Chesapeake.

Black strivings, however laudable, did not themselves end slavery or put it on the road to mid-century extinction. Over half a million slaves populated the Chesapeake in 1860, far more than had toiled there in the 1770s. Yet slaves had proven to their masters that were not and never would be lifelong children, contentedly accepting the rule of white patriarchs. The realization that slaves truly wanted to be free, and would risk their lives to gain freedom, influenced the thoughts and deeds of the slaveholding master class, other Chesapeake whites, and the anti-slavery elements of the North.

Slave unrest was not the sole cause of the Civil War, but if slaves had never challenged their bondage it is virtually impossible to imagine the political disputes of the antebellum period escalating into secession and war.

Without Gabriel or Nat Turner southerners would have found it far easier for to ignore antislavery critics and to dismiss the notion that outside agitators might stir up a slave rebellion. If no slaves had run to the North, no Fugitive Slave Law would have been necessary, confrontations between slavecatchers and northern opponents would never have occurred, and Harriet Beecher Stowe would perhaps be remembered, if at all, as a minor regional novelist of New England country life. Had free blacks passively accepted deportation to Africa's supposedly more suitable environment, colonization might have significantly reduced the free black population in the Chesapeake, thereby shoring up slavery in the region. Finally, if blacks had truly been happy as slaves, southern hopes for victory in the Civil War might well have proven to be realistic. Challenging slavery in the Chesapeake lay at the heart of ending slavery in America.

References

Chapter 1: The First Africans in the Chesapeake

[1] See Landers, *Black Society in Spanish Florida* and David J. Weber, *The Spanish Frontier in North America* (New Haven: Yale University Press, 1992).

[2] William H. Williams, *Slavery and Freedom in Delaware, 1639–1865* (Wilmington, Del.: SR Books, 1996), 2–3.

[3] Ibid., 4–9.

[4] Death rates on slaving voyages averaged about 15 per cent in the eighteenth-century heyday of the trade, but in the sixteenth and early seventeenth centuries mortality could run as high as one-third of all slaves. See David Eltis, *The Rise of African Slavery in the Americas* (Cambridge, U.K.: Cambridge University Press, 2000), 68, 185–86.

[5] David Eltis argues that by the sixteenth century Europeans had evolved a sense of inclusiveness as Christians that rendered enslavement of each other for economic exploitation unacceptable, but that Africans lay outside this culturally defined boundary. See Eltis, *Rise of African Slavery*, 57–84, and "Europeans and the Rise and Fall of African Slavery in the Americas," *American Historical Review*, 98 (1993): 1399–1423.

[6] For the concept of a charter generation of Africans in America see Ira Berlin, *Many Thousands Gone: The First Two Centuries of Slavery in America* (Cambridge, Mass.: Harvard University Press, 1998), 1–92, especially 29–46 for the Chesapeake and for the life of Anthony Johnson.

[7] For accounts of Johnson's life, see J. Douglas Deal, *Race and Class in Colonial Virginia: Indians, Africans, and Englishmen on the Eastern Shore of Virginia during the Seventeenth Century* (New York: Garland, 1993), 217–50; T. H. Breen and Stephen Innes, *"Myne Owne Ground": Race and Freedom on Virginia's Eastern Shore, 1640–1676* (New York: Oxford University Press, 2004); Susie M. Ames, *Studies of the Virginia Eastern Shore in the Seventeenth Century* (Richmond: The Dietz Press, 1940); and, Ross Kimmel, "Free Blacks in Seventeenth-Century Maryland," *Maryland Historical Magazine*, 71 (1976): 19–25.

[8] Berlin, *Many Thousands Gone*, 36–37.

[9] See Kathleen M. Brown, *Good Wives, Nasty Wenches, and Anxious Patriarchs: Race, Gender, and Power in Colonial Virginia* (Chapel Hill: University of North Carolina Press, 1996).

[10] Eltis, *Rise of African Slavery*, 208.

[11] See Jack P. Greene, *Pursuits of Happiness: The Social Development of Early Modern British Colonies and the Formation of American Culture* (Chapel Hill: University of North Carolina Press, 1988), 178–79; Allan Kulikoff, *Tobacco and Slaves: The Development of Southern Cultures in the Chesapeake, 1680–1800* (Chapel Hill: University North Carolina Press, 1986), 319–20; Edmund S. Morgan, *American Slavery, American Freedom: The Ordeal of Colonial Virginia* (New York: W. W. Norton, 1975), 305–8, 422–23; James Horn, *Adapting to a New World: English Society in the Seventeenth Century Chesapeake* (Chapel Hill: University North Carolina Press, 1994), 149–50.

[12] The following discussion draws heavily on Thomas D. Morris, *Southern Slavery and the Law, 1619–1860* (Chapel Hill: University of North Carolina Press, 1996), as well as Berlin, *Many Thousands Gone*. Other important accounts include Warren M. Billings, "The Law of Servants and Slaves in Seventeenth Century Virginia," *Virginia Magazine of History and Biography*, 99 (1991): 45–62; David T. Konig, "'Dale's Laws' and the Non-Common Law Origins of Criminal Justice in Virginia," *American Journal of Legal History*, 26 (1982): 354–75; and, Robert McColley, *Slavery in Jeffersonian Virginia*, second ed. (Urbana: University of Illinois Press, 1973), 11–23.

[13] Morris, *Southern Slavery*, 40–42.

[14] Ibid., 43–45; Williams, *Slavery and Freedom in Delaware*, 18; Morgan, *American Slavery, American Freedom*, 327–37.

[15] Morris, *Southern Slavery*, 163–69.

[16] Morgan, *American Slavery, American Freedom*, 311.

[17] See Morgan, *American Slavery, American Freedom*, 250–70, and Wilcomb Washburn, *The Governor and the Rebel* (Chapel Hill: University North Carolina Press, 1957).

[18] Berlin, *Many Thousands Gone*, 109–41; Morgan, *American Slavery, American Freedom*, 311–13.

[19] Michael Nicholls makes this point in "Passing Through This Troublesome World: Free Blacks in the Early Southside," *Virginia Magazine of History and Biography*, 92 (1984), 51–53.

[20] Maryland passed a similar law in 1715. See *Laws of Maryland*, 1715, ch. 44.

[21] See Douglas Deal, "A Constricted World: Free Blacks on Virginia's Eastern Shore, 1680–1750," in *Colonial Chesapeake Society*, Lois Carr, Philip D. Morgan, and Jean B. Russo, eds. (Chapel Hill: University of North Carolina Press, 1988), 275–305.

[22] Deal, "Constricted World," 278–79, with citations to William Waller Hening, "The Statutes at Large: Being a Collection of All the Laws of Virginia, from the first Session of the Legislature in the Year 1619," (Richmond, 1809–1823).

[23] Deal, "Constricted World," 299–302.

[24] Ibid., 281–85.

[25] See Anthony S. Parent Jr., *Foul Means: The Formation of a Slave Society in Virginia, 1660–1740* (Chapel Hill: University of North Carolina Press, 2003) for Virginia.

[26] Berlin, *Many Thousands Gone*, 109–12.

[27] See Michael Tadman, "The Demographic Cost of Sugar: Debates on Slave Societies and Natural Increase in the Americas," *American Historical Review*, 105 (2000): 1534–75.

[28] Lorena Walsh, "Slave Life, Slave Society, and Tobacco Production in the Tidewater Chesapeake, 1620–1820," in Ira Berlin and Philip D. Morgan, eds., *Cultivation and Culture: Labor and the Shaping of Slave Life in the Americas* (Charlottesville: University Press of Virginia, 1993), 170–202; Williams, *Slavery and Freedom in Delaware*, xv.

[29] See Jean Elliott Russo, "'Fifty-Four Days Work of Two Negroes': Enslaved Labor in Colonial Somerset County Maryland," *Agricultural History*, 78 (2004): 466–92.

[30] Walsh, "Slave Life," 184–88.

[31] Berlin, *Many Thousands Gone*, 117–19.

[32] See Philip D. Morgan, *Slave Counterpoint: Black Culture in the Eighteenth-Century Chesapeake & Lowcountry* (Chapel Hill: University North Carolina Press, 1998), 102–45.

[33] "Eighteenth-Century Maryland as Portrayed in the 'Itinerant Observations' of Edward Kimber," *Maryland Historical Magazine*, 51 (1956): 327–28.

[34] Morgan, *Slave Counterpoint*, 341–42, 349.

[35] Berlin, *Many Thousands Gone*, 120–21.

[36] Philip Schwarz, *Twice Condemned: Slaves and the Criminal Laws of Virginia, 1705–1865* (Baton Rouge: Louisiana State University Press, 1988), 171–75. First quote from 1736, second from Brunswick County Court, 1752.

[37] Schwarz, *Twice Condemned*, 175–79; Stegmaier, "Maryland Fear of Insurrection at the Time of Braddock's Defeat," 467–83.

[38] The following discussion relies principally on Morgan, *Slave Counterpoint*, 498–557 Berlin, *Many Thousands Gone*, 109–41, Kulikoff, *Tobacco and Slaves*, 317–420, and Lorena Walsh, *From Calabar to Carter's Grove: The History of a Slave Community* (Charlottesville: University Press of Virginia, 1997).

[39] See Walsh, *From Calabar to Carter's Grove*, 204–19, on the breakup of slave communities occasioned by the removal of one branch of the wealthy Burwell family from the Williamsburg area to the piedmont in the 1760s and 1770s.

[40] Morgan, *Slave Counterpoint*, 526.

[41] Ibid., 503–5.

[42] For an explication of this issue in a South Carolina setting, see Larry E. Hudson, *To Have and to Hold: Slave Work and Family in Antebellum South Carolina* (Athens: University of Georgia Press, 1997).

[43] Morgan, *Slave Counterpoint*, 462–77.

[44] See Mechal Sobel, *The World They Made Together: Black and White Values in Eighteenth Century Virginia* (Princeton: Princeton University Press, 1987).

Chapter 2: Slavery and the American Revolution

[1] See William W. Freehling, "The Founding Fathers and Slavery," in *The Reinterpretation of American History* (New York: Oxford University Press, 1994), and Gordon S. Wood, *The Radicalism of the American Revolution* (New York: Alfred A. Knopf, 1992), 186–87, for recent evocations of the view that the revolution weakened slavery.

[2] See Douglas Egerton, "Black Independence Struggles and the Tale of Two Revolutions: A Review Essay," *Journal of Southern History*, 64 (1998): 98–116, for a recent interpretation that discounts the idea of the American Revolution as a catalyst of social change. Also see McColley, *Slavery and Jeffersonian Virginia* for a thorough elaboration of this perspective with respect to Virginia. See Michael Morrison, *Slavery and the American West: The Eclipse of Manifest Destiny and the Coming of the Civil War* (Chapel Hill: University of North Carolina Press, 1997), 252–81, on the historical legacy of the American Revolution in the era of secession.

[3] See David Brion Davis, *The Problem of Slavery in the Age of Revolution, 1770–1823* (Ithaca: Cornell University Press, 1975), especially 255–342.

[4] See Jack P. Greene, *Pursuits of Happiness*, 170–206.

[5] Quoted in Schwarz, *Twice Condemned*, 187.

[6] Arthur Zilversmit, *The First Emancipation: The Abolition of Slavery in the North* (Chicago: University of Chicago Press, 1967); Gary B. Nash, *Forging Freedom: The Formation of Philadelphia's Black Community, 1720–1840* (Cambridge: Harvard University Press, 1988); Nash and Jean R. Soderlund, *Freedom by Degrees: Emancipation in Pennsylvania and Its Aftermath* (Oxford: Oxford University Press, 1991); Shane White, *Somewhat More Independent: The End of Slavery in New York City, 1770–1810* (Athens: University of Georgia Press, 1991); Graham Russell Hodges, *Root and Branch: African Americans in New York and East Jersey, 1613–1863* (Chapel Hill: University of North Carolina Press, 1999) and *Slavery and Freedom in the Rural North: African Americans in Monmouth County, New Jersey, 1665–1865* (Madison, Wis.: Madison House, 1996); John Wood Sweet, "Bodies Politic: Colonialism, Race and the Emergence of American North Rhode Island, 1730–1830" (Ph.D. diss., Princeton University, 1995); Joanne Pope Melish, *Disowning Slavery: Gradual Emancipation and 'Race' in New England, 1780–1860* (Ithaca: Cornell University Press, 1998).

[7] See Rachel N. Klein, *Unification of a Slave State: The Rise of the Planter Class in the South Carolina Backcountry, 1760–1808* (Chapel Hill: University of North Carolina Press, 1990), and Sylvia Frey, *Water from the Rock: Black Resistance in a Revolutionary Age* (Princeton: Princeton University Press, 1991).

[8] For the origins of the southern free black population, see Ira Berlin, *Slaves without Masters: The Free Negro in the Antebellum South* (New York: Pantheon Books, 1974), 15–51. City and state studies in the Chesapeake include Patience Essah, *A House Divided: Slavery and Emancipation in Delaware, 1638–1865* (Charlottesville: Univer-

sity Press of Virginia, 1996); Williams, *Slavery and Freedom in Delaware*; Christopher Phillips, *Freedom's Port: The African American Community of Baltimore, 1790–1860* (Urbana: University of Illinois Press, 1997); T. Stephen Whitman, *The Price of Freedom: Slavery and Manumission in Baltimore and Early National Maryland* (Lexington: University Press of Kentucky, 1997); James Sidbury, *Ploughshares into Swords: Race, Rebellion, and Identity in Gabriel's Virginia, 1730–1810* (Cambridge, U.K.: Cambridge University Press, 1997); Michael Nicholls, "Passing Through This Troublesome World: Free Blacks in the Early Southside," *Virginia Magazine of History and Biography*, 92 (1984); Tommy L. Bogger, *Free Blacks in Norfolk, Virginia 1790–1860: The Darker Side of Freedom* (Charlottesville: University Press of Virginia, 1997).

⁹ See Peter Wood, "'The Dream Deferred': Black Freedom Struggles on the Eve of White Independence," in Gary Y. Okihiro, ed., *In Resistance: Studies in African, Caribbean, and Afro-American History* (Amherst: University of Massachusetts Press, 1986), 166–87; Robert Olwell, "'Domestick Enemies': Slavery and Political Independence in South Carolina, May 1775–March 1776," *Journal of Southern History*, 55 (1989): 21–48; Frey, *Water from the Rock*, 45–80.

¹⁰ For conspiracy threats and alarms before 1775, see Schwarz, *Twice Condemned*, 173–80, and Mark Stegmaier, "Maryland Fear of Insurrection at the Time of Braddock's Defeat," *Maryland Historical Magazine*, 71 (1976): 467–83. The following account of Dunmore's proclamation and his "Ethiopian Regiment" relies principally on Woody Holton, *Forced Founders* (Chapel Hill: University of North Carolina Press, 1999), 132–54, as well as "'Rebel against Rebel': Enslaved Virginians and the Coming of the American Revolution," *Virginia Magazine of History and Biography*, 105 (1997): 157–92, and Sylvia Frey, "Between Slavery and Freedom: Virginia Blacks in the American Revolution," *Journal of Southern History*, 49 (1983): 375–98. Also see Charles W. Carey Jr., "'These Black Rascals': The Origins of Lord Dunmore's Ethiopian Regiment," *Virginia Social Science Journal*, 31 (1996): 65–77, and Benjamin Quarles, "Lord Dunmore as Liberator," *William and Mary Quarterly*, 15 (1958): 494–507. For African American involvement in the revolution, see Sylvia Frey, *Water from the Rock*. Still valuable is Benjamin Quarles, *The Negro in the American Revolution* (Chapel Hill: University of North Carolina Press, 1961).

¹¹ See, Merton Dillon, *Slavery Attacked: Southern Slaves and Their Allies, 1619 – 1865* (Baton Rouge: Louisiana State University Press, 1990), 29.

¹² Ronald Hoffman, *A Spirit of Dissension: Economics, Politics, and the Revolution in Maryland* (Baltimore: Johns Hopkins University Press, 1973), 147–48.

¹³ Holton, "Rebel against Rebel," 177.

¹⁴ Carey, "These Black Rascals," 71.

¹⁵ Frey, "Between Slavery and Freedom," 378; Quarles *Negro in the American Revolution*, 22. I am indebted to Michael Nicholls for this analysis of the Willoughby slaves' flight.

¹⁶ See Holton, "Rebel against Rebel," 182.

[17] Frey, "Between Slavery and Freedom," 383–86; Hoffman, *A Spirit of Dissension*; Michael Nicholls, "Strangers Setting Among Us: The Sources and Challenges of the Urban Free Black Population in Early Virginia," *Virginia Magazine of History and Biography*, 108 (2000): 155–79.

[18] Holton, "Rebel against Rebel," 182–83; Quarles, "Lord Dunmore as Liberator," 502–4.

[19] For Titus, see Hodges, *Slavery and Freedom in the Rural North*, 92–93 and 97–104, and Quarles, *Negro in the American Revolution*, 147–48. For the Philadelphia incident, see Nash, *Forging Freedom*, 45. For Maryland runaways, see Hoffman, *A Spirit of Dissension*, 184–88.

[20] Frey, *Water from the Rock*, 106–22, 192–93.

[21] See Schwarz, *Twice Condemned*, 183–87.

[22] Frey, *Water from the Rock*, 145–48.

[23] Quarles, *Negro in the American Revolution*, 116–17, 152–53.

[24] See Fritz Hirschfeld, *George Washington and Slavery: A Documentary Portrayal* (Columbia: University of Missouri Press, 1997), 21–29.

[25] Quarles, *Negro in the American Revolution*, 140–47.

[26] See Frey, "Between Slavery and Freedom," 392–94, and *Water from the Rock*, 169–70.

[27] See Quarles, *Negro in the American Revolution*, 160–61; Whitman, *The Price of Freedom*, 63.

[28] Boston King, quoted in James W. St. G. Walker, *The Black Loyalists: The Search for a Promised Land in Nova Scotia and Sierra Leone, 1783–1870* (New York: Africana Publishing Company and Dalhousie, Nova Scotia: Dalhousie University Press, 1976), 10–11.

[29] See Quarles, *Negro in the American Revolution*, 172–80, and Frey, *Water from the Rock*, 174–79.

[30] See Michael McDonnell, "Other Loyalists: A Reconsideration of the Black Loyalist Experience in the American Revolutionary Era," *Southern Historian*, 16 (1995): 5–25; Frey, *Water from the Rock*, 172–75.

[31] See Walker, *The Black Loyalists*, passim.

[32] Frey, "Between Slavery and Freedom," 376.

[33] Frey, *Water from the Rock*, 172–205, discusses state by state estimates of slave losses, as well as probable destinations of black emigrants.

[34] See Luther P. Jackson, "Virginia Negro Soldiers and Seamen in the American Revolution," *Journal of Negro History*, 28 (1942): 250–52.

[35] See Jackson, "Virginia Negro Soldiers," 255.

[36] Ibid., 254.

[37] Hoffman, *A Spirit of Dissension*, 241.

[38] Sidney Kaplan and Emma Nogrady Kaplan, *The Black Presence in the Era of the American Revolution*, rev. ed. (Amherst: University of Massachusetts Press, 1989), 37; Quarles, *Negro in the American Revolution*, 95.

[39] Jackson, "Virginia Negro Soldiers," 272–75, Quarles, *Negro in the American Revolution*, 95, Kaplan and Kaplan, *Black Presence*, 59–60.

[40] Kaplan and Kaplan, *Black Presence*, 60.

[41] Jackson, "Virginia Negro Soldiers," 273.

[42] Landers, *Black Society in Spanish Florida*, 23–60.

[43] Orlando Patterson, *Freedom: Volume I: Freedom in the Making of Western Culture* (New York: Basic Books, 1991), 1–8, 36–41.

[44] John P. Kaminski, ed., *A Necessary Evil?: Slavery and the Debate Over the Constitution* (Madison, Wis.: Madison House, 1995), 187–88.

[45] *Maryland Gazette*, July 9, 30, August 20, and September 10, 1767, quoted in Duncan MacLeod, *Slavery, Race, and the American Revolution* (Cambridge, U.K.: Cambridge University Press, 1974), 31–40.

[46] Matthew E. Mason, "Slavery Overshadowed: Congress Debates Prohibiting the Atlantic Slave Trade to the United States, 1806–1807," *Journal of the Early Republic*, 20 (2000): 59–82.

[47] Whitman, *Price of Freedom*, 11.

[48] Peter S. Onuf, *Statehood and Union: A History of the Northwest Ordinance* (Bloomington: Indiana University Press, 1987); Paul Finkelman, "Slavery and the Northwest Ordinance: A Study in Ambiguity," and "Evading the Ordinance: The Persistence of Bondage in Indiana and Illinois," both in *Slavery and the Founders: Race and Liberty in the Age of Jefferson* (Armonk: M. E. Sharpe, 1996), 34–56 and 57–79.

[49] Donald Robinson, *Slavery in the Structure of American Politics* (New York: W. W. Norton & Company, 1971), 302–15.

Chapter 3: Manumitters and Would-Be Emancipators

[1] Jean Soderlund, *Quakers and Slavery: A Divided Spirit* (Princeton: Princeton University Press, 1985).

[2] Warner Mifflin, *The Defence of Warner Mifflin against Aspersions cast on him on Account of his endeavours to promote Righteousness, Mercy, and Peace Among Mankind* (Philadelphia, 1796), 3–10.

[3] Michael Nicholls's study of manumissions in Norfolk, Williamsburg, Petersburg, Richmond, Frederick, and Alexandria between 1782 and 1810 found that at least one in five urban manumissions were explicit self-purchases or featured payments to a slaveholder by a free person of color. Nicholls, "Strangers Setting Among Us: The Sources and Challenges of the Urban Free Black Population in Early Virginia," *Virginia Magazine of History and Biography*, 108 (2000): 164–65, Over one-third of manumissions registered in the Norfolk area between 1790 and 1820 were self-purchases according to Tommy L. Bogger, *Free Blacks in Norfolk, Virginia*, 2, 11. An early study of Petersburg revealed similar patterns. See Luther P. Jackson, "Manumission

in Certain Virginia Cities," *Journal of Negro History*, 15 (1930): 278–314. About one-quarter of some twelve thousand manumissions examined in early national Maryland record payments to the manumitter; virtually none show ex-slaves receiving goods or money. See Whitman, *Price of Freedom*, 97. For a similar pattern in Delaware, see Williams, *Slavery and Freedom in Delaware*, 82.

⁴ Nicholls, "Strangers Setting Among Us," 155.

⁵ Manumissions in several Maryland counties exhibit this pattern, including Harford, Kent, Queen Anne's, and Talbot.

⁶ Williams, *Slavery and Freedom in Delaware*, 10–12.

⁷ See George Buchanan, *An Oration upon the moral and political evil of Slavery. Delivered at a public meeting of the Maryland Society for Promoting the Abolition of Slavery, and the Relief of Free Negroes, and others unlawfully held in Bondage* (Baltimore, 1791), 17.

⁸ Berlin, *Slaves without Masters*, 29–32; Williams, *Slavery and Freedom in Delaware*, 141–76; Whitman, *Price of Freedom*, 10–11, 67.

⁹ For a general account of anti-slavery in the Upper South see Ira Berlin, *Slaves without Masters*, 79–107. For Virginia, see Douglas R. Egerton, *Gabriel's Rebellion: The Virginia Slave Conspiracies of 1800–1802* (Chapel Hill: University of North Carolina Press, 1993). Quotation is from David Meade, c. 1799, cited in Egerton, *Gabriel's Rebellion*, 15. For a more positive assessment of Maryland's consideration of gradual emancipation, see William L. Calderhead, "Slavery in Maryland in the Age of the Revolution, 1775–1790," *Maryland Historical Magazine*, 98 (2003): 303–24.

¹⁰ Egerton, *Gabriel's Rebellion*, 10–11.

¹¹ Kenneth Carroll, "An Eighteenth Century Episcopalian Attack on Quaker and Methodist Manumission of Slaves," *Maryland Historical Magazine*, 80 (1985): 139–50; Richard K. MacMaster, "Liberty or Property? The Methodists' Petition for Emancipation in Virginia, 1785," *Methodist History*, 10 (1971): 44–55; Fredrika Teute Schmidt and Barbara Ripel Wilhelm, "Early Proslavery Petitions in Virginia," *William and Mary Quarterly*, 30 (1973): 133–46.

¹² See David Brion Davis, *The Problem of Slavery in Western Culture* (Ithaca: Cornell University Press, 1966), for an extended discussion of religious and philosophical thought on slavery and the slave trade in early modern Europe and the Americas.

¹³ Soderlund, *Quakers and Slavery;* Kenneth Carroll, "Maryland Quakers and Slavery," *Quaker History*, 72 (1983): 27–42; Philip J. Schwarz, *Migrants against Slavery: Virginians and the Nation* (Charlottesville: University Press of Virginia, 2001), 82–83.

¹⁴ McColley, *Slavery and Jeffersonian Virginia*, 158–59.

¹⁵ John S. Tyson, *The Life of Elisha Tyson* (Baltimore, n.p., 1825), 126.

¹⁶ Monte Calvert, "The Abolition Society of Delaware, 1801–1807," *Delaware History*, 10 (1963): 295–321.

¹⁷ Williams, *Slavery and Freedom in Delaware*, 141–43.

¹⁸ Ibid., 149–55.

[19] Patience Essah, *A House Divided: Slavery and Emancipation in Delaware, 1638–1865* (Charlottesville: University Press of Virginia, 1996), 82.

[20] Hodges, *Root and Branch*, 187–226, and Hodges, *Slavery and Freedom in the Rural North*, 147–70.

[21] Calvert, "The Abolition Society of Delaware, 1801–1807," 309.

[22] The society was founded in 1789. See Ira Berlin, *Slaves without Masters*, 28, for an occupational breakdown of the society's original members. See Gordon Finnie, "The Anti-Slavery Movement in the Upper South Before 1840," *Journal of Southern History*, 35 (1969): 322–25, for a discussion of the society.

[23] Peter Wallenstein, "Indian Foremothers: Race, Sex, Slavery and Freedom in Early Virginia," in Catherine Clinton and Michele Gillespie, *The Devil's Lane: Sex and Race in the Early South* (New York: Oxford University Press, 1997), 57–73, describes how bi- and tri-racial enslaved people came into being in the early Chesapeake.

[24] John D. Cushing, "The Cushing Court and the Abolition of Slavery in Massachusetts: More Notes on the 'Quock Walker Case,'" *American Journal of Legal History*, 5 (1961): 118–44; Melish, *Disowning Slavery*, 64–65.

[25] "Report of a meeting of the Maryland Society for promoting the abolition of slavery and the relief of free negroes, and others unlawfully held in bondage," Joseph Townsend, 1792, Enoch Pratt Free Library, Baltimore.

[26] *Laws of Maryland*, 1796, ch. 67, sections 21–27. The law also restricted petition filings to county courts, likely to provide a cheaper and friendlier venue for slaveholders than the appellate courts.

[27] Speech of William Pinkney in the Maryland House of Delegates, November, 1789 session (Philadelphia, 1790).

[28] *Maryland Gazette*, November 12, 1790. Bettye Gardner has tentatively identified "A Freeman," as Ezekiel Cooper, a Methodist preacher. See her "The Free Blacks of Baltimore" (Ph.D. diss., George Washington University, 1973).

[29] *Maryland Gazette*, November 26, 1790.

[30] Ibid., December 2 and 16, 1790.

[31] For Abaris, see the *Maryland Gazette,* January 13, 1791. The Freeman's reply appeared on January 20.

[32] See *The American Museum*, May 10 and May 23, 1788, 414–17 and 509–12. "Othello" signed himself as being "of Baltimore."

[33] Drew McCoy, *The Elusive Republic: Political Economy in Jeffersonian America* (Chapel Hill: University of North Carolina Press, 1980), especially 13–47.

[34] The 1790 census listed 8,043 free blacks in the entire state of Maryland, 7 per cent of the black population of the state.

[35] See Jeffrey R. Brackett, *The Negro in Maryland: A Study of the Institution of Slavery* (Baltimore: Johns Hopkins University Press, 1889), 53–54 and Eric Papenfuse, "From Redcompense to Revolution: Mahoney v. Ashton and the Transfiguration of Maryland Culture, 1791–1802," *Slavery and Abolition*, 15 (1994): 38–62.

[36] See MacLeod, *Slavery, Race, and Revolution*, 93, and Kay McKelvey, "Early Black Dorchester, 1776–1870: A history of the struggle of African-Americans in Dorchester County, Maryland, to be free to make their own choices" (Ph.D. diss., University of Maryland, College Park, 1991), 158–63.

[37] Matthew E. Mason, "Slavery Overshadowed: Congress Debates Prohibiting the Atlantic Slave Trade to the United States, 1806–1807," *Journal of the Early Republic*, 20 (2000): 59–82, quote p. 72, from Kaminski, *Necessary Evil?*, 225–26.

[38] Fredrika Teute Schmidt and Barbara Ripel Wilhelm, "Early Proslavery Petitions in Virginia," *William and Mary Quarterly*, 30 (1973): 133–46.

[39] McColley, *Slavery and Jeffersonian Virginia*, 151.

[40] Jefferson's famous condemnations of slavery in his *Notes on the State of Virginia*, written in 1781–82, were originally intended for the private enjoyment of French friends and colleagues, and not for publication in the United States.

[41] For an explication of Jefferson's views, see Peter S. Onuf, "'To Declare Them a Free and Independent People': Race, Slavery and National Identity in Jefferson's Thought," *Journal of the Early Republic*, 18 (1998): 1–46; and, Onuf, "Every Generation Is and 'Independant Nation': Colonization, Miscegenation, and the Fate of Jefferson's Children," *William and Mary Quarterly*, 67 (2000): 153–70.

[42] See Paul Finkelman, "Jefferson and Slavery: Treason against the Hopes of the World," in Peter S. Onuf, ed., *Jeffersonian Legacies* (Charlottesville: University Press of Virginia, 1993), 181–224, and Alexander O. Boulton, "The American Paradox: Jeffersonian Equality and Racial Science," *American Quarterly*, 47 (1995): 467–92.

[43] For Patrick Henry, see Henry Mayer, *A Son of Thunder: Patrick Henry and the American Republic* (New York and Toronto: Franklin Watts, 1986), 166–70, 433–34, 4721–75; for Jefferson, Lucia Stanton, "'Those Who Labor for my Happiness': Thomas Jefferson and His Slaves," and Paul Finkelman, "Jefferson and Slavery: 'Treason against the Hopes of the World,'" in Onuf, ed., *Jeffersonian Legacies*, 147–80 and 181–221; for Washington, Henry Wiencek, *An Imperfect God: George Washington, His Slaves, and the Creation of America* (New York: Farrar, Straus, and Giroux, 2003), 311–62; for Madison, Drew R. McCoy, *The Last of the Fathers: James Madison and the Republican Legacy* (Cambridge: Cambridge University Press, 1989), 253–322.

[44] For Carter, Andrew Levy, *First Emancipator: The Forgotten Story of Robert Carter, the Founding Father Who Freed His Slaves* (New York: Random House, 2005), 136–73. For Randolph, Melvin Patrick Ely, *Israel on the Appomattox: A Southern Experiment in Black Freedom from the 1790s through the Civil War* (New York: Alfred A. Knopf, 2004), 7–8 and 27–33.

[45] See Duncan MacLeod, *Slavery, Race, and the American Revolution*, 73, quoting one Henry Bedinger.

[46] See population tables in Richard Wright, *The Free Negro in Maryland* (New York: Columbia University Press, 1921), 86–88.

[47] For discussion of interstate slave "indentures" see *Report of the Committee Ap-*

pointed in the Senate of Pennsylvania to investigate the cause of an Increased Number of Slaves being returned for that Commonwealth, by the Census of 1830, over that of 1820 (Harrisburg, 1833), 3–6.

[48] Orlando Patterson, *Slavery and Social Death: A Comparative Study* (Cambridge: Harvard University Press, 1982), 211–18, outlines the theory of manumission as a gift exchange.

[49] Michael L. Nicholls, "'The Squint of Freedom': African-American Freedom Suits in Post-Revolutionary Virginia," *Slavery & Abolition*, 20 (1999): 47–62.

[50] One recent study of Virginia superior court records found that twenty-six persons won freedom in the 1790s, of whom nineteen were determined to be Indians, rather than black. See Christopher Doyle, "Judge St. George Tucker and the Case of *Tom* vs. *Roberts*: Blunting the Revolution's Radicalism from Virginia's District Courts," *Virginia Magazine of History and Biography*, 106 (1998): 419–42.

[51] McColley, *Slavery in Jeffersonian Virginia*, 157–59; Doyle, "Judge St. George Tucker," 430–31; Egerton, *Gabriel's Rebellion*, 15; Nicholls, "Squint of Freedom," 55–58.

[52] Nicholls, "Squint of Freedom," 56.

[53] Doyle, "Judge St. George Tucker," passim.

[54] Ibid., 432–33.

[55] St. George Tucker, *A Dissertation on Slavery with a Proposal for the Gradual Abolition of it, in the State of Virginia* (Philadelphia: Matthew Carey, 1796), 82; Thomas Jefferson, *Notes on the State of Virginia* (originally published, 1782; Charlottesville, Va.: 1993, electronic text, University of Virginia Library), 264.

[56] Philip Hamilton, "Revolutionary Principles and Family Loyalties: Slavery's Transformation in the St. George Tucker Household of Early National Virginia," *William and Mary Quarterly*, 55 (1998): 531–56.

[57] Nicholls, "Strangers Setting Among Us," 168–72.

[58] See St. George Tucker, *Dissertation on Slavery*, 91–98.

[59] McColley, *Slavery in Jeffersonian Virginia*, 135.

[60] Ira Berlin, *Slaves without Masters*, 84–85.

[61] Schwarz, *Migrants against Slavery*, espec. 18–84; MacLeod, *Slavery, Race, and the American Revolution*, 143–46, and John Parrish, *Remarks on the Slavery of the Black People; Addressed to the Citizens of the United States, particularly to those in legislative or executive stations in the general or state government and also to such individuals as hold them in bondage* (Philadelphia, 1806).

[62] Dee E. Andrews, *The Methodists and Revolutionary America, 1760–1800: The Shaping of an Evangelical Culture* (Princeton: Princeton University Press, 2000), 130–31.

[63] Whitman, *Price of Freedom*, 93–118; Nicholls, "Strangers Setting Among Us," 165–67.

[64] See *Robert Pleasants, son and heir of John Pleasants, deceased, Plaintiff, against Mary Logan et al. . . . in the High Court of Chancery, Virginia, March 16, 1798* (Philadelphia, 1802).

⁶⁵ The standard account is Donald Matthews, *Slavery and Methodism: A Chapter in American Morality, 1780–1865* (Princeton: Princeton University Press, 1965). For an excellent new discussion of the issue, see Andrews, *The Methodists*, 124–53.

⁶⁶ Andrews, *The Methodists*, 126–27; Jesse Lee, *A Short History of the Methodists in the United States of America; Beginning in 1766, and Continued till 1809* (Baltimore, 1810), 102; and, Francis Asbury, *Journals of Francis Asbury*, 3 vols. (New York 1821; reprint, Nashville, 1958), entry of February 1, 1809.

⁶⁷ See the Journal of the Baltimore Annual Conference, Methodist Episcopal Church, Vols. 1–2 (1800–16, and 1817–44), for examples of church trials of slaveholders.

⁶⁸ See Matthews, *Slavery and Methodism*, 8–28, and Christine Heyrman, *Southern Cross: The Beginnings of the Bible Belt* (Chapel Hill: University of North Carolina Press, 1998), 92–94.

⁶⁹ Andrews, *The Methodists*, 128–31.

⁷⁰ Kenneth Carroll, "Religious Influences on Manumission of Slaves in Caroline, Dorchester, and Talbot Counties," *Maryland Historical Magazine*, 56 (1961): 176–97.

⁷¹ W. Harrison Daniel, "Virginia Baptists and the Negro in the Early Republic," *Virginia Magazine of History and Biography*, 80 (1972): 59–69.

Chapter 4: Early Black Challenges to Slavery

¹ Richard Allen, *The Life, Experience, and Gospel Labors of the Right Reverend Richard Allen* (Philadelphia: Martin and Boden, 1833), 5–10; Gary Nash, "New Light on Richard Allen: The Early Years of Freedom," *William and Mary Quarterly*, 46 (1989): 332–40.

² For the role of Quakers, Methodists, and Nicholites in manumission on the Eastern Shore, see Carroll, "Religious Influences on the Manumission of Slaves in Caroline, Dorchester, and Talbot Counties," 176–95, and Carroll, "Maryland Quakers and Slavery," *Quaker History*, 72 (1983): 27–42.

³ Ronald Hoffman, *A Spirit of Dissension: Economics, Politics, and the Revolution in Maryland* (Baltimore: Johns Hopkins University Press, 1973), 126–95.

⁴ Women in early national Maryland granted a share of all manumissions twice as large as the proportion of slaves they held. Whitman, *Price of Freedom*, 110.

⁵ Matthias's narrative appears as an appendix in John Joyce, *The Confession of John Joyce, alias Davis, who was executed on Monday, the 14th of March, 1808, for the Murder of Mrs. Sarah Cross; with an Address to the Public and People of Colour, together with the substance of the Trial, and the address of Chief Justice Tilghman on his condemnation* (Philadelphia, 1808). The pamphlet was "printed for the benefit of Bethel Church," and registered for copyright by Richard Allen. For Grandy, see Bogger, *Free Blacks in Norfolk, Virginia*, 17–22.

⁶ Whitman, *Price of Freedom*, 75, 82–86.

⁷ For analyses of slaveholders' motivation in the Chesapeake, see Whitman, *Price of*

Freedom, chapters 3 and 4; Eva Sheppard, "The Liberty of Emancipating Their Slaves: Manumission in Virginia, 1782–1806," and Sean Condon, "The Slaveowner's Family and Manumission in the Post Revolutionary Chesapeake: Evidence from Anne Arundel County Wills, 1790 to 1820," papers presented at "From Slavery to Freedom: Manumission in the Atlantic World," conference held at Charleston, S.C., October 4–7, 2000. See also Robert L. Hall, "Slave Resistance in Baltimore City and County, 1747–1790," *Maryland Historical Magazine*, 84 (1989): 305–18.

[8] *Laws of Maryland*, 1663, ch. 30.

[9] Ibid., 1681, ch. 4.

[10] Harris and McHenry, *Maryland Reports*, Butler v. Boarman, September, 1770.

[11] Butler lived in St. Mary's County where a courthouse fire had destroyed all records from the relevant period.

[12] Harris & McHenry, *Maryland Reports*, 1787, v. 2, p. 214.

[13] Ibid., v. 4, p. 295. For a recent and thorough examination of this case, see Papenfuse, "From Recompense to Revolution." Papenfuse contends that the St. Domingue revolt keyed a reaction against freedom petitions that worked against the Mahoneys.

[14] Helen Catterall, *Judicial Cases Concerning American Slavery and the Negro* (Washington, D.C.: Carnegie Institution, 1936), *Maryland Cases*, IV, 53.

[15] This practice was struck down by the United States Supreme Court in 1813. Caterall, *Judicial Cases Concerning American Slavery and the Negro*, IV, 45.

[16] See the *Maryland Gazette*, January 19, 1792, advertisement of G. R. Brown for the runaway Jemima. Nine runaway advertisers of the 1790s noted that an escapee would try to pass for free "as a Butler." Compiled from Baltimore newspapers and the *Maryland Gazette*.

[17] Catterall, *Judicial Cases*, IV, 54.

[18] Ibid., IV, 5, concerning the case of Mima v. Queen.

[19] Caterall, *Judicial Cases*, IV, passim.

[20] The *Maryland Gazette* carried ads for eighteen runaways in conjunction with a pending or unsuccessful freedom petition between 1791 and 1800. Rawlings's ads appeared in issues of July 1797, and October 1800, respectively.

[21] See Anne Arundel County, Manumissions, Maryland State Archives. Carrollton's manumission of five Mahoney brothers and two other slaves occurred in 1808, that of John Joice in 1802. Ashton manumitted Daniel Mahoney in 1806. See also Papenfuse, "From Recompense to Revolution," 53–54, for Carroll's interest in the Ashton-Mahoney case.

[22] See Manumission of James Chaplain to Negro Job, Dorchester County Land Records, 1823, MSA; Peter Wallenstein, "Indian Foremothers," 61–62, for examples from Virginia.

[23] *Maryland Journal and Baltimore Advertiser*, June 14, 1793, quoted in John Hope Franklin and Loren Schweninger, *Runaway Slaves: Rebels on the Plantation* (New York: Oxford University Press, 1999), 35; Cynthia Lyerly, "Religion, Gender, and Iden-

tity: Black Methodist Women in a Slave Society, 1770–1810," in Patricia Morton, ed., *Discovering the Women in Slavery: Emancipating Perspectives on the American Past* (Athens: University of Georgia Press, 1996), 205.

[24] The following account of Gabriel's rebellion draws principally on Douglas Egerton's *Gabriel's Rebellion* and James Sidbury, *Ploughshares into Swords*. For a detailed investigation of the 1799 trial for hog stealing and its implications, see Philip J. Schwarz, "Gabriel's Challenge: Slaves and Crime in Late Eighteenth-Century Virginia," *Virginia Magazine of History and Biography*, 90 (1982): 283–309.

[25] See Julius Sherrard Scott III, "A Common Wind: Currents of Afro-American Communication in the Era of the Haitian Revolution" (Ph.D. diss., Duke University, 1986).

[26] This line of thinking is drawn out by James Sidbury, *Ploughshares into Swords*, 71–81.

[27] Egerton, *Gabriel's Rebellion*, 102, quoting Sutcliff, *Travels in North America*.

[28] See William G. Merkel, "To See Oneself as a Target of a Justified Revolution: Thomas Jefferson and Gabriel's Uprising," *American Nineteenth Century History*, 4 (2003): 1–31.

[29] Douglas Egerton speculates that had no rainstorm occurred, Gabriel and his recruits might well have caused enough bloodshed to goad Virginia's lawmakers into passing a gradual emancipation law. (Letter from Douglas Egerton, March 11, 2001, in the author's possession.)

[30] See Egerton, *Gabriel's Rebellion*, 102, and George Tucker, *A Letter to A Member of the General Assembly of Virginia, on the Subject of the Late Conspiracy of the Slaves; with a Proposal for their Colonization* (Baltimore, 1801), 7.

[31] George Tucker, "Letter to a Member . . . ," 6–8.

[32] Ibid., 11; Egerton, *Gabriel's Rebellion*, 51.

[33] Sidbury, *Ploughshares into Swords*, 135–37.

[34] Egerton, *Gabriel's Rebellion*, 150–51.

[35] Sidbury, *Ploughshares into Swords*, 113–40.

[36] For Hosier, see Andrews, *The Methodists*, 139–40; Frey and Wood, *Come Shouting to Zion*, 124, and Heyrman, *Southern Cross*, 219–19. For Toogood, see Andrews, *The Methodists*, 35.

[37] Andrews, *The Methodists*, 139–42.

[38] Allen, *Life, Experience, and Gospel Labors of the Rt. Rev. Richard Allen*, 13–15.

[39] Andrews, *The Methodists*, 133–34, 137.

[40] Ibid., 137–38.

[41] See Phillips, *Freedom's Port*, 129–35; Andrews, *The Methodists*, 150–52; and Frey and Wood, *Come Shouting to Zion*, 179.

[42] Frey and Wood, *Come Shouting to Zion*, 150–59.

[43] The following account of military activities during the War of 1812 draws on Frank A. Cassell, "Slaves of the Chesapeake Bay Area and the War of 1812," *Journal of*

Negro History, 57 (1972): 144–55, and Christopher T. George, "Mirage of Freedom: African Americans in the War of 1812," *Maryland Historical Magazine*, 91 (1996): 426–50.

⁴⁴ John Hope Franklin and Loren Schweninger discuss runaways in the War of 1812 in *Runaway Slaves*, 27–30.

⁴⁵ Quoted from George, "Mirage of Freedom," 432–33.

⁴⁶ Ibid., 433.

⁴⁷ John N. Grant, "Black Immigrants into Nova Scotia, 1776–1815," *Journal of Negro History*, 58 (1973): 253–70.

⁴⁸ Quote of Tobias Stansbury in George, "Mirage of Freedom," 440.

⁴⁹ See John McNish Weiss, "The Corps of Colonial Marines 1814–16: A Summary," *Immigrants and Minorities*, 15 (1996): 80–90.

⁵⁰ Grant, "Black Immigrants," 269–70.

Chapter 5: A Flickering Candle

¹ Douglas Egerton, "Averting a Crisis: The Proslavery Critique of the American Colonization Society," *Civil War History*, 43 (1997): 142–56.

² See David Brian Davis, *The Problem of Slavery in the Age of Revolution, 1770–1823* (Ithaca: Cornell University Press, 1975), 180–82, and Paul Finkelman, "Thomas Jefferson and Slavery II: Historians and Myths," in *Slavery and the Founders: Race and Liberty in the Age of Jefferson* (Armonk, N.Y.: M. E. Sharpe, 1996), 165–67.

³ For the Gist case, see Schwarz, *Migrants against Slavery*, 122–48 and Michael Trotti, "Freedmen and Enslaved Soil: A Case Study of Manumission, Migration, and Land," *Virginia Magazine of History and Biography*, 104 (1996): 455–70. For Randolph, see Schwarz, *Migrants against Slavery*, 75–78; for York, Pennsylvania, *York Daily Recorder*, June 26, 1827; for Columbia, Leroy T. Hopkins, "Black Eldorado on the Susquehanna: The Emergence of Black Columbia, 1726–1861," *Journal of the Lancaster County Historical Society*, 89 (1985): 110–31.

⁴ For a contemporary account of kidnappings of free blacks in the Chesapeake, see Jesse Torrey, *A Portraiture of Domestic Slavery in the United States* (Philadelphia: Jesse Torrey, 1817), 31–58.

⁵ *Baltimore American*, November 30, 1816.

⁶ Ibid., November 30, 1816.

⁷ Ibid., July 18, 1818.

⁸ Kidnapping flared up again in the 1820s, leading to an unsuccessful proposal to allow slaves and free blacks to testify against whites in kidnapping cases. See the *Baltimore American* of August 9, 1822. Also see "A Further Supplement to the Act entitled, an Act Relating to Servants and Slaves," Pamphlet #2708, MdHS.

⁹ For southern attitudes toward free black labor after the Civil War, see James L. Roark, *Masters without Slaves: Southern Planters in the Civil War and Reconstruction*

(New York: W. W. Norton, 1977), 111–56. For Cuba, see Rebecca J. Scott, *Slave Emancipation in Cuba: The Transition to Free Labor* (Princeton: Princeton University Press, 1985). For a good overview also see Scott, "Exploring the Meaning of Freedom: Postemancipation Societies in Comparative Perspective," *Hispanic American Historical Review*, 68 (1988): 407–28. For Pennsylvania, see Gary Nash, *Forging Freedom*, 219–27. Graham Hodges's *Root and Branch*, covers this subject for New York and New Jersey, and Joanne Pope Melish's *Disowning Slavery* discusses white reaction to gradual abolition in southern New England. For white assessments of free blacks in Maryland, see Whitman, *Price of Freedom*, 140–66. George Fredrickson, *The Black Image in the White Mind: The Debate on Afro-American Character and Destiny, 1817–1914* (New York: Harper and Row, 1971) remains a valuable overview of this question.

[10] The literature on conceptualization of waged labor and laboring people in nineteenth-century America is extensive. See Jonathan Glickstein, *Concepts of Free Labor in Antebellum America* (New Haven: Yale University Press, 1991) and Christopher Tomlins, *Law, Labor and Ideology in the Early American Republic* (Cambridge: Cambridge University Press, 1993) for two excellent recent treatments.

[11] See *A Letter from General Harper, of Maryland, to Elias B. Caldwell, Esquire, Secretary of the American Society for Colonizing the Free People of Color, in the United States with Their Own Consent* (Baltimore, 1817). The letter is reprinted in Eric Robert Papenfuse, *The Evils of Necessity: Robert Goodloe Harper and the Moral Dilemma of Slavery* (Philadelphia: American Philosophical Society, 1997). Papenfuse provides a sensitive analysis of Harper's evolving views on slavery from the 1780s to his death in 1825.

[12] "Letter from General Harper," 6–7.

[13] From "A Discourse on Learning," 1788, reprinted in Papenfuse, *The Evils of Necessity*, 81–97, quoted material, 82.

[14] "Letter from General Harper," 8–9.

[15] Ibid., 9–11.

[16] Ibid., 8, 13–14.

[17] See Douglas Egerton, *Charles Fenton Mercer and the Trial of National Conservatism* (Jackson: University Press of Mississippi, 1989), 111.

[18] "Letter from General Harper," 25.

[19] See Fredrickson, *The Black Image in the White Mind*, 3–22, and Gordon Finnie, "The Anti-Slavery Movement in the Upper South Before 1840," *Journal of Southern History*, 35 (1969): 324, for more embracing discussions of colonization.

[20] For Niles on the slave trade and kidnapping, see the *Weekly Register* of 1817–18, v. 12, 287 and 323; v. 13, 80, 332, and 377, v. 14, 280, and v. 15, 267–68, 384.

[21] Ibid., v. 16, May 8 and 22, and August 14, 1819.

[22] Ibid., August 14, 1819.

[23] Niles had been raised in Wilmington, Delaware, in the 1780s and 1790s, where private manumission had all but extinguished slavery. In 1810, Niles reported a slave

in his household in the census but had none according to the 1813 tax roll. He may have served for a few years as the master of a term slave. For attitudes toward women as inculcators of republican virtues see Linda K. Kerber's *Women of the Republic: Intellect and Ideology in Revolutionary America* (Chapel Hill: University of North Carolina Press, 1980), especially 283–87.

[24] *Niles' Weekly Register*, August 21, 1819.

[25] Jesse T. Torrey, *A Portraiture of Domestic Slavery*.

[26] George Bourne, *The Book and Slavery Irreconcilable* (Philadelphia, 1816).

[27] John D. Paxton, *Letters on Slavery, Addressed to the Cumberland Congregation, Virginia* (Lexington, Ky.: Abram T. Skillman, 1833).

[28] See Randolph Scully, "'Somewhat Liberated': Baptist Discourses of Race and Slavery in Nat Turner's Virginia, 1777–1840," unpublished paper presented at the McNeill Center for Early American Studies, March, 2000.

[29] Schwarz, *Migrants against Slavery*, 83–84.

[30] Merton Dillon, *Benjamin Lundy and the Struggle for Negro Freedom* (Urbana: University of Illinois Press, 1966), 45–58, 85, 88–94, and 162.

[31] Baltimore *Genius of Universal Emancipation*, September 12, 1825, volume 1, no. 3.

[32] Lundy frequently voiced the suspicion that masters of term slaves collaborated with abductors to cheat slaves of freedom.

[33] *Genius*, August 12, 1826.

[34] For coartacion, see Herbert S. Klein, *Slavery in the Americas: A Comparative Study of Virginia and Cuba* (Chicago: University of Chicago Press, 1967); Whitman, *Price of Freedom*, p. 113–14.

[35] *Genius*, July 7, 1827.

[36] William Lloyd Garrison, *A Brief Sketch of the Trial of Wm. L. Garrison, for an Alleged Libel on Francis Todd, of Massachusetts* (Boston, 1834).

[37] Raymond's best known work is his *Elements of Political Economy* (Baltimore, 1820). For his role in the Protection Society, see the *Baltimore American* of November 6, 1816. For the Baltimore meeting opposing the unrestricted admission of Missouri, see the *American* of December 30, 1819, and January 1, 1820, and his *The Missouri Question* (Baltimore, 1819). For Raymond as a political economist, see Paul Keith Conkin, *Prophets of Prosperity: America's First Political Economists* (Bloomington: Indiana University Press, 1980), 77–111.

[38] Raymond, *Missouri Question*, 8–20. For other anti-slavery writers who had compared northern growth to southern stagnation, see Merton Dillon, *Slavery Attacked: Southern Slaves and Their Allies, 1619–1865* (Baton Rouge: Louisiana State University Press, 1990), 120–22.

[39] Raymond, *Missouri Question*, 18–19 and 25.

[40] Ibid., 26–29.

[41] *Genius*, September 24 and October 8, 1825.

[42] Ibid., September 12, 1826.

[43] Ibid., September 16 and October 7, 1826.

[44] Ibid., October 14, 1826.

[45] *Laws of Maryland*, 1825, ch. 93. For criticism of this law, see the *Genius* of January 20, February 10 and 24, and March 24 and 31, 1827.

[46] Adams would win six of Maryland's electoral votes to Jackson's five, and gain a plurality of about 1,000 votes out of 50,000 cast. See Robert V. Remini, *The Election of Andrew Jackson* (Philadelphia: Lippincott, 1963), p.187.

[47] Eric Burin, *Slavery and the Peculiar Solution: A History of the American Colonization Society* (Gainesville: University Press of Florida, 2005), 48–49, and Elizabeth R. Varon, *We Mean to Be Counted: White Women and Politics in Antebellum Virginia* (Chapel Hill: University of North Carolina Press, 1998), 45

[48] See Varon, *We Mean to Be Counted,* 11 and 46.

[49] Elizabeth R. Varon, "Evangelical Womanhood and the Politics of the African Colonization Movement in Virginia," in John R. McKivigan and Mitchell Snay, eds., *Religion and the Antebellum Debate over Slavery* (Athens: University of Georgia Press, 1998) 169–93, and Varon, *We Mean to Be Counted,* 7–62.

[50] Burin, *Slavery and the Peculiar Solution,* 75–77.

[51] Ellen Eslinger, "Liberation in a Rural Context: The Valley of Virginia, 1800–1860," paper presented at "From Slavery to Freedom: Manumission in the Atlantic World," Charleston, S.C., October 4–7, 2000.

[52] Thomas C. Parramore, "Covenant in Jerusalem," in Kenneth S. Greenberg, ed., *Nat Turner: A Slave Rebellion in History and Memory* (Oxford: Oxford University Press, 2003), 58–78.

[53] Varon, "Evangelical Womanhood," 179.

[54] William G. Shade, *Democratizing the Old Dominion: Virginia and the Second Party System, 1824–1861* (Charlottesville: University Press of Virginia, 1996), 195–96.

[55] *Speech of Thomas Jefferson Randolph (of Albemarle) in the House of Delegates of Virginia on the Abolition of Slavery, delivered January 21, 1832* (Richmond, 1832).

[56] For two excellent treatments of Virginia's slavery debate of 1832, as well as the struggle over constitutional revision that preceded it in 1829–30, see William W. Freehling, *The Road to Disunion: Secessionists at Bay, 1776–1854* (Oxford: Oxford University Press, 1990), 162–210, and Shade, *Democratizing the Old Dominion,* 191–224.

[57] Alison Freehling, *Drift Toward Dissolution: The Virginia Slavery Debate of 1831–32* (Baton Rouge: Louisiana State University Press, 1982) sees the debates as a missed opportunity to end slavery in Virginia. William Freehling, *Road to Disunion,* 178–96, and William G. Shade, *Democratizing the Old Dominion,* 191–224, offer differing interpretations but share a view that the anti-slavery content of the debates was colonizationist rather than emancipationist, and anti-black and deportationist in nature.

[58] Shade, *Democratizing the Old Dominion,* 204–6; Freehling, *Road to Disunion,* 190–95.

[59] Thomas R. Dew, *Review of the Debate in the Virginia Legislature of 1831 and 1832*

(Richmond, 1832); Shade, *Democratizing the Old Dominion*, 192–99. For Madison on slavery, see Drew McCoy, *The Last of the Fathers: James Madison and the Republican Legacy* (Cambridge; New York: Cambridge University Press, 1989), 253–322. Harrison's essay, "The Slavery Question in Virginia," appeared in 1832 and is contained in *Aris Sonis Focisque: Being a Memoir of an American Family: The Harrisons of Skimino*, Fairfax Harrison, ed (privately printed, 1910).

⁶⁰ Varon, "Evangelical Womanhood," 180–84.

⁶¹ *The Trial of Reuben Crandall, M.D., charged with Publishing and Circulating Sedition and Incendiary Papers, &c in the District of Columbia, with the intent of Exciting Servile Insurrection, by a member of the Bar* (Washington, D.C., 1836).

⁶² Phillips, *Freedom's Port*, 191–92.

⁶³ *Report of the Committee on Grievances and Courts of Justice of the House of Delegates relative to the Colored Population of Maryland*, Henry Brawner, Chair (Annapolis, 1832).

⁶⁴ Phillips, *Freedom's Port*, 191–95.

⁶⁵ Essah, *A House Divided*, 155–61.

⁶⁶ Williams, *Slavery and Freedom in Delaware*, 198–201.

⁶⁷ Ibid., 189–97.

⁶⁸ For Janney's life, see Patricia Hickin, "Gentle Agitator: Samuel M. Janney and the Antislavery Movement in Virginia, 1842–1851," *Journal of Southern History*, 37 (1971): 159–88.

⁶⁹ Hickin, "Gentle Agitator," 179, from Pleasants, *Richmond Whig*, January 27, 1846

⁷⁰ Elwood L. Bridner, "Joseph E. Snodgrass and Freedom of the Press in Antebellum Maryland," *Maryland Historical Magazine*, 92 (2003): 456–65.

⁷¹ Henry Ruffner, *Address to the People of West Virginia, showing that slavery is injurious to the public welfare, and that it may be gradually abolished, without detriment to the rights and interests of slaveholders* ... (Lexington, Va., 1847), 41.

⁷² See Stanley Harrold, *Abolitionists and the South: 1831–1861* (Lexington: University Press of Kentucky, 1995), 28–29, 41–42.

⁷³ John L. Carey, *Some Thoughts concerning Domestic Slavery in a Letter to ⁻⁻* (Baltimore, 1838), and *Slavery in Maryland Briefly Considered* (Baltimore, 1845).

⁷⁴ Carey, *Slavery Briefly Considered*, 37.

⁷⁵ William Freehling, *The Reintegration of American History: Slavery and the Civil War* (New York: Oxford University Press, 1994), 138–57.

⁷⁶ Burin, *Slavery and the Peculiar Solution*, 100–20.

Chapter 6: We Got This Far by Faith

¹ Accounts of the rise of African American churches include Albert J. Raboteau, *Fire in the Bones: Reflections on African-American Religious History* (Boston: Beacon Press, 1995), Timothy E. Fulop and Albert J. Raboteau, eds., *African-American Reli-*

gion: Interpretive Essays in History and Culture (New York: Routledge, 1997), Sylvia R. Frey and Betty Wood, *Come Shouting to Zion: African American Protestantism in the American South and British Caribbean to 1830* (Chapel Hill: University of North Carolina Press, 1998), and Milton C. Sernett, *Black Religion and American Evangelicalism* (Metuchen, N.J.: Scarecrow Press, 1975). For a comparative overview of white and black nineteenth-century evangelicalism, see Curtis D. Johnson, *Redeeming America: Evangelicals and the Road to Civil War* (New York: Ivan R. Dee, 1990). For the origins of African American Methodism, see Dee E. Andrews, *The Methodists and Revolutionary America, 1760–1800* (Princeton: Princeton University Press, 2000), especially ch. 5.

[2] On the symbolic importance of Exodus in African American religion, see Alfred Raboteau, "African Americans, Exodus, and the American Israel," in Paul E. Johnson, ed., *African American Christianity: Essays in History* (Berkeley: University of California Press, 1994), 1–18.

[3] The standard institutional history of the American Colonization Society remains P. J. Staudenraus, *The African Colonization Movement, 1816–1865* (New York: Columbia University Press, 1961). For black views and actions on colonization, see Floyd J. Miller, *The Search for a Black Nationality: Black Emigration and Colonization, 1787–1863* (Urbana: University of Illinois Press, 1975), and Wilson J. Moses, *The Golden Age of Black Nationalism* (Oxford: Oxford University Press, 1988). For an excellent recent treatment focusing on free blacks in the northern states, see James Oliver Horton and Lois E. Horton, *In Hope of Liberty: Culture, Community, and Protest among Northern Free Blacks, 1700–1860* (Oxford: Oxford University Press, 1997), 177–202.

[4] See Gary Nash, *Forging Freedom*, 237–38, for an account of the Philadelphia meeting. Horton and Horton, *In Hope of Liberty*, 181–87, summarize Paul Cuffe's attempts to promote colonization from 1800 until his death in 1817.

[5] Marie Tyler McGraw, "Richmond Free Blacks and African Colonization, 1816–1832," *Journal of American Studies*, 21 (1987): 207–24. McGraw cites compilations by William Lloyd Garrison of black anti-colonization publications; only the Philadelphia, Richmond, and District of Columbia statements pre-date the late 1820s. For the Richmond and Philadelphia petitions, see Herbert Aptheker, ed., *A Documentary History of the Negro People in the United States* (New York: Citadel Press, 1951), 70–72.

[6] This account of Cary and Teage's activities is drawn from McGraw, "Richmond Free Blacks," 213–21. See also Mechal Sobel, *Trabelin' On: The Black Journey to an Afro-Baptist Faith* (Westport, Conn.: Greenwood Press, 1979), 263.

[7] For a brief biography of Daniel Coker and his role in creating the African Methodist Episcopal Church in Maryland, see Phillips, *Freedom's Port*, 131–38, Leroy Graham, *Baltimore: The Nineteenth-Century Black Capital* (Washington, D.C.: University Press of America, 1982), 63–76, and Bettye Gardner, "Free Blacks in Baltimore, 1800–1860" (Ph.D. diss., George Washington University, 1974), passim. Coker's deal-

ings with Richard Allen are covered by Allen's biographers. See Carol George, *Segregated Sabbaths* (Oxford: Oxford University Press, 1980), and Charles H. Wesley, *Richard Allen: Apostle of Freedom* (Washington, D.C.: The Associated Publishers, 1935).

[8] A revision of Maryland's slave code in 1790 eliminated this provision, but a savings clause kept it in force for those born before the new law's enactment. *Laws of Maryland,* 1715, ch. 44, and 1790, ch. 9.

[9] Daniel Coker, "A Dialogue between a Virginian and an African Minister," in Dorothy Porter, ed., *Negro Protest Pamphlets* (New York: Arno Press, 1969).

[10] The Baltimore Conference included circuits in Pennsylvania, Maryland, and northern Virginia. By 1813 the Conference had adopted a local option approach that all but wiped out its rules against slaveholding for church officials in Virginia, e.g., with provisions that allowed slave sales for life in cases of "necessity." See *Journal of the Baltimore Annual Conference, Methodist Episcopal Church*, vol. 1, 1800–1816, 54–70.

[11] On the foundation of African churches, in addition to Graham and Phillips, see Daniel A. Payne, *A History of the African Methodist Episcopal Church* (Nashville: Publishing House of the A.M.E. Sunday School Union, 1891), Will B. Gravely, "Rise of African Churches in America (1786–1822)," *Journal of Religious Thought*, 14 (1984): 315–32, and Albert J. Raboteau, "Richard Allen and the African Church Movement," in August Meier and Leon Litwack, eds., *Black Leaders of the Nineteenth Century* (Urbana: University of Illinois Press, 1988).

[12] Horton and Horton, *In Hope of Liberty*, 141; Phillips, *Freedom's Port*, 134–35. Harry Reed, *Platform for Change: The Foundations of the Northern Free Black Community, 1775–1865* (East Lansing: Michigan State University Press, 1994), 32–33, sees Richard Allen as organizing a power grab and forcing Coker to resign.

[13] Paul A. Gilje, "The Baltimore Riots of 1812 and the Breakdown of the Anglo-American Mob Tradition," *Journal of Social History*, 13 (1980): 547–64, and Gilje, "'Le Menu Peuple' in America: Identifying the Mob in the Baltimore Riots of 1812," *Maryland Historical Magazine*, 80 (1985): 50–66.

[14] Whitman, *Price of Freedom*, 80–81. For a general treatment of kidnapping of free blacks, see Carol Wilson, *Freedom at Risk: The Kidnapping of Free Blacks in America, 1780–1865* (Lexington: University Press of Kentucky, 1994).

[15] *Journal of the Baltimore Annual Conference, Methodist Episcopal Church*, 1 (1800–1844): 109.

[16] Phillips, *Freedom's Port*, 136–38; Graham, *Baltimore . . . Black Capital*, 73–76; *Baltimore Federal Gazette*, September 4, 1817; Murray N. Rothbard, *The Panic of 1819: Reactions and Policies* (New York: Columbia University Press, 1962).

[17] The account of black resistance to colonization in Maryland is largely drawn from Christopher Phillips, *Freedom's Port*, 211–25. For the history of colonization in Maryland, see Penelope Campbell, *Maryland in Africa: The Maryland State Colonization Society, 1831–1857* (Urbana: University of Illinois Press, 1971); and Richard L.

Hall, *On Afric's Shore: A History of Maryland in Liberia, 1834–1857* (Baltimore: Maryland Historical Society, 2003).

[18] "Report of the Committee on Colored Population," Maryland House of Delegates, quotation from John H. B. Latrobe, President, Maryland Colonization Society (Annapolis, 1840).

[19] Phillips, *Freedom's Port*, 220.

[20] This account of Watkins draws on Graham, *Baltimore . . . Black Capital*, 93–127, Phillips, *Freedom's Port*, 220–24, Bettye Gardner, "William Watkins: Antebellum Black Teacher and Anti-slavery Writer," *Negro History Bulletin*, 39 (1976): 623–25, and "Opposition to Emigration: A Selected Letter of William Watkins (The Colored Baltimorean)," *Journal of Negro History*, 67 (1982): 155–58.

[21] David Walker, *Appeal to the Colored Citizens of America* (New York: Hill and Wang, 1969), 4–5, quoted in Graham, *Baltimore . . . Black Capital*, 108.

[22] William Lloyd Garrison, *Thoughts on African Colonization: or an impartial exhibition of the Doctrines, Principles & Purposes of the American Colonization Society* (Boston, 1832), 55–56; Horton and Horton, *In Hope of Liberty*, p. 212. For letters from Watkins to Garrison, see C. Peter Ripley, ed., *The Black Abolitionist Papers* (Chapel Hill: University of North Carolina Press, 1991), vol. 3, 92–102.

[23] *The Liberator*, June 4, 1831.

[24] *Genius of Universal Emancipation*, November 27, 1829; second quote from Gardner, "Opposition to Emigration . . . ," 155–58.

[25] Grice proposed the idea of a convention in the spring of 1830 in a circular letter to prominent blacks, including Richard Allen. The latter issued the call for a convention which duly met in Philadelphia in September 1830. See the *Anglo-African*, October, 1859, for an article based on an interview with Grice, reprinted in Aptheker, *Documentary History of the Negro People*, 98–102.

[26] On black interest in colonizing Haiti or Canada, see Horton and Horton, *In Hope of Liberty*, 199–211. On the conventions themselves, Howard Bell, *A Survey of the Negro Convention Movement, 1830–1861* (New York: Arno Press, 1969).

[27] *Minutes and Proceedings of the First Annual Convention of the People of Colour, 1831* (Philadelphia: Published by the Convention, 1831). See also Minutes and Proceedings for 1833 and 1835, also in Philadelphia.

[28] On Whipper, Horton and Horton, *In Hope of Liberty*, 221–23. For Watkins's involvement, Graham, *Baltimore . . . Black Capital*, 120.

[29] Donald Yacovone, "The Transformation of the Black Temperance Movement, 1827–1854: An Interpretation," *Journal of the Early Republic*, 8 (1988): 281–97. Yacovone sees black commitment to temperance as virtually coterminous with support for abolition, and views both activities as important elements in building urban black communities. Benjamin Lundy supported a short-lived free produce store on Calvert Street in Baltimore in 1826–27; see *Genius of Universal Emancipation*, August 5, 1826.

[30] Phillips, *Freedom's Port*, 220–24; Graham, *Baltimore . . . Black Capital*, 93–127.

31 Graham, *Baltimore . . . Black Capital*, 124–26.

32 McGraw, "Richmond Free Blacks," 207–24; Phillips, *Freedom's Port*, 211–26; Hall, *On Afric's Shore* includes a list of more than one thousand black colonists to Maryland in Liberia, including information on whether persons were freed on condition of migrating there.

33 Hall, *On Afric's Shore*, 17–27, 136–50, 392–418.

34 Horton and Horton, *In Hope of Liberty*, 192–95. David Walker's *Appeal to Colored Citizens* criticized Haitian colonization in an anti-Catholic vein.

35 Nathaniel Peck and Thomas Price, *Report of Messrs. Peck and Price who were appointed at a meeting of the free colored people of Baltimore, held on November 25, 1839, Delegates to Visit British Guiana and the Island of Trinidad for the purposes of ascertaining the advantages to be derived by colored people migrating to those places* (Baltimore, 1840).

36 Phillips, *Freedom's Port*, 215–20.

37 Mitch Kachun, *Festivals of Freedom: Memory and Meaning in African American Emancipation Celebrations, 1808–1915* (Amherst and Boston: University of Massachusetts Press, 2003), 54–96.

38 Sobel, *Trabelin' On*, 191–92.

39 Williams, *Slavery and Freedom in Delaware*, 224–27; Frey and Wood, *Come Shouting to Zion*, 154.

40 Jean Libby, ed., *From Slavery to Salvation: The Autobiography of Rev. Thomas W. Henry of the A.M.E. Church* (Jackson: University Press of Mississippi, 1994), xxvii–xxix.

41 See Noah Davis, *A Narrative of the Life of the Rev. Noah Davis, a Colored Man* (Baltimore, 1859). Diane Batts Morrow, *Persons of Color and Religious at the Same Time: The Oblate Sisters of Providence, 1828–1860* (Chapel Hill: University of North Carolina Press, 2002) and Willa Banks, "A Contradiction in Antebellum Baltimore: A Competitive School for Girls of 'Color' within a Slave State," *Maryland Historical Magazine*, 99 (2004): 133–63.

42 Sobel, *Trabelin' On*, 169, 205–9.

43 Frey and Wood, *Come Shouting to Zion*, 201.

44 See Betty Wood, "'For Their Satisfaction or Redress': African Americans and Church Discipline in the Early South," in Catherine Clinton and Michelle Gillespie, *The Devil's Lane: Sex and Race in the Early South* (Oxford: Oxford University Press, 1997), 109–23.

45 Frey and Wood, *Come Shouting to Zion*, 202–3. Jacob Gruber, quoted in William P. Strickland, *The Life of Jacob Gruber* (New York, 1860), 329.

46 Andrews, *The Methodists*, 129–30.

47 John Boles, "Tension in a Slave Society: The Trial of Reverend Jacob Gruber," *Southern Studies*, 18 (1979): 179–97; William P. Strickland, *The Life of Jacob Gruber* (New York; Carlton & Porter: se, 1860), 130–259.

[48] See William L. Andrews, ed., *Sisters of the Spirit: Three Black Women's Autobiographies of the Nineteenth Century* (Bloomington: University of Indiana Press, 1986), on women evangelists.

[49] This account is drawn from Jarena Lee, *Religious Experiences and Journal of Mrs. Jarena Lee* (Philadelphia, 1849).

[50] Zilpha Elaw, *Memoirs of the Life, Religious Experience, ministerial travels and labours of Mrs. Zilpha Elaw . . .* (London, 1846). Lee and Elaw's memoirs appear together in William Andrews, ed., *Sisters of the Spirit*.

[51] See Noah Davis, *A Narrative of the Life*.

[52] Earl Ofari Hutchinson, *"Let Your Motto be Resistance": The Life and Thought of Henry Highland Garnet* (Boston: Beacon Press, 1972); Herman E. Thomas, *James W. C. Pennington: African American Churchman and Abolitionist* (New York: Garland Publishing, 1995).

[53] Ofari, *"Let Your Motto be Resistance,"* 144–53.

[54] William McFeely's *Frederick Douglass* (New York: W. W. Norton & Company, 1991) is the best biography. Douglass wrote no fewer than three versions of his autobiography; *Narrative of the Life of Frederick Douglass* (Boston, 1845) was the first.

[55] Melba Joyce Boyd, *Discarded Legacy: Politics and Poetics in the Life of Frances E. W. Harper 1825–1911* (Detroit: Wayne St. University Press, 1994). See also William Still, *The Underground Railroad* (Philadelphia, 1872; repr., New York: Arno Press, 1968), 755–81.

[56] Joyce, *Discarded Legacy*, passim.

[57] Libby, *From Slavery to Salvation*.

[58] See Washington County Orphans' Court Proceedings, 1807, Manumission of the Slaves of Richard Barnes, John T. Mason, Executor.

[59] Libby, *From Slavery to Salvation*, 73.

[60] Ibid., 14–16.

[61] Ibid., 18–23.

[62] Frey and Wood, *Come Shouting to Zion*, 212.

[63] Thomas R. Gray, *The Confessions of Nat Turner, the leader of the late Insurrection in Southampton, Virginia* (Baltimore, 1831); David F. Almendinger, Jr., "The Construction of *The Confessions of Nat Turner*," in Greenberg, ed., *Nat Turner: A Slave Rebellion in History and Memory*, 24–42.

[64] Sobel, *Trabelin' On*, 163.

[65] Freehling, *Road to Disunion*, 180–81.

[66] French's views are taken from Tony Horwitz, "Urban Confessions," *The New Yorker*, December 13, 1999, 80–89.

[67] Freehling, *Road to Disunion*, 178–86.

[68] Quoted material in Raboteau, "Exodus and the American Israel," 13–14.

Chapter 7: The Two Underground Railroads:

¹ See David W. Blight, ed., *Passages to Freedom: The Underground Railroad in History and Memory* (Washington, D.C.: Smithsonian Books, 2004). For an older treatment that downplays the significance of white abolitionists and emphasizes black agency, see Larry Gara, *The Liberty Line: The Legend of the Underground Railroad* (1961; repr. Lexington: University Press of Kentucky, 1996).

² Stanley Harrold, *Subversives: Antislavery Community in Washington, D.C., 1828–1865* (Baton Rouge: Louisiana State University Press, 2003), and *Abolitionists and the South*, 66–79 and passim.

³ Harriet Beecher Stowe, *Uncle Tom's Cabin, or Life Among the Lowly*, first published in installments, 1851–1852 in *The Washington National Era*. Also see Josiah Henson: *Truth Stranger than Fiction: Father Henson's Story of His Own Life* (Boston, 1858).

⁴ Julie Winch, "Philadelphia and the Other Underground Railroad," *Pennsylvania Magazine of History and Biography,* 111 (1987): 3–25.

⁵ Virginia first legislated against kidnapping in 1788 and stipulated capital punishment for offenders; by 1819 the penalty had been reduced to two years in prison. See Bogger, *Free Blacks in Norfolk, Virginia*, 99. Maryland pardoned half of the kidnappers (thirteen of twenty-six) sentenced to its penitentiary in the period 1811–1830, compared to a 16 per cent rate for all inmates (365 of 2260). Nearly 70 per cent of those pardoned for kidnapping had their sentences commuted after serving less than half the time imposed at trial (nine of thirteen), versus 38 per cent of all persons pardoned (139 of 365). See Maryland Penitentiary, Prisoner Records, 1811–1840. Franklin and Schweninger, *Runaway Slaves*, discuss kidnapping, 192–94 and 273–74.

⁶ Todd A. Herring, "Kidnapped and Sold in Natchez: The Ordeal of Aaron Cooper, a Free Black Man," *Journal of Mississippi History,* 60 (1998): 341–53. Herring attributes Cooper's liberation to Mississippians' fair-mindedness. Carol Wilson argues that slaveholders also wanted to rid their community of blacks who had been free, fearing them as an element that would breed discontent among other slaves. Wilson, *Freedom at Risk,* 30.

⁷ Carol Wilson, *Freedom at Risk,* 9–40; Phillips, *Freedom's Port,* 230–31; Solomon Northup, *Twelve Years a Slave* (1853; repr., Baton Rouge: Louisiana State University Press, 1968); Jesse Torrey, *A Portraiture of Domestic Slavery in the United States* (Philadelphia, 1817), 57.

⁸ Wilson, *Freedom at Risk,* 43–44.

⁹ Ibid., 19–37; Williams, *Slavery and Freedom in Delaware*, 238–40; Winch, "Two Underground Railroads," and M. Sammy Miller, "Patty Cannon: Murderer and Kidnapper of Free Blacks: A Review of the Evidence," *Maryland Historical Magazine,* 72 (1977): 419–23.

¹⁰ Phillips, *Freedom's Port,* 204.

[11] Manumissions in Loudoun County, Virginia, declined by 80 per cent for the period 1806–18, as compared to the years 1790–1806. See Brenda Stevenson, *Life in Black and White: Family and Community in the Slave South* (Oxford: Oxford University Press, 1996), 264. Stevenson attributes the decline to increased slave trading activity.

[12] Eslinger, "Liberation in a Rural Context: The Valley of Virginia, 1800–1860," paper presented at "From Slavery to Freedom: Manumission in the Atlantic World," Charleston, S.C., October 4–7, 2000.

[13] In Norfolk, more than forty free people of color were indicted as illegal residents and threatened with re-enslavement in the first half of the 1830s. Bogger, *Free Blacks in Norfolk, Virginia,* 41; Stevenson, *Life in Black and White,* 259. Commonwealth Attorney Richard Henderson complained in 1836 of efforts by some local courts to frustrate his enforcement of the expulsion law by granting continuances and extensions to free blacks seeking to remain. Stevenson, *Life in Black and White,* 269–70.

[14] On the domestic slave trade generally, see Michael Tadman, *Speculators and Slaves: Masters, Traders, and Slaves in the Old South* (Madison: University of Wisconsin Press, 1989), *Slave Trade and Migration,* Paul Finkelman, ed. (New York: Garland Publishing, 1989), and Frederic Bancroft, *Slave Trading in the Old South* (Baltimore: J. H. Furst Company, 1931). On slave-trading in the nineteenth-century Chesapeake, William Calderhead, "How Extensive Was the Border State Slave Trade?: A New Look," reprinted in Finkelman, 42–55, and "The Role of the Professional Slave Trader in a Slave Economy: Austin Woolfolk, a Case Study," *Civil War History,* 23 (1977): 195–211.

[15] Franklin and Schweninger, *Runaway Slaves,* 106–7, 142–45.

[16] See for example the narratives of Moses Grandy, Venture Smith, or Equiano from the pre-1830 period. William Still's *The Underground Railroad* recounts many stories in which slaves fled masters who had cheated them out of self-purchase, or were perceived as preparing to sell someone in violation of a self-purchase bargain.

[17] Josiah Henson, *Truth Stranger than Fiction,* 59–61.

[18] Henry "Box" Brown, *Narrative of Henry Box Brown, Who Escaped from Slavery Enclosed in a Box 3 Feet Long and 2 Wide* (Boston, 1849), 15, 49–58. See also Still, *Underground Railroad,* 81–85.

[19] Franklin and Schweninger, *Runaway Slaves,* 107–8, 264–66; Whitman, *Price of Freedom,* 86.

[20] Franklin and Schweninger, *Runaway Slaves,* 279–82.

[21] Ervin L. Jordan, *Black Confederates and Afro-Yankees in Civil War Virginia* (Charlottesville: University Press of Virginia, 1995), 69.

[22] See Whitman, *Price of Freedom,* 78–81.

[23] Franklin and Schweninger offer a thorough discussion of runaway demographics in *Runaway Slaves,* 209–33.

[24] Franklin and Schweninger, *Runaway Slaves,* 17–74; Whitman, *Price of Freedom,* 61–92; and Bogger, *Free Blacks in Norfolk, Virginia,* 7–32.

[25] James W. C. Pennington, "The Fugitive Blacksmith," in William L. Katz, ed., *Five Slave Narratives* (New York: Arno Press, 1969), 14. See also Thomas, *James W. C. Pennington*, 37–62.

[26] Pennington, *Fugitive Blacksmith*, 15–41.

[27] See William Otter, *History of My Own Times*, Richard B. Stott, ed. (Ithaca: Cornell University Press, 1995) for accounts of slavecatching as a part-time occupation of white craftsmen or laborers in Maryland and southern Pennsylvania.

[28] Thomas, *J. W. C. Pennington*, 56.

[29] William McFeely, *Frederick Douglass*, 70; Shirley Yee, *Black Women Abolitionists*, 28–29. Douglass's wife's earnings helped finance his escape by train, and family history credited her both with conceiving the idea of Douglass passing as a free black sailor, and with altering a set of clothes to suit this role.

[30] James Watkins, *Narrative of the Life of James Watkins* (Bolton, England, 1852), 11–38.

[31] William Whipper, a black lumber merchant in Columbia stated that 943 African Americans resided in Columbia in 1850, nearly one-fifth of the town's population. See his letter to William Still in *Underground Railroad*, 735–40.

[32] On Columbia, see Willis L. Shirk, Jr., "Testing the Limits of Tolerance: Blacks and the Social Order in Columbia, Pennsylvania, 1800–1851," *Pennsylvania History*, 60 (1993): 35–50; for Lancaster, see the many articles on its black community by Leroy Hopkins, including "The Negro Entry Book: A Document of Lancaster City's Antebellum Afro-American Community," *Journal of the Lancaster County Historical Society*, 88 (1984): 142–75, and also Carl Oblinger, "In Recognition of Their Prominence: A Case Study of the Economic and Social Backgrounds of an Ante-Bellum Negro Business and Farming Class in Lancaster County," *Journal of the Lancaster County Historical Society*, 72 (1968): 65–83. On Whipper, Richard P. McCormick, "William Whipper: Moral Reformer," *Pennsylvania History*, 43 (1976): 23–48. On Whipper's estimate, see Still, *Underground Railroad*, 738–39.

[33] See advertisement of Christopher Hughes, *Federal Gazette and Baltimore Daily Advertiser*, May 17, 1798.

[34] See *Baltimore Sun*, February 18, 1841, for the arraignment of a free black for purchasing a railway ticket and conveying it to a runaway slave.

[35] Earl Conrad, *Harriet Tubman* (Washington, D.C.: Associated Publishers, 1943), 57. Regarding the propensity of runaways to seek cities, see Franklin and Schweninger, *Runaway Slaves*, 124–48.

[36] Horton and Horton, *In Hope of Liberty*, 203–31; William and Ellen Craft, *Running a Thousand Miles for Freedom* (London: William Tweedie, 1860; repr., New York: Arno Press, 1969), Still, *Underground Railroad*, 368–77. For a delineation of the routes used by escapees, see William J. Switala, *Underground Railroad in Delaware, Maryland, and West Virginia* (Mechanicsburg, Pa.: Stackpole Books, 2004).

[37] See Essah, *House Divided*, 54–56; Williams, *Slavery and Freedom in Delaware*, 167–

68; Still, *Underground Railroad*, 623–41, and passim for individual stories of Delaware escapes. For a biography of Garrett, see James A. McGowan, *Station Master on the Underground Railroad: The Life and Letters of Thomas Garrett* (Moylan, Pa.: Whimsie Press, 1977). For Garrett's ties to Harriet Tubman, see Priscilla Thompson, "Harriet Tubman, Thomas Garrett, and the Underground Railroad," *Delaware History*, 22 (1986): 1–21.

[38] Thompson, "Harriet Tubman," 13–16. For John Hunn, see Still, *Underground Railroad*, 712–18.

[39] See Thompson, "Harriet Tubman," 3–5.

[40] William Green, *Narrative of Events in the Life of William Green (formerly a slave)* (Springfield, Mass., 1853).

[41] See Essah, *House Divided*, 55; Thompson, "Harriet Tubman," 8–9.

[42] This account of Tubman's life draws on Kate Clifford Larson's *Bound for the Promised Land: Harriet Tubman˜Portrait of an American Hero* (New York: One World–Ballantine Books, 2004), 62–114. See also Catherine Clinton, *Harriet Tubman: The Road to Freedom* (New York and Boston: Little, Brown and Co., 2004).

[43] Thompson, "Harriet Tubman," 12–21, notes that contemporary estimates of how many blacks Tubman assisted varied from sixty to three hundred, with no definitive records to resolve the matter. Kate Larson suggests that Tubman rescued between seventy and eighty persons and gave detailed instructions for escape to fifty or sixty more. Larson, *Bound for the Promised Land*, 100.

[44] See Howard Jones, *Mutiny on the Amistad: The Saga of a Slave Revolt and Its Impact on American Abolition, Law, and Diplomacy* (Oxford: Oxford University Press, 1986). For a general discussion of the decline of non-resistant sentiment among abolitionists, see Merton Dillon, *Slavery Attacked: Southern Slaves and Their Allies, 1619–1865* (Baton Rouge: Louisiana State University Press, 1990), 219–42.

[45] Howard Jones, "The Peculiar Institution and National Honor: The Case of the *Creole* Slave Revolt," *Civil War History*, 21 (1975): 28–50; Edward D. Jervey and C. Harold Huber, "The *Creole* Affair," *Journal of Negro History*, 65 (1980): 196–211; Dillon, *Slavery Attacked*, 201–3; Horton and Horton, *In Hope of Liberty*, 244–46. Americans protested the freeing of the slaves; a claims commission awarded compensation to the slaveowners in 1853.

[46] Harrold in *Abolitionists and the South* argues for strong and continuous support by abolitionists of slave escapes and rescuers, from the early 1830s onward, in contrast to Larry Gara, who portrayed most abolitionists as largely indifferent to rescues and the underground railroad in *The Liberty Line: The Underground Railroad*. Merton Dillon sees abolitionists shifting toward embracing slaves as allies in the wake of the shipboard risings on the *Amistad* and *Creole* in 1839 and 1841, in *Slavery Attacked*, 201–23.

[47] Stanley Harrold, "John Brown's Forerunners: Slave Rescue Attempts and the Abolitionists, 1841–1851," *Radical History Review*, 55 (1989): 92, 97, and *Subversives*,

64–93; Joseph C. Lovejoy, *Memoir of Charles T. Torrey* (Boston, 1847; repr., New York, Negro Universities Press, 1969); Thomas Smallwood, *A Narrative of Thomas Smallwood* (Toronto, 1851).

⁴⁸ See Lovejoy, *Memoir of Charles T. Torrey*, 287–301.

⁴⁹ Harrold, "John Brown's Forerunners," 94.

⁵⁰ Harrold, *Subversives*, 96, 106–7, 211–19; Still, *Underground Railroad*, 182–86.

⁵¹ Daniel Drayton, *Personal Memoir of Daniel Drayton* (Boston, 1855), 20–23. The description of Drayton as a "soldier of fortune" is from Stanley Harrold, "John Brown's Forerunners," 89–110, quote from p. 93. See also Harrold, *Subversives*, 116–45.

⁵² Drayton, *Personal Memoir*, 25–38. The prosecution was led by Philip Barton Key, son of the author of *The Star-Spangled Banner*.

⁵³ Still, *Underground Railroad*, 165–72.

⁵⁴ Bogger, *Free Blacks in Norfolk, Virginia*, 164, quoting an 1854 article in the Norfolk *Argus*.

⁵⁵ See Still, *Underground Railroad*, 150–52, 165–72.

⁵⁶ *Narrative of the Facts in the Case of Passmore Williamson* (Philadelphia: Pennsylvania Abolition Society, 1855).

⁵⁷ Harrold, "John Brown's Forerunners," 104.

⁵⁸ Freehling, *Road to Disunion*, 93–95, 502–5.

⁵⁹ See ibid., especially 93–95, 502–7.

⁶⁰ *Laws of Maryland*, 1798, Resolution no. 43.

⁶¹ *Mr. Nicholson's Motion, referred to a committee in the House of Reps, on January 22, 1801*, pamphlet, American Antiquarian Society, Worcester, Mass.

⁶² Laws of Maryland, 1816, Resolution no. 68; 1817, Resolution no. 43; 1820, Resolution no. 28; 1821, Resolution no. 53; 1822, Resolution no. 58. Julie Winch, "Philadelphia and the Other Underground Railroad," *Pennsylvania Magazine of History and Biography*, 111 (1987): 1–25; Paul Finkelman, "Prigg v. Pennsylvania and Northern State Courts: Anti-Slavery Use of a Pro-Slavery Decision," *Civil War History*, 25 (1979): 5–35.

⁶³ Finkelman, "Prigg v. Pennsylvania," 7–21.

⁶⁴ Freehling, *Road to Disunion*, 499–501; Shade, *Democratizing the Old Dominion*, 256–259.

⁶⁵ Gerald Eggert, "The Impact of the Fugitive Slave Law on Harrisburg: A Case Study," *Pennsylvania Magazine of History and Biography*, 109 (1985): 537–69; Elwood L. Bridner, Jr., "The Fugitive Slaves of Maryland," *Maryland Historical Magazine*, 66 (1970): 33–50.

⁶⁶ See Shirk, "Testing the Limits of Tolerance," 47–49.

⁶⁷ Thomas P. Slaughter's *Bloody Dawn: The Christiana Riot and Racial Violence in the Antebellum North* (New York: Oxford University Press, 1991) offers a stimulating and comprehensive treatment of the incident. Also see W. U. Hensel, *The Christiana Riot and the Treason Trials of 1851: An Historical Sketch*, 2nd ed. (Lancaster, Pa., 1911).

[68] Slaughter, *Bloody Dawn*, 28–29.

[69] Whitman, *Price of Freedom*, 51–52, 102–9, 156.

[70] William Parker, "The Freedman's Story. In Two Parts," *The Atlantic Monthly*, 17 (1866): 152–66 and 276–95; electronic edition, University of North Carolina at Chapel Hill, metalab.unc.edu/docsouth/parker.

[71] Parker, "The Freedman's Story," 285.

[72] Slaughter, *Bloody Dawn*, 104–5.

[73] See Ibid., 112–38 for an analysis of the trial.

[74] Still, *Underground Railroad*, 551–55.

[75] Burns had escaped from a Virginia slave owner. When Boston antislaveryites threatened violence to prevent Burns's rendition, President Franklin Pierce dispatched a navy cruiser and federal troops to Boston to underline his determination to enforce the Fugitive Slave Law. Burns was returned to Virginia, but subsequently became free when supporters purchased and freed him from his master. See Albert J. Von Frank, *The Trials of Anthony Burns: Freedom and Slavery in Emerson's Boston* (Cambridge: Harvard University Press, 1998).

[76] Horton and Horton, *In Hope of Liberty*, 257.

Chapter 8: Civil War and the Destruction of Slavery

[1] Ira Berlin provides an overview of the free black experience in the 1850s in *Slaves without Masters*, 343–81. For Virginia, see Shade, *Democratizing the Old Dominion*, 262–91; Lynda J. Morgan, *Emancipation in Virginia's Tobacco Belt, 1850–1870* (Athens: University of Georgia Press, 1992), 1–78; Midori Takagi, *"Rearing Wolves to Our Own Destruction": Slavery in Richmond, Virginia, 1782–1865* (Charlottesville: University Press of Virginia, 1999), 71–123; and, Jordan, *Black Confederates*, 1–68. For Maryland, Barbara Jeanne Fields, *Slavery and Freedom on the Middle Ground: Maryland during the Nineteenth Century* (New Haven: Yale University Press, 1985), 90–130; Phillips, *Freedom's Port*, 177–210; and, Jean Baker, *The Politics of Continuity: Maryland Politics from 1858 to 1870* (Baltimore: Johns Hopkins University Press, 1973), 1–47. For Delaware, Williams, *Slavery and Freedom in Delaware*, 185–218, and Essah, *A House Divided*, 108–86. For Washington, D.C., Harrold, *Subversives*.

[2] William A. Link, *Roots of Secession: Slavery and Politics in Antebellum Virginia* (Chapel Hill: University of North Carolina Press, 2003), 51–61, 100. William Oakes, *Slavery and Freedom: An Interpretation of the Old South* (New York: Alfred A. Knopf, 1990), 181.

[3] William A. Link "The Jordan Hatcher Case: Politics and 'A Spirit of Insubordination' in Antebellum Virginia," *Journal of Southern History*, 64 (1998): 615–48, reprised in Link, *Roots of Secession*, 80–89; Shane White and Graham White, *The Sounds of Slavery: Discovering African American History through Song, Sermons, and Speech* (Boston: Beacon Press, 2005), 168–86.

[4] Berlin, *Slaves without Masters*, 360–61.

[5] Phillips, *Freedom's Port*, 224–25; Berlin, *Slaves without Masters*, 356–58.

[6] Richard Morris, "Labor Controls in Maryland in the Nineteenth Century," *Journal of Southern History*, 14 (1948): 385–400.

[7] Phillips, *Freedom's Port*, 199.

[8] Frank Towers, "Job Busting at Baltimore Shipyards: Racial Violence in the Civil War–Era South," *Journal of Southern History*, 66 (2000): 221–56.

[9] Williams, *Slavery and Freedom in Delaware*, 196–97.

[10] Berlin, *Slaves without Masters*, 345–47.

[11] Patricia Hickin, "John C. Underwood and the Antislavery Movement in Virginia, 1847–1860," *Virginia Magazine of History and Biography*, 73 (1965): 156–68; George Winston Smith, "Antebellum Attempts of Northern Business Interests to 'Redeem' the Upper South," *Journal of Southern History*, 11 (1945): 177–213; James Redpath, *The Roving Editor: or Talks with Slaves in the Southern States* (New York, 1859), 227; Link, *Roots of Secession*, 162–65.

[12] See Charles B. Dew, "Black Ironworkers and the Slave Insurrection Panic of 1856," *Journal of Southern History*, 41 (1975): 321–37.

[13] Link, *Roots of Secession*, 110–19.

[14] See Kenneth M. Stampp, *America in 1857: A Nation on the Brink* (New York: Oxford University Press, 1992).

[15] Berlin, *Slaves without Masters*, 351–52.

[16] Ibid., 369–70; Link, *Roots of Secession*, 138–44, 145–57.

[17] Fields, *Slavery and Freedom on the Middle Ground*, 71–82.

[18] The counties voting on the 1860 re-enslavement referendum were: Baltimore, Calvert, Charles, Howard, Kent, Prince George's, Queen Anne's, Somerset, St. Mary's, Talbot, and Worcester. Jeffrey R. Brackett, *The Negro in Maryland: A Study of the Institution of Slavery* (1889; repr., Freeport, N.Y.: Books for Libraries Press, 1969), 260–62.

[19] Phillips, *Freedom's Port*, 204–9, 232–34.

[20] For a biography of Brown, see Stephen B. Oates, *To Purge This Land with Blood: A Biography of John Brown* (Amherst: University of Massachusetts Press, 1984). Russell Banks's *Cloudsplitter* (New York: Harper Collins, 1999) treats Brown in an historical novel.

[21] Redpath, *The Roving Editor*, 11–15.

[22] Berlin, *Slaves without Masters*, 375.

[23] See www.multied.com/elections/1860Pop.html for state-by-state totals for each candidate. Breckinridge's margin of victory was 722 votes out of more than 90,000 cast in Maryland. Bell won Virginia by 156 votes out of 166,000 cast.

[24] Quoted in Fields, *Slavery and Freedom on the Middle Ground*, 114.

[25] See Ira Berlin, Barbara J. Fields, Thavolia Glymph, Joseph P. Reidy, and Leslie S. Rowland, eds., *Freedom: A Documentary History of Emancipation, 1861–1867*, Series I,

Volume I, *The Destruction of Slavery* (Cambridge: Harvard University Press, 1985), 159–67; William C. Harris, *With Charity for All: Lincoln and the Restoration of the Union* (Lexington: University Press of Kentucky, 1997), 33–57; Eric Foner, *Reconstruction: America's Unfinished Revolution, 1863–1877* (New York: Harper Collins, 1988), 17.

[26] Otis K. Rice, *West Virginia: A History* (Lexington: University Press of Kentucky, 1985), 99–153; Richard O. Curry, *A House Divided: A Study of Statehood Politics and the Copperhead Movement in West Virginia* (Pittsburgh: University of Pittsburgh Press, 1964), 69–105; Milton Gerofsky, "Reconstruction in West Virginia, Part I," *West Virginia History,* 6 (1945): 295–360; John Alexander Williams, "The New Dominion and the Old: Ante-Bellum and Statehood Politics as the Background of West Virginia's 'Bourbon Democracy,'" *West Virginia History,* 33 (1972): 317–407; Harris, *With Charity for All,* 18–24.

[27] See Harris, *Charity for All,* 100–103, 161–70.

[28] Berlin et al., eds., *Freedom: The Destruction of Slavery,* 46–47.

[29] Williams, *Slavery and Freedom in Delaware,* 173–76; Essah, *A House Divided,* 153–90.

[30] The First Confiscation Act passed in August 1861; the ban on returning fugitive slaves took effect in March 1862; the Second Confiscation Act became law in July 1862.

[31] Fields, *Slavery and Freedom on the Middle Ground,* 90–130, emphasizes black agency in achieving emancipation in Maryland. For an account that stresses white political activity, see Charles Lewis Wagandt, *The Mighty Revolution: Negro Emancipation in Maryland, 1862–1864* (1964; repr., Baltimore: Maryland Historical Society, 2005), passim.

[32] Fields, *Slavery and Freedom on the Middle Ground,* 111.

[33] *New York World,* April 15, 1862, quoted in Baker, *Politics of Continuity,* 80.

[34] Ira Berlin, et al., *Black Military Experience,* 200–202.

[35] Ibid., 184–87.

[36] *Cecil Whig,* February 6, 1864, quoted in Fields, *Slavery and Freedom on the Middle Ground,* 129.

[37] Baker, *Politics of Continuity,* 77–110, Wagandt, *Mighty Revolution,* 133–245, Fields, *Slavery and Freedom on the Middle Ground,* 90–130.

[38] See Richard Paul Fuke, *Imperfect Equality: African Americans and the Confines of White Racial Attitudes in Postemancipation Maryland* (New York: Fordham University Press, 1999), for a discussion of post-emancipation struggles in Maryland.

[39] Accounts of Afro-Virginians during the Civil War include Jordan, *Black Confederates and Afro-Yankees*; Morgan, *Emancipation in Virginia's Tobacco Belt*; Robert F. Engs, *Freedom's First Generation: Black Hampton, Virginia, 1861–1890* (Philadelphia: University of Pennsylvania Press, 1979), and Berlin, et al., *Documentary History of Emancipation,* Series 1, Volume 1, 57–101, and Series 1, Volume 2, 83–240.

[40] Charles L. Perdue Jr., Thomas E. Barden, and Robert K. Phillips et al., eds., *Wee-*

vils in the Wheat: Interviews with Virginia Ex-Slaves (Bloomington: Indiana University Press, 1980), 228.

[41] Joseph Reidy, "Coming From the Shadow of the Past: The Transition from Slavery to Freedom at Freedmen's Village, 1863–1900," *Virginia Magazine of History and Biography,* 95 (1987): 403–28.

[42] See Berlin et al., *Freedom: The Destruction of Slavery,* 70–73, and 91; Jordan, *Black Confederates,* 81–83.

[43] Wilder quotes from testimony before the American Freedman's Inquiry Commission, May 9, 1863, in Berlin et al., *The Destruction of Slavery,* 88–90; Jordan, *Black Confederates,* 71–72, 85–87.

[44] Berlin et al., *The Black Military Experience,* 114–15.

[45] Jordan, *Black Confederates and Afro-Yankees,* 271.

[46] Sylvia Frey describes the Revolutionary War in the South thus, in *Water from the Rock.*

[47] For black body servants in the armies, see Jordan, *Black Confederates and Afro-Yankees,* 185–201; for a general discussion of black labor in Confederate Virginia, Morgan, *Emancipation in Virginia's Tobacco Belt,* 89–103.

[48] Ulysses S. Grant, *Personal Memoirs of U.S. Grant* (New York, 1885–1886), 2:501, quoted in Morgan, *Emancipation in Virginia's Tobacco Belt,* 87.

[49] See Charles B. Dew, *Ironmaker to the Confederacy: Joseph R. Anderson and the Tredegar Iron Works* (New Haven: Yale University Press, 1966); Morgan, *Emancipation in Virginia's Tobacco Belt,* 97.

[50] Diary of Lucy Rebecca Buck, quoted in Jordan, *Black Confederates and Afro-Yankees,* 201.

[51] Morgan, *Emancipation in Virginia's Tobacco Belt,* 100–104, 119.

[52] Jordan, *Black Confederates and Afro-Yankees,* 217–32.

[53] Ibid., 237–43.

[54] Berlin, et al., *The Destruction of Slavery,* 68, 339; Jordan, *Black Confederates and Afro-Yankees,* 267.

Bibliography

Books, Articles, and Dissertations from the
Twentieth and Twenty-first Centuries

Almendinger, David F. Jr. "The Construction of *The Confessions of Nat Turner.*" In *Nat Turner: A Slave Rebellion in History and Memory*, edited by Kenneth S. Greenberg, 24–42. Oxford and New York: Oxford University Press, 2003.

Ames, Susie M. *Studies of the Virginia Eastern Shore in the Seventeenth Century.* Richmond: The Dietz Press, 1940.

Andrews, Dee E. *The Methodists and Revolutionary America, 1760–1800: The Shaping of an Evangelical Culture.* Princeton: Princeton University Press, 2000.

Andrews, William L., ed. *Sisters of the Spirit: Three Black Women's Autobiographies of the Nineteenth Century.* Bloomington: University of Indiana Press, 1986.

Aptheker, Herbert, ed. *A Documentary History of the Negro People in the United States.* New York: Citadel Press, 1951.

Baker, Jean H. *The Politics of Continuity: Maryland Politics from 1858 to 1870.* Baltimore: Johns Hopkins University Press, 1973.

Bancroft, Frederic. *Slave Trading in the Old South.* Baltimore: J. H. Furst Company, 1931.

Banks, Russell. *Cloudsplitter.* New York: Harper Collins, 1999.

Banks, Willa. "A Contradiction in Antebellum Baltimore: A Competitive School for Girls of 'Color' within a Slave State." *Maryland Historical Magazine,* 99 (2004): 133–63.

Bell, Howard. *A Survey of the Negro Convention Movement, 1830–1861.* New York: Arno Press, 1969.

Berlin, Ira. *Many Thousands Gone: The First Two Centuries of Slavery in America.* Cambridge, Mass.: Harvard University Press, 1998.

———. *Slaves without Masters: The Free Negro in the Antebellum South.* New York: Pantheon Books, 1974.

Berlin, Ira, Barbara Jeanne Fields, Thavolia Glymph, Joseph P. Reidy, and Leslie S. Rowland, eds. *Freedom: A Documentary History of Emancipation, 1861–1867.* Series I, Volume I, *The Destruction of Slavery.* Cambridge: Harvard University Press, 1985.

Billings, Warren M. "The Law of Servants and Slaves in Seventeenth Century Virginia." *Virginia Magazine of History and Biography,* 99 (1991): 45–62.

Blight, David W. ed. *Passages to Freedom: The Underground Railroad in History and Memory*. Washington, D.C.: Smithsonian Books, 2004.

Bogger, Tommy L. *Free Blacks in Norfolk, Virginia 1790–1860: The Darker Side of Freedom*. Charlottesville: University Press of Virginia, 1997.

Boles, John. "Tension in a Slave Society: The Trial of Reverend Jacob Gruber." *Southern Studies*, 18 (1979): 179–97.

Boulton, Alexander O. "The American Paradox: Jeffersonian Equality and Racial Science." *American Quarterly*, 47 (1995): 467–92.

Boyd, Melba Joyce. *Discarded Legacy: Politics and Poetics in the Life of Frances E. W. Harper 1825–1911*. Detroit: Wayne St. University Press, 1994.

Breen, T. H. and Stephen Innes. *"Myne Owne Ground": Race and Freedom on Virginia's Eastern Shore, 1640–1676*. New York: Oxford University Press, 2004.

Bridner, Elwood L. "The Fugitive Slaves of Maryland." *Maryland Historical Magazine*, 66 (1970): 33–50.

———. "Joseph E. Snodgrass and Freedom of the Press in Antebellum Maryland." *Maryland Historical Magazine*, 92 (2003).

Brown, Kathleen M. *Good Wives, Nasty Wenches, and Anxious Patriarchs: Race, Gender, and Power in Colonial Virginia*. Chapel Hill: University of North Carolina Press, 1996.

Burin, Eric. *Slavery and the Peculiar Solution: A History of the American Colonization Society*. Gainesville: University Press of Florida, 2005.

Calderhead, William L. "How Extensive Was the Border State Slave Trade?: A New Look." In *Slave Trade and Migration*, edited by Paul Finkleman, 42–55. New York: Garland Press, 1989.

———. "The Role of the Professional Slave Trader in a Slave Economy: Austin Woolfolk, a Case Study." *Civil War History*, 23 (1977): 195–211.

———. "Slavery in Maryland in the Age of the Revolution, 1775–1790." *Maryland Historical Magazine*, 98 (2003).

Calvert, Monte. "The Abolition Society of Delaware, 1801–1807." *Delaware History*, 10 (1963): 295–321.

Campbell, Penelope. *Maryland in Africa: The Maryland State Colonization Society, 1831–1857*. Urbana: University of Illinois Press, 1971.

Carey, Charles W. Jr. "'These Black Rascals': The Origins of Lord Dunmore's Ethiopian Regiment." *Virginia Social Science Journal*, 31 (1996): 65–77.

Carroll, Kenneth. "An Eighteenth Century Episcopalian Attack on Quaker and Methodist Manumission of Slaves." *Maryland Historical Magazine*, 80 (1985).

———. "Maryland Quakers and Slavery. *Quaker History*, 72 (1983): 27–42.

———. "Religious Influences on Manumission of Slaves in Caroline, Dorchester, and Talbot Counties." *Maryland Historical Magazine*, 56 (1961): 176–97.

Cassell, Frank A. "Slaves of the Chesapeake Bay Area and the War of 1812." *Journal of Negro History*, 57 (1972): 144–55.

Catterall, Helen. *Judicial Cases Concerning American Slavery and the Negro.* Washington, D.C.: Carnegie Institution, 1936.

Clinton, Catherine. *Harriet Tubman: The Road to Freedom.* New York and Boston: Little, Brown and Co., 2004.

Condon, John Joseph Jr. "Manumission, Slavery, and Family in the Post Revolutionary Rural Chesapeake: Anne Arundel County, Maryland, 1781–1831." Ph.D. dissertation, University of Minnesota, 2001.

Conkin, Paul Keith. *Prophets of Prosperity: America's First Political Economists.* Bloomington: Indiana University Press, 1980.

Conrad, Earl. *Harriet Tubman.* Washington, D.C.: Associated Publishers, 1943.

Curry, Richard O. *A House Divided: A Study of Statehood Politics and the Copperhead Movement in West Virginia.* Pittsburgh: University of Pittsburgh Press, 1964.

Cushing, John D. "The Cushing Court and the Abolition of Slavery in Massachusetts: More Notes on the 'Quock Walker Case.'" *American Journal of Legal History,* 5 (1961): 118–44.

Daniel, W. Harrison. "Virginia Baptists and the Negro in the Early Republic." *Virginia Magazine of History and Biography,* 80 (1972): 59–69.

Davis, David Brion. *The Problem of Slavery in the Age of Revolution, 1770–1823.* Ithaca: Cornell University Press, 1975.

Davis, David Brion. *The Problem of Slavery in Western Culture.* Ithaca: Cornell University Press, 1966

Deal, J. Douglas. "A Constricted World: Free Blacks on Virginia's Eastern Shore, 1680–1750." In *Colonial Chesapeake Society,* edited by Lois Carr, Philip D. Morgan, and Jean B. Russo. Chapel Hill: University of North Carolina Press, 1988.

———. *Race and Class in Colonial Virginia: Indians, Africans, and Englishmen on the Eastern Shore of Virginia during the Seventeenth Century.* New York: Garland, 1993.

Charles B. Dew. "Black Ironworkers and the Slave Insurrection Panic of 1856." *Journal of Southern History,* 41 (1975): 321–37.

———. *Ironmaker to the Confederacy: Joseph R. Anderson and the Tredegar Iron Works.* New Haven: Yale University Press, 1966.

Dillon, Merton. *Benjamin Lundy and the Struggle for Negro Freedom.* Urbana: University of Illinois Press, 1966.

———. *Slavery Attacked: Southern Slaves and Their Allies, 1619–1865.* Baton Rouge: Louisiana State University Press, 1990.

Doyle, Christopher. "Judge St. George Tucker and the Case of *Tom* vs. *Roberts*: Blunting the Revolution's Radicalism from Virginia's District Courts." *Virginia Magazine of History and Biography,* 106 (1998): 419–442.

Egerton, Douglas R. "Averting a Crisis: The Proslavery Critique of the American Colonization Society." *Civil War History,* 43 (1997).

———. "Black Independence Struggles and the Tale of Two Revolutions: A Review Essay." *Journal of Southern History,* 64 (1998): 98–116.

————. *Charles Fenton Mercer and the Trial of National Conservatism.* Jackson: University Press of Mississippi, 1989.

————. *Gabriel's Rebellion: The Virginia Slave Conspiracies of 1800–1802.* Chapel Hill: University of North Carolina Press, 1993.

Eggert, Gerald. "The Impact of the Fugitive Slave Law on Harrisburg: A Case Study." *Pennsylvania Magazine of History and Biography,* 109 (1985): 537–69;

Eltis, David. *The Rise of African Slavery in the Americas.* Cambridge, U.K.: Cambridge University Press, 2000.

————. "Europeans and the Rise and Fall of African Slavery in the Americas." *American Historical Review,* 98 (1993): 1399–1423.

Ely, Melvin Patrick. *Israel on the Appomattox: A Southern Experiment in Black Freedom from the 1790s through the Civil War.* New York: Alfred A. Knopf, 2004.

Engs, Robert F. *Freedom's First Generation: Black Hampton, Virginia, 1861–1890.* Philadelphia: University of Pennsylvania Press, 1979.

Eslinger, Ellen. "Liberation in a Rural Context: The Valley of Virginia, 1800–1860." Paper presented at "From Slavery to Freedom: Manumission in the Atlantic World," Charleston, S.C., October 4–7, 2000.

Essah, Patience. *A House Divided: Slavery and Emancipation in Delaware, 1638–1865.* Charlottesville: University Press of Virginia, 1996.

Fields, Barbara Jeanne. *Slavery and Freedom on the Middle Ground: Maryland during the Nineteenth Century.* New Haven: Yale University Press, 1985.

Finkelman, Paul. "Jefferson and Slavery: Treason against the Hopes of the World." In *Jeffersonian Legacies,* edited by Peter S. Onuf, 181–224. Charlottesville: University Press of Virginia, 1993.

————. "Prigg v. Pennsylvania and Northern State Courts: Anti-Slavery Use of a Pro-Slavery Decision." *Civil War History,* 25 (1979): 5–35.

————, ed. *Slave Trade and Migration.* New York: Garland Press, 1989.

————, ed. *Slavery and the Founders: Race and Liberty in the Age of Jefferson.* Armonk, N.Y.: M. E. Sharpe, 1996.

Finnie, Gordon. "The Anti-Slavery Movement in the Upper South Before 1840." *Journal of Southern History,* 35 (1969): 319–342.

Foner, Eric. *Reconstruction: America's Unfinished Revolution, 1863–1877.* New York: Harper Collins, 1988.

Franklin, John Hope, and Loren Schweninger. *Runaway Slaves: Rebels on the Plantation.* New York: Oxford University Press, 1999.

Fredrickson, George M. *The Black Image in the White Mind: The Debate on Afro-American Character and Destiny, 1817–1914.* New York: Harper & Row, 1971.

Freehling, Alison, *Drift Toward Dissolution: The Virginia Slavery Debate of 1831–32.* Baton Rouge: Louisiana State University Press, 1982.

Freehling, William W. *The Reinterpretation of American History.* New York: Oxford University Press, 1994.

————. *The Reintegration of American History: Slavery and the Civil War.* New York: Oxford University Press, 1994.

————. *The Road to Disunion: Secessionists at Bay, 1776–1854.* Oxford: Oxford University Press, 1990.

Frey, Sylvia. "Between Slavery and Freedom: Virginia Blacks in the American Revolution." *Journal of Southern History,* 49 (1983): 375–98.

————. *Water from the Rock: Black Resistance in a Revolutionary Age.* Princeton: Princeton University Press, 1991.

Frey, Sylvia R. and Betty Wood. *Come Shouting to Zion: African American Protestantism in the American South and British Caribbean to 1830.* Chapel Hill: University of North Carolina Press, 1998.

Fuke, Richard Paul. *Imperfect Equality: African Americans and the Confines of White Racial Attitudes in Postemancipation Maryland.* New York: Fordham University Press, 1999.

Fulop, Timothy E., and Albert J. Raboteau, eds. *African-American Religion: Interpretive Essays in History and Culture.* New York: Routledge, 1997.

Gara, Larry. *The Liberty Line: The Legend of the Underground Railroad.* 1961; repr. Lexington: University Press of Kentucky, 1996.

Gardner, Bettye. "The Free Blacks of Baltimore." Ph.D. dissertation, George Washington University, 1973.

————. "Opposition to Emigration: A Selected Letter of William Watkins (The Colored Baltimorean)." *Journal of Negro History,* 67 (1982): 155–58.

————. "William Watkins: Antebellum Black Teacher and Anti-slavery Writer." *Negro History Bulletin,* 39 (1976): 623–25.

George, Carol. *Segregated Sabbaths.* Oxford: Oxford University Press, 1980.

George, Christopher T. "Mirage of Freedom: African Americans in the War of 1812." *Maryland Historical Magazine,* 91 (1996): 426–50.

Gerofsky, Milton. "Reconstruction in West Virginia, Part I." *West Virginia History,* 6 (1945): 295–360.

Gilje, Paul A. "The Baltimore Riots of 1812 and the Breakdown of the Anglo-American Mob Tradition." *Journal of Social History,* 13 (1980): 547–64.

————. "'Le Menu Peuple' in America: Identifying the Mob in the Baltimore Riots of 1812." *Maryland Historical Magazine,* 80 (1985): 50–66.

Glickstein, Jonathan. *Concepts of Free Labor in Antebellum America.* New Haven: Yale University Press, 1991.

Grant, John N. "Black Immigrants Immigrants into Nova Scotia, 1776–1815." *Journal of Negro History,* 58 (1973): 253–70.

Gravely, Will B. "Rise of African Churches in America (1786–1822)." *Journal of Religious Thought,* 14 (1984): 315–32.

Greene, Jack P. *Pursuits of Happiness: The Social Development of Early Modern Brit-*

ish Colonies and the Formation of American Culture. Chapel Hill: University of North Carolina Press, 1988.

Hall, Richard L. *On Afric's Shore: A History of Maryland in Liberia, 1834–1857.* Baltimore: Maryland Historical Society, 2003.

Hall, Robert L. "Slave Resistance in Baltimore City and County, 1747–1790." *Maryland Historical Magazine,* 84 (1989): 305–18.

Hamilton, Philip. "Revolutionary Principles and Family Loyalties: Slavery's Transformation in the St. George Tucker Household of Early National Virginia." *William and Mary Quarterly,* 55 (1998): 531–56.

Harris, William C. *With Charity for All: Lincoln and the Restoration of the Union.* Lexington: University Press of Kentucky, 1997

Harrold, Stanley. *Abolitionists and the South: 1831–1861.* Lexington: University Press of Kentucky, 1995.

———. "John Brown's Forerunners: Slave Rescue Attempts and the Abolitionists, 1841–1851." *Radical History Review,* 55 (1989): 92, 97,

———. *Subversives: Antislavery Community in Washington, D.C., 1828–1865.* Baton Rouge: Louisiana State University Press, 2003.

Hensel, W. U. *The Christiana Riot and the Treason Trials of 1851: An Historical Sketch.* Second edition. Lancaster, Pa., 1911.

Herring, Todd A. "Kidnapped and Sold in Natchez: The Ordeal of Aaron Cooper, a Free Black Man." *Journal of Mississippi History,* 60 (1998): 341–53.

Heyrman, Christine. *Southern Cross: The Beginnings of the Bible Belt.* Chapel Hill: University of North Carolina Press, 1998.

Hickin, Patricia. "Gentle Agitator: Samuel M. Janney and the Antislavery Movement in Virginia, 1842–1851," *Journal of Southern History,* 37 (1971).

———. "John C. Underwood and the Antislavery Movement in Virginia, 1847–1860." *Virginia Magazine of History and Biography,* 73 (1965): 156–68.

Hirschfeld, Fritz. *George Washington and Slavery: A Documentary Portrayal.* Columbia: University of Missouri Press, 1997, 21–29.

Hodges, Graham Russell. *Root and Branch: African Americans in New York and East Jersey, 1613–1863.* Chapel Hill: University of North Carolina Press, 1999.

———. *Slavery and Freedom in the Rural North: African Americans in Monmouth County, New Jersey, 1665–1865.* Madison, Wis.: Madison House, 1996.

Hoffman, Ronald. *A Spirit of Dissension: Economics, Politics, and the Revolution in Maryland.* Baltimore: Johns Hopkins University Press, 1973.

Holton, Woody. *Forced Founders.* Chapel Hill: University of North Carolina Press, 1999.

———. "'Rebel Against Rebel': Enslaved Virginians and the Coming of the American Revolution." *Virginia Magazine of History and Biography,* 105 (1997): 157–92.

Hopkins, Leroy T. "Black Eldorado on the Susquehanna: The Emergence of Black Columbia, 1726–1861," *Journal of the Lancaster County Historical Society,* 89 (1985), 110–31.

————. "The Negro Entry Book: A Document of Lancaster City's Antebellum Afro-American Community." *Journal of the Lancaster County Historical Society,* 88 (1984): 142–75

Horn, James, *Adapting to a New World: English Society in the Seventeenth-Century Chesapeake.* Chapel Hill: University North Carolina Press, 1994.

Horton, James Oliver and Lois E. Horton. *In Hope of Liberty: Culture, Community, and Protest among Northern Free Blacks, 1700–1860.* Oxford: Oxford University Press, 1997.

Horwitz, Tony. "Urban Confessions." *The New Yorker,* December 13, 1999, 80–89.

Hudson, Larry, E. *To Have and To Hold: Slave Work and Family in Antebellum South Carolina.* Athens: University of Georgia, 1997.

Hutchinson, Earl Ofari. *"Let Your Motto be Resistance": The Life and Thought of Henry Highland Garnet.* Boston: Beacon Press, 1972.

Jackson, Luther P. "Manumission in Certain Virginia Cities." *Journal of Negro History,* 15 (1930): 278–314.

————. "Virginia Negro Soldiers and Seamen in the American Revolution." *Journal of Negro History,* 28 (1942): 250–52.

Jervey, Edward D. and C. Harold Huber. "The *Creole* Affair." *Journal of Negro History,* 65 (1980): 196–211.

Johnson, Curtis D. *Redeeming America: Evangelicals and the Road to Civil War.* New York: Ivan R. Dee, 1990.

Jones, Howard. *Mutiny on the Amistad: The Saga of a Slave Revolt and Its Impact on American Abolition, Law, and Diplomacy.* Oxford: Oxford University Press, 1986.

————. "The Peculiar Institution and National Honor: The Case of the *Creole* Slave Revolt." *Civil War History,* 21 (1975): 28–50.

Jordan, Ervin L. *Black Confederates and Afro-Yankees in Civil War Virginia.* Charlottesville: University Press of Virginia, 1995.

Kachun, Mitch. *Festivals of Freedom: Memory and Meaning in African American Emancipation Celebrations, 1808–1915.* Amherst and Boston: University of Massachusetts Press, 2003.

Kaminski, John P., ed. *A Necessary Evil?: Slavery and the Debate Over the Constitution.* Madison, Wis.: Madison House, 1995, 187–88.

Kaplan, Sidney, and Emma Nogrady Kaplan. *The Black Presence in the Era of the American Revolution.* Revised edition. Amherst: University of Massachusetts Press, 1989.

Katz, William L., ed. *Five Slave Narratives.* New York: Arno Press, 1969.

Kerber, Linda K. *Women of the Republic: Intellect and Ideology in Revolutionary America.* Chapel Hill: University of North Carolina Press, 1980.

Kimber, Edward. "Eighteenth-Century Maryland as Portrayed in the 'Itinerant Observations' of Edward Kimber." *Maryland Historical Magazine,* 51 (1956): 327–28.

Kimmel, Ross. "Free Blacks in Seventeenth-Century Maryland." *Maryland Historical Magazine*, 71 (1976): 19–25.

Klein, Herbert S. *Slavery in the Americas: A Comparative Study of Virginia and Cuba.* Chicago: University of Chicago Press, 1967.

Klein, Rachel N. *Unification of a Slave State: The Rise of the Planter Class in the South Carolina Backcountry, 1760–1808.* Chapel Hill: University of North Carolina Press, 1990.

Konig, David T. "'Dale's Laws' and the Non-Common Law Origins of Criminal Justice in Virginia." *American Journal of Legal History*, 26 (1982).

Kulikoff, Allan. *Tobacco and Slaves: The Development of Southern Cultures in the Chesapeake, 1680–1800.* Chapel Hill: University North Carolina Press, 1986.

Landers Jane. *Black Society in Spanish Florida.* Urbana: University of Illinois Press, 1999.

Larson, Kate Clifford. *Bound for the Promised Land: Harriet Tubman˗Portrait of an American Hero.* New York: One World–Ballantine Books, 2004.

Levy, Andrew. *First Emancipator: The Forgotten Story of Robert Carter, the Founding Father Who Freed His Slaves.* New York: Random House, 2005.

Libby, Jean, ed. *From Slavery to Salvation: The Autobiography of Rev. Thomas W. Henry of the A.M.E. Church.* Jackson: University Press of Mississippi, 1994.

Link, William A. "The Jordan Hatcher Case: Politics and 'A Spirit of Insubordination' in Antebellum Virginia." *Journal of Southern History*, 64 (1998): 615–48.

Link, William A. *Roots of Secession: Slavery and Politics in Antebellum Virginia.* Chapel Hill: University of North Carolina Press, 2003.

Lyerly, Cynthia. "Religion, Gender, and Identity: Black Methodist Women in a Slave Society, 1770–1810." In *Discovering the Women in Slavery: Emancipating Perspectives on the American Past,* edited by Patricia Morton. Athens: University of Georgia Press, 1996.

MacLeod, Duncan. *Slavery, Race, and the American Revolution.* Cambridge, U.K.: Cambridge University Press, 1974.

MacMaster, Richard K. "Liberty or Property? The Methodists' Petition for Emancipation in Virginia, 1785." *Methodist History*, 10 (1971).

Mason, Matthew E. "Slavery Overshadowed: Congress Debates Prohibiting the Atlantic Slave Trade to the United States, 1806–1807." *Journal of the Early Republic*, 20 (2000): 59–82.

Mayer, Henry. *A Son of Thunder: Patrick Henry and the American Republic.* New York and Toronto: Franklin Watts, 1986.

McColley, Robert. *Slavery in Jeffersonian Virginia.* Second edition. Urbana: University of Illinois Press, 1973.

McCormick, Richard P. "William Whipper: Moral Reformer." *Pennsylvania History*, 43 (1976): 23–48.

McCoy, Drew R. *The Elusive Republic: Political Economy in Jeffersonian America.* Chapel Hill: University of North Carolina Press, 1980.

————. *The Last of the Fathers: James Madison and the Republican Legacy*. Cambridge: Cambridge University Press, 1989.

McDonnell, Michael. "Other Loyalists: A Reconsideration of the Black Loyalist Experience in the American Revolutionary Era." *Southern Historian*, 16 (1995).

McGowan, James A. *Station Master on the Underground Railroad: The Life and Letters of Thomas Garrett*. Moylan, Pa.: Whimsie Press, 1977.

McGraw, Marie Tyler. "Richmond Free Blacks and African Colonization, 1816–1832." *Journal of American Studies*, 21 (1987): 207–24.

McKelvey, Kay. "Early Black Dorchester, 1776–1870: A history of the struggle of African-Americans in Dorchester County, Maryland, to be free to make their own choices." Ph.D. dissertation, University of Maryland, College Park, 1991.

Melish, Joanne Pope. *Disowning Slavery: Gradual Emancipation and "Race" in New England, 1780–1860*. Ithaca: Cornell University Press, 1998.

Merkel, William G. "To See Oneself as a Target of a Justified Revolution: Thomas Jefferson and Gabriel's Uprising." *American Nineteenth Century History*, 4 (2003): 1–31.

Miller, Floyd J. *The Search for a Black Nationality: Black Emigration and Colonization, 1787–1863*. Urbana: University of Illinois Press, 1975.

Miller, M. Sammy. "Patty Cannon: Murderer and Kidnapper of Free Blacks: A Review of the Evidence." *Maryland Historical Magazine*, 72 (1977): 419–23.

Morgan, Edmund S. *American Slavery, American Freedom: The Ordeal of Colonial Virginia*. New York: W. W. Norton, 1975.

Morgan, Lynda. *Emancipation in Virginia's Tobacco Belt, 1850–1870*. Athens: University of Georgia Press, 1992.

Morgan, Philip D. *Slave Counterpoint: Black Culture in the Eighteenth-Century Chesapeake and Lowcountry*. Chapel Hill: University of North Carolina Press, 1998.

Morris, Richard. "Labor Controls in Maryland in the Nineteenth Century." *Journal of Southern History*, 14 (1948): 385–400.

Morris, Thomas D. *Southern Slavery and the Law, 1619–1860*. Chapel Hill: University of North Carolina Press, 1996.

Morrison, Michael. *Slavery and the American West: The Eclipse of Manifest Destiny and the Coming of the Civil War*. Chapel Hill: University of North Carolina Press, 1997.

Morrow, Diane Batts. *Persons of Color and Religious at the Same Time: The Oblate Sisters of Providence, 1828–1860*. Chapel Hill: University of North Carolina Press, 2002.

Moses, Wilson J. *The Golden Age of Black Nationalism*. Oxford: Oxford University Press, 1988.

Nash, Gary B. *Forging Freedom: The Formation of Philadelphia's Black Community, 1720–1840*. Cambridge: Harvard University Press, 1988.

————. "New Light on Richard Allen: The Early Years of Freedom." *William and Mary Quarterly*, 46 (1989): 332–40.

Nash, Gary B. and Jean R. Soderlund. *Freedom by Degrees: Emancipation in Pennsylvania and Its Aftermath*. Oxford: Oxford University Press, 1991.

Nicholls, Michael. "Passing Through This Troublesome World: Free Blacks in the Early Southside." *Virginia Magazine of History and Biography*, 92 (1984).

———. "'The Squint of Freedom': African-American Freedom Suits in Post-Revolutionary Virginia." *Slavery & Abolition*, 20 (1999): 47–62.

———. "Strangers Setting Among Us: The Sources and Challenges of the Urban Free Black Population in Early Virginia." *Virginia Magazine of History and Biography*, 108 (2000).

Oakes, William. *Slavery and Freedom: An Interpretation of the Old South*. New York: Alfred A. Knopf, 1990.

Oates, Stephen B. *To Purge This Land With Blood: A Biography of John Brown*. Amherst: University of Massachusetts Press, 1984.

Oblinger, Carl. "In Recognition of Their Prominence: A Case Study of the Economic and Social Backgrounds of an Ante-Bellum Negro Business and Farming Class in Lancaster County." *Journal of the Lancaster County Historical Society*, 72 (1968): 65–83.

Olwell, Robert. "'Domestick Enemies': Slavery and Political Independence in South Carolina, May 1775–March 1776." *Journal of Southern History*, 55 (1989): 21–48.

Onuf, Peter S. "Every Generation Is and 'Independant Nation': Colonization, Miscegenation, and the Fate of Jefferson's Children." *William and Mary Quarterly*, 67 (2000): 153–70.

———. *Statehood and Union: A History of the Northwest Ordinance*. Bloomington: Indiana University Press, 1987.

———. "'To Declare Them a Free and Independent People': Race, Slavery and National Identity in Jefferson's Thought." *Journal of the Early Republic*, 18 (1998): 1–46.

Papenfuse, Eric Robert. *The Evils of Necessity: Robert Goodloe Harper and the Moral Dilemma of Slavery*. Philadelphia: American Philosophical Society, 1997.

———. "From Redcompense to Revolution: Mahoney v. Ashton and the Transfiguration of Maryland Culture, 1791–1802." *Slavery and Abolition*, 15 (1994).

Parent, Anthony S. Jr. *Foul Means: The Formation of a Slave Society in Virginia, 1660–1740*. Chapel Hill: University of North Carolina Press, 2003.

Parramore, Thomas C. "Covenenat in Jerusalem." In *Nat Turner: A Slave Rebellion in History and Memory*, edited by Kenneth S. Greenberg. Oxford: Oxford University Press, 2003.

Patterson, Orlando. *Freedom: Volume I: Freedom in the Making of Western Culture*. New York: Basic Books, 1991.

———. *Slavery and Social Death: A Comparative Study*. Cambridge: Harvard University Press, 1982.

Perdue, Charles L. Jr., Thomas E. Barden, and Robert K., Phillips, eds. *Weevils in the*

Wheat: Interviews with Virginia Ex-Slaves. Bloomington: Indiana University Press, 1980.

Phillips, Christopher. *Freedom's Port: The African American Community of Baltimore, 1790–1860.* Urbana: University of Illinois Press, 1997.

Porter, Dorothy, ed. *Negro Protest Pamphlets.* New York: Arno Press, 1969.

Quarles, Benjamin. "Lord Dunmore as Liberator." *William and Mary Quarterly,* 15 (1958): 494–507.

———. *The Negro in the American Revolution.* Chapel Hill: University of North Carolina Press, 1961.

Raboteau, Alfred J. "African Americans, Exodus, and the American Israel." In *African American Christianity: Essays in History,* edited by Paul F. Johnson. 1–18. Berkeley: University of California Press, 1994.

———. *Fire in the Bones: Reflections on African-American Religious History.* Boston: Beacon Press, 1995.

———. "Richard Allen and the African Church Movement." In *Black Leaders of the Nineteenth Century,* edited by August Meier and Leon Litwack. Urbana: University of Illinois Press, 1988.

Reed, Harry, *Platform for Change: The Foundations of the Northern Free Black Community, 1775–1865.* East Lansing: Michigan State University Press, 1994.

Reidy, Joseph. "Coming from the Shadow of the Past: The Transition from Slavery to Freedom at Freedmen's Village, 1863–1900." *Virginia Magazine of History and Biography,* 95 (1987): 403–28.

Remini, Robert V. *The Election of Andrew Jackson.* Philadelphia: Lippincott, 1963.

Rice, Otis K. *West Virginia: A History.* Lexington: University Press of Kentucky, 1985.

Ripley, C. Peter, ed. *The Black Abolitionist Papers.* Chapel Hill: University of North Carolina Press, 1991.

Roark, James L. *Masters without Slaves: Southern Planters in the Civil War and Reconstruction.* New York: W. W. Norton, 1977.

Robinson, Donald. *Slavery in the Structure of American Politics.* New York: W. W. Norton & Company, 1971.

Rothbard, Murray N. *The Panic of 1819: Reactions and Policies.* New York: Columbia University Press, 1962.

Russo, Jean Elliott. "'Fifty-Four Days Work of Two Negroes'": Enslaved Labor in Colonial Somerset County Maryland." *Agricultural History,* 78 (2004): 466–92.

Schmidt, Frederika Teute, and Barbara Ripel Wilhelm. "Early Proslavery Petitions in Virginia." *William and Mary Quarterly,* 30 (1973): 133–46.

Schwarz, Philip J. "Gabriel's Challenge: Slaves and Crime in Late Eighteenth-Century Virginia." *Virginia Magazine of History and Biography,* 90 (1982): 283–309.

Schwarz, Philip J. *Migrants Against Slavery: Virginians and the Nation.* Charlottesville: University Press of Virginia, 2001.

————. *Twice Condemned: Slaves and the Criminal Laws of Virginia, 1705–1865.* Baton Rouge: Louisiana State University Press, 1988.

Scott, Julius Sherrard III. "A Common Wind: Currents of Afro-American Communication in the Era of the Haitian Revolution." Ph.D. dissertation, Duke University, 1986.

Scott, Rebecca J. "Exploring the Meaning of Freedom: Post-emancipation Societies in Comparative Perspective." *Hispanic American Historical Review,* 68 (1988): 407–28.

————. *Slave Emancipation in Cuba: The Transition to Free Labor.* Princeton: Princeton University Press, 1985.

Scully, Randolph. "'Somewhat Liberated': Baptist Discourses of Race and Slavery in Nat Turner's Virginia, 1777–1840." Unpublished paper presented at the McNeill Center for Early American Studies, March, 2000.

Sernett, Milton C. *Black Religion and American Evangelicalism.* Metuchen, N.J.: Scarecrow Press, 1975.

Shade, William G. *Democratizing the Old Dominion: Virginia and the Second Party System, 1824–1861.* Charlottesville: University Press of Virginia, 1996.

Shirk, Willis L. Jr. "Testing the Limits of Tolerance: Blacks and the Social Order in Columbia, Pennsylvania, 1800–1851." *Pennsylvania History,* 60 (1993): 35–50

Sidbury, James. *Ploughshares into Swords: Race, Rebellion, and Identity in Gabriel's Virginia, 1730–1810.* Cambridge: Cambridge University Press, 1997.

Slaughter, Thomas P. *Bloody Dawn: The Christiana Riot and Racial Violence in the Antebellum North.* Oxford: Oxford University Press, 1991.

Smith, George Winston, "Antebellum Attempts of Northern Business Interests to 'Redeem' the Upper South," *Journal of Southern History,* 11 (1945): 177–213.

Sobel, Mechal. *Trabelin' On: The Black Journey to an Afro-Baptist Faith.* Westport, Conn.: Greenwood Press, 1979.

————. *The World They Made Together: Black and White Values in Eighteenth Century Virginia.* Princeton, N.J.: Princeton University Press, 1987.

Soderlund, Jean. *Quakers and Slavery: A Divided Spirit.* Princeton: Princeton University Press, 1985.

Stampp, Kenneth. *America in 1857: A Nation on the Brink.* Oxford: Oxford University Press, 1992.

Stanton, Lucia. "'Those Who Labor for my Happiness': Thomas Jefferson and His Slaves." In *Jeffersonian Legacies,* edited by Peter S. Onuf, 147–80. Charlottesville: University Press of Virginia, 1993.

Staudenraus, P. J. *The African Colonization Movement, 1816–1865.* New York: Columbia University Press, 1961.

Stegmaier, Mark. "Maryland Fear of Insurrection at the Time of Braddock's Defeat." *Maryland Historical Magazine,* 71 (1976): 467–83.

Stevenson, Brenda. *Life in Black and White: Family and Community in the Slave South.* Oxford: Oxford University Press, 1996.

Stott, Richard B. ed. William Otter, *History of My Own Times*. Ithaca: Cornell University Press, 1995.

Sweet, John Wood. "Bodies Politic: Colonialism, Race and the Emergence of American North Rhode Island, 1730–1830." Ph.D. dissertation, Princeton University, 1995.

Switala, William J. *Underground Railroad in Delaware, Maryland, and West Virginia*. Mechanicsburg, Pa.: Stackpole Books, 2004.

Tadman, Michael. "The Demographic Cost of Sugar: Debates on Slave Societies and Natural Increase in the Americas." *American Historical Review*, 105 (2000): 1534–75.

Tadman, Michael. *Speculators and Slaves: Masters, Traders, and Slaves in the Old South*. Madison: University of Wisconsin Press, 1989.

Takagi, Midori. *"Rearing Wolves to Our Own Destruction": Slavery in Richmond, Virginia, 1782–1865*. Charlottesville: University Press of Virginia, 1999.

Thomas, Herman E. *James W. C. Pennington: African American Churchman and Abolitionist*. New York: Garland Publishing, 1995.

Thompson, Priscilla. "Harriet Tubman, Thomas Garrett, and the Underground Railroad." *Delaware History*, 22 (1986): 1–21.

Tomlins, Christopher. *Law, Labor and Ideology in the Early American Republic*. Cambridge: Cambridge University Press, 1993.

Towers, Frank. "Job Busting at Baltimore Shipyards: Racial Violence in the Civil War–Era South." *Journal of Southern History*, 66 (2000): 221–56.

Trotti, Michael. "Freedmen and Enslaved Soil: A Case Study of Manumission, Migration, and Land." *Virginia Magazine of History and Biography*, 104 (1996): 455–70.

Varon, Elizabeth R. "Evangelical Womanhood and the Politics of the African Colonization Movement in Virginia." In *Religion and the Antebellum Debate over Slavery*, edited by John R. McKivigan and Mitchell Snay. Athens: University of Georgia Press, 1998.

———. *We Mean to Be Counted: White Women and Politics in Antebellum Virginia*. Chapel Hill: University of North Carolina Press, 1998.

Walker, James W. St. G. *The Black Loyalists: The Search for a Promised Land in Nova Scotia and Sierra Leone, 1783–1870*. New York: Africana Publishing Company and Dalhousie, Nova Scotia: Dalhousie University Press, 1976.

Von Frank, Albert J. *The Trials of Anthony Burns: Freedom and Slavery in Emerson's Boston*. Cambridge: Harvard University Press, 1998.

Wagandt, Charles Lewis. *The Mighty Revolution: Negro Emancipation in Maryland, 1862–1864*. 1964; repr., Baltimore: Maryland Historical Society, 2005.

Wallenstein, Peter. "Indian Foremothers: Race, Sex, Slavery and Freedom in Early Virginia." In *The Devil's Lane: Sex and Race in the Early South*, edited by Catherine Clinton and Michele Gillespie. New York: Oxford University Press, 1997.

Walsh, Lorena. *From Calabar to Carter's Grove: The History of a Slave Community.* Charlottesville: University Press of Virginia, 1997.

———. "Slave Life, Slave Society, and Tobacco Production in the Tidewater Chesapeake, 1620–1820." In *Cultivation and Culture: Labor and the Shaping of Slave Life in the Americas,* edited by Ira Berlin and Philip D. Morgan. Charlottesville: University Press of Virginia, 1993.

Washburn, Wilcomb, *The Governor and the Rebel.* Chapel Hill: University North Carolina Press, 1957.

Weber, David J. *The Spanish Frontier in North America.* New Haven: Yale University Press, 1992.

Weiss, John McNish. "The Corps of Colonial Marines 1814–16: A Summary." *Immigrants and Minorities,* 15 (1996): 80–90.

Wesley, Charles H. *Richard Allen: Apostle of Freedom.* Washington, D.C.: The Associated Publishers, 1935.

White, Shane. *Somewhat More Independent: The End of Slavery in New York City, 1770–1810.* Athens: University of Georgia Press, 1991.

White, Shane, and Graham White. *The Sounds of Slavery: Discovering African American History through Song, Sermons, and Speech.* Boston: Beacon Press, 2005.

Whitman, T. Stephen. *The Price of Freedom: Slavery and Manumission in Baltimore and Early National Maryland.* Lexington: University Press of Kentucky, 1997.

Wiencek, Henry. *An Imperfect God: George Washington, His Slaves, and the Creation of America.* New York: Farrar, Straus, and Giroux, 2003.

Williams, John Alexander. "The New Dominion and the Old: Ante-Bellum and Statehood Politics as the Background of West Virginia's 'Bourbon Democracy.'" *West Virginia History,* 33 (1972): 317–407.

Williams, William H. *Slavery and Freedom in Delaware, 1639–1865.* Wilmington, Del.: Scholarly Resources Books, 1996.

Winch, Julie. "Philadelphia and the Other Underground Railroad." *Pennsylvania Magazine of History and Biography,* 111 (1987): 3–25.

Wilson, Carol. *Freedom at Risk: The Kidnapping of Free Blacks in America, 1780–1865.* Lexington: University Press of Kentucky, 1994.

Wolf, Eva Sheppard. *Race and Liberty in the New Nation: Emancipation in Virginia from the Revolution to Nat Turner's Rebellion.* Baton Rouge: Louisiana State University Press, 2006.

Wood, Betty. "'For Their Satisfaction or Redress': African Americans and Church Discipline in the Early South." In *The Devil's Lane: Sex and Race in the Early South,* edited by Catherine Clinton and Michelle Gillespie, 109–23. Oxford: Oxford University Press, 1997.

Wood, Gordon S. *The Radicalism of the American Revolution.* New York: Alfred A. Knopf, 1992.

Wood, Peter. "'The Dream Deferred': Black Freedom Struggles on the Eve of White

Independence." In *In Resistance: Studies in African, Caribbean, and Afro-American History,* edited by Gary Y. Okihiro, 166–87. Amherst: University of Massachusetts Press, 1986.

Wright, Richard. *The Free Negro in Maryland.* New York: Columbia University Press, 1921.

Yacovone, Donald. "The Transformation of the Black Temperance Movement, 1827–1854: An Interpretation." *Journal of the Early Republic,* 8 (1988): 281–97.

Zilversmit, Arthur. *The First Emancipation; the Abolition of Slavery in the North.* Chicago: University of Chicago Press, 1967.

Books, Articles, and Pamphlets of the Eighteenth and Nineteenth Centuries:

Allen, Richard. *The Life, Experience, and Gospel Labors of the Right Reverend Richard Allen.* Philadelphia: Martin and Boden, 1833.

Asbury, Francis. *Journals of Francis Asbury.* 3 vols. New York 1821; reprint, Nashville, 1958.

Bourne, George. *The Book and Slavery Irreconcilable.* Philadelphia: J. M. Sanderson & Co., 1816.

Brackett, Jeffrey R. *The Negro in Maryland: A Study of the Institution of Slavery.* Baltimore: Johns Hopkins University Press, 1889.

Brown, Henry "Box." *Narrative of Henry Box Brown, Who Escaped from Slavery Enclosed in a Box 3 Feet Long and 2 Wide.* Boston: Brown and Stearns, 1849.

Buchanan, George. *An Oration upon the moral and political evil of Slavery. Delivered at a public meeting of the Maryland Society for Promoting the Abolition of Slavery, and the Relief of Free Negroes, and others unlawfully held in Bondage.* Baltimore, 1791.

Carey, John L. *Slavery in Maryland Briefly Considered.* Baltimore: Joseph N. Lewis, 1845.

———. *Some Thoughts concerning Domestic Slavery in a Letter to ⎯⎯* Baltimore, 1838.

Craft, William and Ellen. *Running a Thousand Miles for Freedom.* London: William Tweedie, 1860; repr., New York: Arno Press, 1969.

Davis, Noah. *A Narrative of the Life of the Rev. Noah Davis, a Colored Man.* Baltimore: J. S. Weishampel, Jr., 1859.

Dew, Thomas R. *Review of the Debate in the Virginia Legislature of 1831 and 1832.* Richmond, 1832.

Douglas, Frederick. *Narrative of the Life of Frederick Douglass.* Boston, 1845.

Drayton, Daniel. *Personal Memoir of Daniel Drayton.* Boston: Bela Marsh, 1855.

Elaw, Zilpha. *Memoirs of the Life, Religious Experience, ministerial travels and labours of Mrs. Zilpha Elaw. . . .* London: Charter-House Lane, 1846.

Garrison, William Lloyd. *A Brief Sketch of the Trial of Wm. L. Garrison, for an Alleged Libel on Francis Todd, of Massachusetts.* Boston: Garrison and Knapp, 1834.

Garrison, William Lloyd. *Thoughts on African Colonization: or an impartial exhibition of the Doctrines, Principles & Purposes of the American Colonization Society.* Boston: Garrison and Knapp, 1832.

Grant, Ulysses S. *Personal Memoirs of U. S. Grant.* New York, 1885–1886.

Gray, Thomas R. *The Confessions of Nat Turner, the leader of the late Insurrection in Southampton, Virginia.* Baltimore: Lucas & Deaver, 1831.

Green, William. *Narrative of Events in the Life of William Green (formerly a slave).* Springfield, Mass: L. M. Guernsey., 1853.

Harper, Robert. *A Letter from General Harper, of Maryland, to Elias B. Caldwell, Esquire, Secretary of the American Society for Colonizing the Free People of Color, in the United States with Their Own Consent.* Baltimore, 1817.

Harrison, Jesse Burton. *The Slavery Question in Virginia,* in *Aris Sonis Focisque: Being a Memoir of an American Family: The Harrisons of Skimino,* Fairfax Harrison, ed. privately printed, 1910.

Henson, Josiah. *Truth Stranger than Fiction: Father Henson's Story of His Own Life.* Boston: John P. Jewett, 1858.

Jefferson, Thomas. *Notes on the State of Virginia.* Originally published 1782; Charlottesville: 1993, electronic text, University of Virginia Library.

Journal of the Baltimore Annual Conference, Methodist Episcopal Church. Vols. 1–2. Baltimore: 1817 and 1844.

Joyce, John. *The Confession of John Joyce, alias Davis, who was executed on Monday, the 14th of March, 1808, for the Murder of Mrs. Sarah Cross; with an Address to the Public and People of Colour, together with the substance of the Trial, and the address of Chief Justice Tilghman on his condemnation.* Philadelphia: Richard Allen, 1808.

Lee, Jarena. *Religious Experiences and Journal of Mrs. Jarena Lee.* Philadelphia: The author, 1849.

Lee, Jesse. *A Short History of the Methodists in the United States of America; Beginning in 1766, and Continued till 1809 .* Baltimore, 1810.

Lovejoy, Joseph C. *Memoir of Charles T. Torrey.* Boston: John Pl. Jewett, 1847; repr., New York, Negro Universities Press, 1969.

Mifflin, Warner. *The Defence of Warner Mifflin Against Aspersions cast on him on Account of his endeavours to promote Righteousness, Mercy, and Peace Among Mankind.* Philadelphia: Samuel Sansom, 1796.

Minutes and Proceedings of the First Annual Convention of the People of Colour, 1831. Philadelphia: Published by the Convention, 1831. See also Minutes and Proceedings for 1833 and 1835, also in Philadelphia.

Narrative of the Facts in the Case of Passmore Williamson. Philadelphia: Pennsylvania Abolition Society, 1855.

Mr. Nicholson's Motion, referred to a committee in the House of Representatives, on January 22, 1801. Pamphlet, American Antiquarian Society, Worcester, Mass.

Northup, Solomon. *Twelve Years a Slave.* 1853; repr., Baton Rouge: Louisiana State University Press, 1968.

Parker, William. "The Freedman's Story. In Two Parts." *The Atlantic Monthly,* 17 (1866): 152–66 and 276–95; electronic edition, University of North Carolina at Chapel Hill, metalab.unc.edu/docsouth/parker.

Paxton, John D. *Letters on Slavery, Addressed to the Cumberland Congregation, Virginia.* Lexington, Ky.: Abram T. Skillman, 1833.

Parrish, John. *Remarks on the Slavery of the Black People; Addressed to the Citizens of the United States, particularly to those in legislative or executive stations in the general or state government and also to such individuals as hold them in bondage.* Philadelphia: Kimber, Conrad, 1806.

Payne, Daniel A. *A History of the African Methodist Episcopal Church.* Nashville: Publishing House of the A.M.E. Sunday School Union, 1891.

Peck, Nathaniel, and Thomas Price. "*Report of Messrs. Peck and Price who were appointed at a meeting of the free colored people of Baltimore, held on November 25, 1839, Delegates to Visit British Guiana and the Island of Trinidad for the purposes of ascertaining the advantages to be derived by colored people migrating to those places.*" Baltimore; Woods & Crane, 1840.

Pinkney, William. *Speech of William Pinkney in the Maryland House of Delegates, November, 1789 session.* Philadelphia, 1790.

Randolph, Thomas Jefferson. *Speech of Thomas Jefferson Randolph (of Albemarle) in the House of Delegates of Virginia on the Abolition of Slavery, delivered January 21, 1832.* Richmond: Thomas White, 1832.

Raymond, Daniel. *Elements of Political Economy.* Baltimore: F. Lucas and E.J. Coale,, 1820.

———. *The Missouri Question.* Baltimore, 1819.

Redpath, James. *The Roving Editor: or Talks with Slaves in the Southern States.* New York, 1859.

Report of the Committee Appointed in the Senate of Pennsylvania to investigate the cause of an Increased Number of Slaves being returned for that Commonwealth, by the Census of 1830, over that of 1820. Harrisburg, 1833.

Report of the Committee on Colored Population. Maryland House of Delegates. Annapolis, 1840.

Report of the Committee on Grievances and Courts of Justice of the House of Delegates relative to the Colored Population of Maryland, Henry Brawner, Chair. Annapolis, 1832.

Robert Pleasants, son and heir of John Pleasants, deceased, Plaintiff, against Mary Logan et al. . . . in the High Court of Chancery, Virginia, March 16, 1798. Philadelphia, 1802.

Ruffner, Henry. *Address to the People of West Virginia, showing that slavery is injurious to the public welfare, and that it may be gradually abolished, without detriment to the rights and interests of slaveholders* . . . . Lexington, Va.: R.C. Noel, 1847.

Smallwood, Thomas. *A Narrative of Thomas Smallwood*. Toronto: James Stephens, 1851.

Still, William. *The Underground Railroad*. Philadelphia: Porter & Coates, 1872; repr., New York: Arno Press, 1968.

Stowe, Harriet Beecher. *Uncle Tom's Cabin, or Life Among the Lowly*. Washington, D.C.: *The Washington National Era*, 1851–1852.

Strickland, William P. *The Life of Jacob Gruber*. New York; Carlton & Porter, 1860.

Torrey, Jesse. *A Portraiture of Domestic Slavery in the United States*. Philadelphia: Jesse Torrey, 1817.

Townsend, Joseph. "Report of a meeting of the Maryland Society for promoting the abolition of slavery and the relief of free negroes, and others unlawfully held in bondage." 1792, Enoch Pratt Free Library, Baltimore.

The Trial of Reuben Crandall, M.D., charged with Publishing and Circulating Sedition and Incendiary Papers, &c in the District of Columbia, with the intent of Exciting Servile Insurrection, by a member of the Bar. Washington, D.C., 1836.

Tucker, George. *A Letter to A Member of the General Assembly of Virginia, on the Subject of the Late Conspiracy of the Slaves; with a Proposal for their Colonization*. Baltimore, 1801.

Tucker, St. George. *A Dissertation on Slavery with a Proposal for the Gradual Abolition of it, in the State of Virginia*. Philadelphia: Matthew Carey, 1796.

Tyson, John S. *The Life of Elisha Tyson*. Baltimore: n.p., 1825.

Walker, David. *Appeal to the Colored Citizens of America*. Boston, 1829; repr., New York: Hill and Wang, 1969.

Watkins, James. *Narrative of the Life of James Watkins*. Bolton, England: Kenyon and Abbatt, 1852.

Index

Abaris (pen name), 57

Abbott, Benjamin, 94

Abrams, Joseph, 149, 150

Act Concerning Negroes (Md. 1663), 80

Adams, John, 86

Adams, John Quincy, 192

Address to the People of West Virginia
(Ruffner), 131–132

advertisements for runaways, 17

African Americans: cultural emergence
during Gabriel's Rebellion, 86;
population growth in early 19th century, 20; sketch of Revolutionary
War soldier, 29; white culture and,
18. *See also* creole(s); slaves; *under*
black

African Methodist Bethel Society, Baltimore, 140

African Methodist Episcopal Church:
Bethel congregation, Baltimore, 97,
140, 149; expansion in Maryland,
148; founding of, 74, 95, 140; Thomas
Henry as elder of, 160

African Union Church, Wilmington,
Del., 148

Africanization of Chesapeake region, 12,
18

agriculture: economic rationale for slavery and, 21; slaves used for work in,
13–14. *See also* tobacco industry

Alexandria Gazette, 130

Allegany County, Md., post–Revolutionary War slavery in, 61–62

Allen, Richard, 74–76, 94, 137, 148, 151–152

Alley (slave), 84

amalgamation, Niles on, 112

American Colonization Society (ACS):
Baltimore, Md. chapter of, 108; black

reactions to founding of, 137–138;
female auxiliaries in Virginia, 121,
126; Key's defense of, 126; Liberia
colony operated by, 145; Liberian
representatives of, 138; John D.
Paxton and Virginia chapter of, 114;
reorganization in Virginia, 121–122

American Convention of abolition societies, 51

American Moral Reform Society, 144, 178

American Museum, 57

American Revolution, 19; African Americans serving with patriots during,
37, 39–40; Richard Allen's liberation
during, 75; blacks fighting for personal freedom in, 135; British raids
on Chesapeake region, 31–32; British recruitment of African Americans during, 30 31, 39; comparisons
of Gabriel's Rebellion to, 86, 88–89;
Paris treaty on runaways, 34; postwar economics, 40; slavery as problem and, 20–22. *See also* Dunmore,
Earl of

American Society of Free Persons of
Color, 143–144

Amistad, 185

Anderson, Joseph, 224

Anderson, William, 148

Anglo-American culture: familiarization
with, 17–18; slaves with no contact
with, 10

Anglo-Dutch War (1664–67), 4

Anne Arundel County, Md., freedom
petitions in, 83

Anthony (slave), 4

Antigua, slave-grown sugar of, 4

Antonio (slave), 5–6